W9-CLR-310

PHILOSOPHY

Philosophy

By

Mortimer J. Adler

and

Seymour Cain

Preface by

Richard McKeon

Distinguished Service Professor of Philosophy

and of Greek

The University of Chicago

ENCYCLOPÆDIA BRITANNICA, INC.

Chicago · London · Toronto · Geneva

PREFACE

Any question which is pushed to its beginning or its end becomes a philosophic question. Prolonged conversations on a subject tend, consequently, to contain reminiscences or parodies of philosophic dialogues, and participants in a discussion defend their positions when challenged by expounding their philosophies. One reason for reading philosophy is to gain insight into the basic questions hidden in everyday experience and in personal convictions and to become aware of answers that have been formulated and of errors that have been exposed in sustained inquiries concerning them. Education in philosophy should not be dogmatic indoctrination into one set of answers propounded by one master, nor should it be skeptical rejection of the questions because no one set of answers has been universally or enduringly accepted.

A newcomer to philosophy sometimes hits happily on a position which seems to him both true and enlightening, but more frequently his first experiences in philosophy are encounters with subtle and unheard-of absurdities. The teacher of philosophy to beginning classes encounters less frequently the problems arising from premature acceptance of philosophic insights by his students than he encounters the problems arising from immediate refutation of Plato, Locke, Kant, or Dewey before even minimal clarity concerning what is in question or what is asserted is achieved. The reading of philosophers is made into a philosophic experience when it contributes to the understanding of basic questions. This is done in two ways. First, since certain basic questions continue to be encountered and raised, with many changes in the manner of their formulation, the reader of a philosophical work, ancient or recent, may make his reading a dialogue with the author about issues which concern them both. Or, since approaches to problems and data relevant to them change, with many indications of continuity and derivation, the reader of a philosophic work, with which he agrees or disagrees, may make his reading an historical exploration into the meanings of terms like "being," "knowledge," "truth," "form," "matter," "cause," "fact," "process," and "decision," which disclose the conditioning circumstances of the questions one raises and of the answers one gives.

Although all questions are based on philosophic assumptions and have philosophic implications, certain questions have taken a central place in philosophical discussion and recur in different forms and sequences in the historical evolution of philosophy. One such question is about the relation of what we say and think to what is. This question was given a dramatic place in early Greek philosophy when Parmenides took the position that what I say and what I think must necessarily be. This conviction determined what he meant by discourse, thought, and being in his exploration of "the way of truth" and "the way of opinion," and whereas few later philosophers accepted his extreme views, alternative theories could be set up only by developing other conceptions and analyses of words, thoughts, and things. Other questions arose in the course of these analyses—questions about the nature and connections of things, the foundations and organization of the sciences, the significance and connections of statements and proof. The answers to these questions depended on altering previous conceptions of being, form, substance, and cause, of assertion and question, of reason and action, of principles and consequences, of reason and sensation, of rational perception and discursive understanding, of facts, actions, and sentences. Sometimes it seemed best to begin these philosophic speculations and adjustments with determinations concerning the nature of reality; sometimes it was argued that the beginning was in the forms or contents of thought; sometimes it was assumed, with no need or possibility of proof, that what is and what is thought is derivative from experience or existence or language.

The three ancient philosophers whose work is included in this Reading Plan took positions on these central basic questions which were to recur frequently in the long history of philosophy after them. Plato held that reality is through and through intelligible, and he named that which most truly is, "Ideas." Dialectic is at once a method of discovering things, of clarifying ideas, and of defining terms. Dialectic is not only the highest of the sciences but it is also in a broader sense the method of all discourse and dialogue. The organization of the sciences is in a hierarchy ranging from opinion through the various branches of mathematics up to dialectic. Virtue is discovered to be knowledge. Aristotle refuted Plato's doctrine of separated ideas, and instituted an inquiry into being as such, which was later to be given the name "metaphysics." It depends on the principles of non-contradiction and excluded middle, which are principles both of argument and of being. It makes use of "causes" to examine substance, form and matter, actuality and potentiality. This inquiry into principles leads to the differentiation of three kinds of sciences —theoretical, practical, and productive. Virtue is not knowledge, but ethics is a part of practical science. Lucretius held that the principles of being were the atoms and the void, and that knowledge too is a motion of atoms. He shared Epicurus' suspicion of verbal logic or dialectic. The foundation of ethics is pleasure, but knowledge can contribute to human well-being by reducing fear and superstition.

The coming of Christianity profoundly influenced the formulation of basic questions in the West. St. Augustine recognized that his statement of Christian doctrines had analogies with the Platonic philosophy. St. Thomas Aquinas worked, eight hundred years later, to bring the newly translated Aristotelian sciences into harmonious relation with the Au-

gustinian theology. He distinguished two modes of truth, one
dependent on revelation and the other on the principles of
natural reason. Since the truths of revealed theology and the
truths of natural theology are both truths, they cannot be in
contradiction. Questions of truth, however, extend beyond
the conformity of understanding and things, which provides
criteria for human ideas, to the conformity of divine understanding and things, which determines the being of things.
Montaigne three hundred years later found in the *Natural
Theology* of Raimond de Sebonde both a refutation of atheism and a support of skepticism.

The philosophers of the seventeenth and eighteenth centuries endeavored to reform philosophical thought by use of
the methods of the new sciences. But science, no less than
philosophy, is conceived in different ways when one raises
basic questions concerning it. Descartes sought to formulate
the method of a universal mathematics, and he thought he
could secure clarity, distinctness, and adequacy in philosophical thought by use of the long chains of reasoning of mathematicians. Bacon sought a new method of discovery of truths
and of sciences, and he projected in detail a program for the
advancement of learning, including sciences and philosophy.
Descartes demonstrated his own existence, and the existence
of God and of the external world; Bacon divided philosophy
into natural theology concerned with God, natural philosophy
concerned with the world, and human philosophy concerned
with man.

Spinoza undertook to demonstrate ethical philosophy in
geometric order, and took his beginning from God, who is nature, substance, cause of himself, and who has two attributes,
thought and extension. Locke, who admired the scientific
method of Newton, analyzed the nature, derivation, and relations of ideas, and thought that he had evidence in them
for the existence of God, the self, and the external world.
Berkeley, who continued to distinguish among our ideas by
means of the activity and the passivity of the mind, argued
that there was no evidence for the separate existence of the
unperceived external world. Hume, who undertook "to in-

troduce the experimental method into moral subjects," showed that there was no basis in the relations of ideas or in the conception of cause for arguments for the existence of God, the self, or the external world.

Kant heralded a second "Copernican revolution," and took his beginning not in dogmatic conceptions of the nature of things but in a critical examination of the forms of thought. His three *Critiques* treat of problems reminiscent of Aristotle's division of knowledge into theoretical, practical, and productive, but he makes use of the so-called "Platonic" division of philosophy into logic, physics, and ethics. William James found new formulations of ancient problems in a context of psychological processes and new criteria of truth in a context of actions and consequences.

The modern reader of philosophy is engaged still in a dialogue with the thirteen philosophers whose answers to fundamental questions are opened up in the Reading Plan, and he is also their descendant and inherits from them modes of statement and conception. The dialogue will become crossed monologues unless the positions are questioned; the history will be disrupted unless the positions are understood. The fashions of formulating questions have changed again: the reader who comes to these thirteen philosophers today will have heard echoes of questions about the significance of metaphysical statements and the soundness of ethical questions, he will have encountered existential and linguistic philosophies, or pragmatics and dialectics, and he will have seen signs of new philosophic problems emerging from the contacts of cultures, peoples, powers, and traditions. He will have some experience of basic questions to bring with him in the discussion of permanent issues and in the examination of newly available facts and data. These are the materials of philosophic inquiry and speculation, and the reading of the works of great philosophers is one initiation to the organization, use, and understanding of these materials.

RICHARD McKEON

FOREWORD

I

This Reading Plan is an aid to the understanding of philosophy. You need not have done the readings in other Reading Plans to follow the discussions in this one. Sometimes a reference is made to another Reading Plan, in order to provide additional understanding of the reading under discussion. For instance, in the Guide to the Tenth Reading, which consists of selections from Spinoza's *Ethics*, we refer to the discussion of his geometrical method in the Reading Plan *Ethics: the Study of Moral Values.*

How to Use the Reading Plan. This Plan contains three parts: a list of readings, guides to each of the readings, and suggestions for additional readings.

1. *The Reading List.* There are fifteen readings. The reading time will vary with the selection and the reader. The First or Second Reading, from Plato's *Republic,* will require much less time than the Eighth Reading, from Bacon's *Advancement of Learning,* or the Tenth Reading, from Spinoza's *Ethics.* The whole course of readings should take about thirty weeks, or an average of two weeks per reading. The reader, however, is well advised to pursue each reading at his own pace, proceeding faster or slower in accordance with his rate of comprehension.

2. *The Guides.* These should prove most helpful to the

reader of *Great Books of the Western World* who is going it alone, without teacher, discussion leader, or other study aids. The purpose of the guide is to help you get started on an assignment by providing you with background material and by stimulating your thinking about the reading. Background material may include information about the particular historical setting—tradition, culture, and contemporary conditions— in which the book was written. It may also include remarks on the form and style of the readings, which range from a Platonic dialogue to a treatise on psychology.

A major portion of each guide describes the content and analyzes the meaning of the reading. Significant and difficult passages are cited and discussed. We consider the basic philosophical concepts and problems discussed in the reading and relate them to perennial philosophical concerns.

The final section of each guide raises questions that are suggested by the reading. You cannot answer such questions merely by repeating what the text says, or by an unqualified "yes" or "no," or by a flat "true" or "false." Hence, a brief discussion follows the statement of a problem, in order to indicate its significance and suggest some of the possible answers. You may be satisfied simply to read the questions and give them a little thought. Or you may want to delve more deeply into them and write out considered answers. The discussions following the questions are intended to stimulate your own inquiry and thought. They are not meant to provide the final or "right" answers. Try to answer the questions yourself.

Each guide concludes with a section entitled SELF-TEST-ING QUESTIONS. These are quite distinct from the discussion questions. They are factual questions about the reading that can be answered by citing a particular part of the text. They give you an opportunity to check how thoroughly you have read and how much you have remembered of what you have read. You can mark your score by referring to the list of answers which appears immediately after the Guide to the Fifteenth Reading.

3. *Additional Readings.* These provide suggestions for

those readers who wish to pursue further their study of philosophy. They include both writings in *Great Books of the Western World* and an extensive list of other works. The latter comprises works in speculative philosophy and epistemology, histories and commentaries, and works on aesthetics. A special attempt has been made to include significant philosophical works written during the past hundred years.

II

In previous Reading Plans we have heard what the philosophers have to say on a wide variety of subjects—politics, law, ethics, religion, and psychology. In this Reading Plan we concentrate on what they have to say about the nature and task of philosophy, and follow their inquiries into metaphysics (the study of first principles) and epistemology (the theory of knowledge). We seek answers to such questions as what it means to be a philosopher, what the philosopher's specific attitude of mind is, what particular role he has in the world. We also seek answers to certain key problems of philosophy—questions about the basic structure of things, about causality, about knowledge and truth, and about philosophical method. We try to get some notion of the nature of philosophy by watching the philosopher at work as he pursues what he conceives to be his major concerns.

We start with Plato's clarion call, summoning the philosopher to bring the light of knowledge of reality to his fellow human beings. This sense of vocation, of the philosopher's prophetic mission to bring light to those who dwell in the darkness, is repeated in one way or another throughout these readings. Plato also treats the perennial philosophical themes of the nature of reality, the modes of human knowledge, the distinction between the sensible and intelligible realms, and the relation of philosophy to the various special sciences, particularly mathematics. The selections from Plato offer us a real beginning, one that has many ramifications and consequences.

The same is true of Aristotle, Plato's most illustrious student and severest critic. Aristotle conveniently provides us with a critical history of philosophy before his time, together with a discussion of "first philosophy" or "metaphysics," and a systematic analysis of the basic causes or principles of things. He also states the basic metaphysical and logical principle of non-contradiction and the "correspondence" theory of truth (that our thoughts or statements are true if and only if they agree with the actual state of things). His vigorous attack upon some of Plato's basic doctrine, as well as his criticism of other great predecessors, is a classic example of the disagreement among eminent philosophers, which many non-philosophers find scandalous.

That there is no unanimity among the great thinkers becomes even more obvious when we read the next author, Lucretius. He presents us with a flatly materialistic account of the nature of things, which makes matter the basis of even the intellectual and spiritual aspects of reality. Materialism, we note, found an eloquent philosophical voice long before Karl Marx.

Another "modern" note is sounded in these selections when Montaigne questions whether human reason can attain certain knowledge. Montaigne's awareness of the variety of human beliefs, of the influence of time, place, and personality on men's opinions, has a familiar sound in the present age. His skepticism about the capacity of the human mind to attain certain truth raises such important philosophical questions as "What do I know?" or "How can I be sure I know?" These questions lead directly to Descartes' famous answer that I can at least be sure that I doubt, and hence, that I am. And after Descartes' historic moment of self-knowledge come the critical inquiries of the great British empiricist philosophers—Locke, Berkeley, and Hume—into the nature and limits of human understanding.

The emphasis of this school on the central role of sense impressions and mental images in the process of knowing leads to Berkeley's startling and brilliant argument that all we can know are our ideas of things, not the things themselves, and to Hume's denial that there is any basis in reason or experience for the idea of necessary causation. After Berkeley and Hume comes Kant, to restore the notion of causal necessity, but now as a basic category of the human mind, rather than as a connection discovered in things. And finally William James attempts a "psychogenetic" explanation of the belief in necessary truths, rooting them in man's organic mental structure.

The selections briefly summarized above mainly emphasize what philosophers have to say about the basic principles of things and about the nature of knowledge and truth, to the neglect not only of ethics (which is handled in a separate Reading Plan), but also of logic and aesthetics. The need for concentration and selectivity explains these omissions. This need also accounts for the absence of such important philosophers as Epictetus, Hobbes, and Hegel, who, however, are well represented in other Reading Plans. The list of additional readings at the end of this volume is intended to repair the omission of these important philosophical points of view.

One of the great satisfactions to be derived from these selections on rather difficult topics is, with a few exceptions, their remarkable readability. Most of the great philosophers write as men talking to other men. The tone of conversation obviously pervades Plato's dramatic dialogue, Descartes' autobiographical confessions, and the virile lucid prose of the English-speaking philosophers. The problems which these thinkers broach are often deep and the solutions they propose often difficult to grasp, but their language for the most part is direct. The great conversation to which these readings invite us is open to any person who wonders about the nature of things and whether we can know the truth about them.

❀ ❀ ❀

This Reading Plan is the product of the over-all collaboration of Mortimer J. Adler with Seymour Cain, Peter Wolff, and V. J. McGill. Dr. Cain is mainly responsible for the guides to the first ten Readings, Mr. Wolff for the guides to the Eleventh, Twelfth, and Thirteenth Readings, and Dr. McGill for the guides to the Fourteenth and Fifteenth Readings.

CONTENTS

A NOTE ON

REFERENCE STYLE

I n referring to *Great Books of the Western World,* the same
style is used as in the *Syntopicon.* Pages are cited by number
and section. In books that are printed in single column, "a" and
"b" refer to the upper and lower halves of the page. In books
that are printed in double column, "a" and "b" refer to the upper and lower halves of the left column, "c" and "d" to the
upper and lower halves of the right column. For example,
"Vol. 53, p. 210b" refers to the lower half of page 210, since
Vol. 53, James's *Principles of Psychology,* is printed in single
column. But "Vol. 7, p. 202b" refers to the lower left quarter
of page 202, since Vol. 7, Plato's *Dialogues,* is printed in double column.

THE READING LIST

PLATO

The Republic

Vol. 7, pp. 369c-383a, 388a-391a

$\mathcal{T}$*he Republic* is the most renowned of Plato's dialogues. Its vision of the ideal human community and of
the harmonious human soul has pervaded the Western
mind for twenty-five centuries. In that vision, it is the
philosopher who plays the central role, for he is the
ruler of the ideal state as reason is the ruler of the perfect soul. Hence this dialogue provides a vivid and
dramatic description of the philosopher and his relation to the community, and at the same time considers
some of the fundamental questions of philosophy.

Plato's literary artistry conveys poignantly the philosopher's human, all-too-human impulse to shrink
from his mission of bringing order to the human soul
and to the human community, and to remain instead
in the perpetual enjoyment of contemplative wisdom.
It shows also the scornful attitude of most men toward
philosophy and the philosopher, and the sad situation
in which the best practical solution is for the philosopher to dwell apart from the common life. And it

depicts the way in which the philosopher may triumph over these obstacles and bring to others the light he himself has attained.

This "light" is the knowledge of reality. Hence Plato deals, in and through this dramatic dialogue, with the basic philosophical themes of the nature of knowledge and the nature of reality. He expounds the basic distinction between knowledge and opinion and between the primary reality of "ideas" and the secondary, reflected reality of concrete experience. He broaches here, in its classical form, the challenging notion that we can have knowledge only of what transcends the level of sense experience—the eternal and universal ideas.

Subsequent generations of philosophers have returned to these basic philosophical themes again and again throughout our tradition, whether to support or refute Plato's views. This reading and the fourteen that follow will acquaint us with the main positions on these fundamental questions of philosophy.

First Reading

I

Plato's *Republic* provides a bewildering richness of themes. As its title indicates, it is a work on the state. But it also is a work on justice, on the human soul, and on education, as well as an inquiry into the basic structure of things and the various levels of human knowledge. Such a richness of subject matter may perplex the reader at first, for the themes all seem to be discussed at the same time. A Platonic dialogue has a structure and a method of its own, but its order is not so obvious as that of the topical, neatly divided presentation of the scholarly dissertation. Reading it is more like reading a story, in which the author treats many different themes and viewpoints together, "synoptically," rather than topically.

In the present reading, for example, Plato presents his view of the nature of the philosopher and his relation to the rest of the world. In the context of *The Republic*, however, the discussion necessarily includes considerations of the state, the soul, and human weakness or corruption, as well as of ultimate reality and philosophical knowledge. A brief summary of the whole argument in the dialogue may help to indicate why this mixture of themes is necessary.

The Republic consists of an imaginary conversation between Socrates, the teacher of Plato, and six interlocutors, including Glaucon and Adeimantus, the brothers of Plato, and Thrasymachus, a famous rhetorician and Sophist. Their original and basic subject is the nature of justice. After discarding the suggested definitions of justice as might, custom, or expediency, they turn to a discussion of the state, which is the individual writ large. Since justice is admittedly a right order or harmony in the soul and in the community, Socrates sketches a portrait

3

of the perfect state to mirror the order of the soul and thus to find out what that right order or harmony consists in.

The ideal state comprises three social classes: the ruling class of guardians or magistrates, the military class of auxiliaries or soldiers, and the producing class of farmers and artisans. Corresponding to these three classes are the three elements of the soul, the rational, the spirited, and the appetitive; and the three virtues, wisdom, courage, and temperance. Justice is the harmony and unity of the classes, elements, or virtues. The just society is the model of the just soul—guided by reason, empowered by a noble will, and controlled in its desires. The opposite of justice is disorder and discord among the various elements of the soul. The educational program of the ideal state and the famous proposal for the community of women and children are designed to achieve harmony in the soul and the state.

This portrait of human perfection is inspiring, but the question arises as to how it is to become a reality. The present state of human affairs (in fifth-century-B.C. Athens, or in twentieth-century America) is utterly at variance with this ideal. It is here that Socrates proposes one "slight" change in human society which will enable us to bring the perfect state into actuality. That is to make philosophers, or rather those who combine the qualities of both political greatness and philosophical wisdom, the rulers of the human community. This proposal leads to a discussion of the nature of the philosopher and his place in the community, which comprises the present reading. A further program of education is sketched for the nurture of the special, advanced intellectual qualities necessary for the philosopher-king.

Socrates goes on to discuss the various forms of corruption, corresponding to various vices of the soul, that will inevitably ensue in the perfect state, and to point out that the just life is a happy life. Thus, justice is rewarded with happiness in this life and with eternal bliss in the afterlife, when all souls are judged. In Book X poetry and art are presented as the antagonists of philosophy, on the grounds that they pretend to a knowledge which they do not possess and that they corrupt morals through their emotional effects. On the other hand, philosophy, which is based on intellectual knowledge rather than imaginative representation, is in touch with basic realities and hence can build virtue and justice in the individual and the state.

II

Our reading begins with Socrates' provocative statement that the perfect human community will be achieved only when philosophers are the rulers of states. Recognizing that this claim for the supreme role of philosophy will be greeted with incredulity, Socrates proceeds to explain what he means by a philosopher. He begins with the simple etymological sense of "philosopher" as a lover of wisdom and then points out that this means a passionate love for the whole of wisdom, for all possible knowledge and learning. The philosopher, he says, is "he who has a taste for every sort of knowledge and who is curious to learn and is never satisfied" (p. 370c).

But this initial definition does not mean quite what it seems to at first glance, for not all that seems to be knowledge is such, and mere indiscriminate curiosity does not make the philosopher. We must distinguish between what is really knowledge and what is not, and hence distinguish between the real and the counterfeit philosopher according as they pursue real knowledge or its counterfeit. For example, the love of the multiplicity of sights and sounds, of the variegated world of sense experience, is not philosophical, although it may be marked by intense desire and restless curiosity. A man who is restricted to this merely aesthetic level and does not go beyond it to the vision of absolute beauty is no philosopher.

The true philosopher concentrates on the eternal essence or "idea" (e.g., beauty) in which the finite objects and forms (e.g., a beautiful human body or work of art) partake, and distinguishes clearly between the idea and the finite things which "participate" in it. The counterfeit philosopher, on the other hand, takes the various tones, colors, forms, and artifacts as the basic reality; he "puts the copy in the place of the real object" (p. 371b), that is, the idea. The mind of the true philosopher takes reality as its object and pattern, whereas the mind of the false philosopher takes a mere copy as its pattern and hence his thought is merely the copy of a copy, twice removed from reality. The mind of the latter is like that of a dreamer, concerned with phantom images, while the mind of the true philosopher is like that of a man who is "wide awake," in touch with substantial reality.

These evocative metaphors lead to the basic distinction between "knowledge" and "opinion." Each is defined as a faculty or power of the human soul, with a special sphere and subject matter, as distinct from one another as sight is from hearing. Knowledge has to do only with what exists absolutely, eternally, immutably; hence it is certain and infallible. This realm (the sphere of eternal ideas) is called "being."

The opposite of being is "non-being," and its correlative mental state is ignorance (a mere blankness). However, there is a state midway between certain knowledge and utter ignorance, because there is a sphere midway between being and non-being. This is the sphere of "becoming," which comprises transitory, changing, relative existence, and its mental correlative is opinion. It is the realm of "the intermediate flux which is caught and detained by the intermediate faculty" (p. 373b). Things which appear beautiful under one aspect may appear ugly under another; acts which appear just in one situation may appear unjust in another; things may be the doubles of some things and the halves of others at the same time. This is the realm where things may be said both to be and not to be; hence, absolute certainty of judgment is impossible here.

The first realm, that of knowledge, is the domain of the philosophers—the "lovers of wisdom." The second realm, that of opinion, is the domain of the imposters—the "lovers of opinion."

III

In Book V Socrates talks about the philosopher's nature in terms of his knowledge, its special sphere and objects. In Book VI he discusses the philosopher's virtues—the kind of person he is, his "character."

First among the philosopher's virtues, of course, is truthfulness, a quality of mind which we would expect in one whose soul is turned toward being, toward what really is. Also associated with the pursuit of knowledge are pleasure in learning and a good memory. Linked with these intellectual qualities are certain moral qualities. The philosopher is temperate, for he is more interested in pleasures of the soul than of the body, and is not covetous of material things. He is also "liberal" or great-souled, as contrasted with the petty and mean-minded person, for he is "the spectator of all time and all existence" (p. 374d).

Thus the man whose mind is turned toward the whole of things is just, gentle, and noble. Above all, his soul is marked by a harmony, a proportion, and a balanced unity of his various qualities, intellectual and moral. The philosopher has "a naturally well-proportioned and gracious mind, which will move spontaneously towards the true being of everything" (p. 375a).

When Socrates, however, goes on from this portrait to infer that philosophy is "a blameless study" and is properly fitted to prepare men to rule the state, Adeimantus breaks in with vigorous objections. He says it is a well-known fact

. . . that the votaries of philosophy, when they carry on the study, not only in youth as a part of education, but as the pursuit of their maturer years, most of them become strange monsters, not to say utter rogues, and that those who may be considered the best of them are made useless to the world by the very study which you extol. (p. 375c)

We note that there are two points to Adeimantus' indictment of philosophy: (1) that most philosophers "become strange monsters, not to say utter rogues," and (2) that even the best of them "are made useless to the world" by the study of philosophy.

Socrates takes the second point first, answering it with a parable about a ship with a strong but dull captain, beset by a crew who claim the right to steer the ship despite their ignorance of the art of navigation. They take over the ship through force and fraud and lead a riotous life of self-indulgence, with no skilled hand to guide the ship's course. They accord the title of pilot only to the kind of man who aids them in their seizure of power, while disdaining the true pilot—the man who really knows the art of navigation—as "a prater, a star-gazer, a good-for-nothing" (p. 376a).

Socrates considers the meaning of this figurative presentation of the philosopher's relation to society as self-evident and requiring no explanation. However, he does explicitly identify the mutinous crew with "the present governors of mankind" and the true pilot with the philosopher. From the context of the dialogue, we may go on to identify the "partisan" who aids the mutineers with the false philosopher or Sophist. Assuming that the Athenian democracy is the particular butt of Plato's satire, we may also identify the strong but imperceptive captain with the people. (We need not be thrown off by Socrates' calling the captain "noble" on p. 376a, for the Greek word might just as well be translated "worthy" and is probably intended ironically.)

In any case, the message of the parable is clear: the best philosophers are useless to the world, but that is the fault of the world, not of philosophy. We must "attribute their uselessness to the fault of those who will not use them" (p. 376b), who foolishly prefer sophistry to philosophy and opinion to knowledge.

Socrates now turns to the other point made by Adeimantus, namely, that most philosophers become evil men. Assuming that the philosopher's nature is originally noble and good, how, then, does it get corrupted? The cause lies, says Socrates, in the community in which the philosopher is brought up and in the peculiar susceptibility of the virtuous and gifted to nurture and education—good or bad.

The philospher's nature is a very rare thing and requires a propitious cultural environment, just as a rare plant requires the right kind of soil, climate, and nutrition. Furthermore, the more potentiality for good there is in man, the more potentiality there is for evil; and when the right kind of environment and nurture is lacking, most of those who start out with the noble nature of a philosopher may well end up as rogues and scoundrels. They have to be *something* in high degree, and if they cannot be good, they are going to be bad, and nothing in between, unless some change or miracle saves them.

And our philosopher follows the same analogy—he is like a plant which, having proper nurture, must necessarily grow and mature into all virtue, but, if sown and planted in an alien soil, becomes the most noxious of all weeds, unless he be preserved by some divine power. (p. 377d)

It is not hard to see what happens to a young man with the soul of a philosopher "in the present evil state of governments." He is impressed by what is commonly held to be good and evil in the community to which he belongs, and by its sanctions "of attainder or confiscation or death" for those who (like the historical Socrates) oppose public opinion. He is seduced by those who wish to use his gifts for their own selfish purposes and who hold out the prospect of place and power without the necessity of treading the rocky road of philosophical knowledge. He sees that the world rewards those who cater to its taste for the multiplicity of temporal things; for the multitude have no vision of the transcendental realm of eternal ideas. The well-paid Sophists do no more than state in a clever and lively way what "the great beast," the multitude, thinks and desires, calling what it likes "good" and what it dislikes "evil." Everything in the present state of society conspires against the young man with the soul of a philosopher to keep him from becoming a philosopher, and aside from rare accidents assures the "ruin and failure" of his virtue and makes his turning to evil almost inevitable.

This gives an opportunity to the false pretenders to usurp the places left empty in the temple of philosophy. Ignoble and unqualified persons assume the name of philosophers and produce a bastard mishmash of glittering but empty sophisms. This leaves the true service of philosophy to the remnant who have been saved by happy chance and have come to treasure philosophy above all other things. They live like aliens in their own communities, keeping themselves apart from the madness and wickedness of the multitude, each keeping his peace and going his own way, seeking only to live a pure and righteous life. This admittedly, in the present condition of things, is "a great work," but not the greatest the philosopher is capable of, nor the fulfillment of his mission. That lies in the creation of a perfect state.

. . . neither cities nor States nor individuals will ever attain perfection until the small class of philosophers whom we termed useless but not corrupt are providentially compelled, whether they will or not, to take care of the State, and until a like necessity be laid on the State to obey them; or until kings, or if not kings, the sons of kings or princes, are divinely inspired with a true love of true philosophy. (p. 381c)

Thus we return to the message proclaimed at the beginning of this reading, having in the meantime been shown the true nature of the philosopher, which can make such a claim possible. The philosopher has his mind fixed on the eternal transcendental realm where all is "in order moving according to reason," and through intercourse with this realm he himself becomes "orderly and divine," as far as a human being can become so. What he has done for himself he can also do for others; he can fashion individuals and states on "the heavenly pattern." Looking for his models to the eternal ideas of absolute beauty, justice, and temperance, he may proceed to make over the human community in the image of the divine order.

I V

Implicit in this view of philosophical knowledge is the belief that the philosopher becomes, or participates in, what he knows. The philosopher's knowledge, being, and character are mutually involved in his progress from darkness to light. Ultimately, then, knowledge is not only the objective apprehension of the eternal ideas but involves a process of spiritual conversion, of becoming like what one knows.

. . . the true lover of knowledge is always striving after being—that is his nature; he will not rest in the multiplicity of individuals which is an appearance only, but will go on—the keen edge will not be blunted, nor the force of his desire abate until he have attained the knowledge of the true nature of every essence by a sympathetic and kindred power in the soul, and by that power drawing near and mingling and becoming incorporate with very being, having begotten mind and truth, he will have knowledge and will live and grow truly, and then, and not till then, will he cease from his travail. (p. 376d)

The lifting of man to this higher stage is presented in a moving and dramatic way in the famous allegory of the cave in Book VII, perhaps the finest of Plato's imaginative inventions. Let us imagine that men are chained from childhood in a dark cave, in such a way that they cannot see the entrance which is open to the light. Behind them is a fire and a kind of stage, along which figures and objects pass, but they can see only the shadows cast by these things upon the back wall of the cave. Never having known real things, they take these shadows for reality, shadows which are doubly removed from reality, since they are shadows of the images, or copies, of the real things.

Suppose one of them were suddenly released and free to turn around toward the fire and the stage. He would be blinded by the light and bewildered by the sight of the moving figures, since he would cling from habit to the belief that the shadows are the real things. At this stage of liberation he is still in the cave, the light is the light of the fire, and the objects which cast the shadows are themselves images.

Imagine him forced now to ascend into the upper world, into the light of day. He would be even more dazzled and would need long practice before he could make out real objects, proceeding gradually from shadows in the sunlight and reflections in the water to the very source of light, the sun itself. Thus he would come to understand the true order of things and to pity his fellows, imprisoned below, whose keenest perception could only be of the shadows of images.

When our imaginary spiritual voyager returned to the cave, he would be blinded at first by the darkness and unable to see the shadows as well as those who had remained below. This temporary dimming of vision would be taken as proof of the evil effect of his liberation from darkness and ascent to light, and hence as a good reason for killing any would-be liberator in the future (which is possibly a reference to the fate of the historical Socrates).

A detailed explanation follows this strange parable. According to it, the cave or "prison-house" corresponds to the material, sensible world, the fire to the physical sun of our ordinary experience, the ascent to the light to the ascent of the soul to the ideal, intelligible world, and the sun to the idea of the good— the supreme idea which is the foundation of all reality. (See pp. 384b-386d.)

It is easy to understand why the man who has had such a vision prefers to dwell in the transcendental realm of ideas and is reluctant to descend to the cave of human affairs; and also why at first he appears so ridiculous and dim-witted when he tries to deal with the images and shadows that are taken for reality in our present political institutions. We realize that just as the whole body in the parable had to be released and turned in order that the eye might turn to the light, so the whole soul must be liberated and turned away from the sensible world in order that the faculty of knowledge, the "eye" of the soul, may apprehend absolute being.

Nevertheless, the philosopher cannot be permitted to remain in the state of the beatific vision of ultimate reality, removed from the situation and plight of his fellows. He must be compelled to descend again and again into the cave of ordinary life, where most men dwell all the days of their life, and to work for the transformation of humanity and society.

Wherefore each of you, when his turn comes, must go down to the general underground abode, and get the habit of seeing in the dark. When you have acquired the habit, you will see ten thousand times better than the inhabitants of the den, and you will know what the several images are, and what they represent, because you have seen the beautiful and just and good in their truth. And thus our State which is also yours will be a reality, and not a dream only, and will be administered in a spirit unlike that of other States, in which men fight with one another about shadows only and are distracted in the struggle for power, which in their eyes is a great good. Whereas the truth is that the State in which the rulers are most reluctant to govern is always the best and most quietly governed, and the State in which they are most eager, the worst. (pp. 390d-391a)

V

What does Plato mean by an "idea"?

Obviously, he does not mean a mere thought—something that exists only in the mind—in the sense that "idea" has in the sentence "He has the wrong idea about me." It is ideas that are really real for Plato and, although they are mentally apprehended, they do not exist merely in the mind.

Do they then exist in things, from which they are abstracted by our minds? Are ideas such as beauty, goodness, justice, etc. abstractions or generalizations from our experience? This seems plausible and understandable, but the difficulty is that the ideas are absolute and eternal, while all the instances of beauty, etc., are relative and temporal.

Where, then, do the Platonic "ideas" exist? Do they exist in some other, transcendental world, above and apart from the world of our experience? There is much in Plato's language about the "divine" and "heavenly" realm of essences and ideas which seems to justify this conclusion. However, it hardly accords with Plato's argument to say that the ideas exist entirely apart from the world of ordinary existence, since the whole object of *The Republic* is to show the connection between the ideal and the actual. The ideas of beauty, goodness, etc. are the models and patterns for the actual world and are somehow present in it; or in Plato's terms, things "participate" in the ideas, which are the ultimate constituents of all existence. Somehow the essential structure of the sensible world resides in purely intelligible realities, of which the sensible world is the "image" or reflection.

What distinguishes the objects and judgments of "opinion" from those of knowledge?

According to the view set forth in this reading, the objects of knowledge are absolute and immutable, while those of opinion are relative and changing. Let us try to apply this distinction to a concrete instance of justice, the key idea of *The Republic*.

Suppose that we say that the political system or constitution of the United States is just. Is this statement an instance of opinion or of knowledge? Certainly the United States and its constitution are historical entities which have changed and may change in the future. They are hardly eternal objects. In this sense, then, any judgment about the justice of the American political system must be relative and qualified.

But suppose that there were a perfect state which fully embodied justice? After all, Plato does hold out the possibility that such a state can be achieved in concrete, historical existence. Would such a historical entity be the proper subject of knowledge? If the United States were an absolutely just community, would the statement "The United States is a just society" be a matter of knowledge or of opinion?

Can particular existence ever be the object of knowledge for Plato? Is the "participation" of particular existence in the eternal ideas a matter of knowledge or opinion? Or is it only the idea itself, which we apprehend in some particular entity or situation, that can be the object of knowledge? Referring to our hypothetical example again, is the embodiment of justice in some particular state or constitution completely irrelevant, so far as philosophical knowledge and valuation are concerned? Do we know justice and the model of the just society before and apart from any empirical instance of it?

Can there be such a thing as "historical knowledge" in Plato's theory of knowledge?

What eternal ideas does the march of history mirror? Is "revolution" an eternal idea which is embodied in particular events, such as the American, French, and Russian Revolutions? What about historical terms like "renaissance," "decline and fall," or "war and peace"? Is the notion of eternal ideas of change self-contradictory and contrary to the whole trend of Plato's thought? Is the notion of history as a reflection or imitation of eternal patterns contrary to the Western secular notion of history? Is it compatible with the biblical notion of Providence?

Would the ideal existence for the philosopher be to live perpetually in the realm of pure essences?

In the present state of things, according to Plato's portrait, the philosopher keeps himself remote from common affairs and enjoys his peaceful isolation. Yet this is not a fully satisfactory life, for his mission is to redeem the human community and to build the perfect state. The individual who has risen from the darkness and shadow images of the cave to the light of day and substantial realities cannot remain in his blessed state. He must return to the level of sense experience and raise other souls to the light.

Certainly the moral of this is quite plain. The philosopher is not a snob, secure in his own superior state and looking down at the rest of mankind. With his nobility and greatness of spirit there goes a fellow feeling for his brother human beings and the impulse to raise them from darkness and ignorance. There is a community of men and of good. The good is to be shared with other men, not enjoyed in isolation.

But do these moral and practical considerations have any bearing on the cognitive and theoretical functions of the philosopher? Would his vision of pure essences be more acute if he did not return to the sensible world? Or is it necessary for him to repeat the process of ascent continually in order to grasp the eternal ideas? Does his immersion in the realm of sense experience and practice aid or impede him as a knower? Or is the philosopher something more than a knower?

Would the pure philosopher be a higher type than the philosopher-king? In his famous statement about the philosopher-king, Plato seems to rank the mere philosopher with the mere governor as a lower type. Is this consistent with Plato's view of philosophy and the philosopher and with the relative rank of contemplation and practice in his thought?

Does philosophy depend on social and political conditions for its existence?

Plato's vivid picture of the corrupting effect of social conditions and culture upon the philosophical spirit comes as a surprise if we think of him as aware only of a transcendent spiritual sphere of reality. Plato's philosopher is not a pure spirit, absolutely free and self-determining, utterly independent of the prevailing cultural atmosphere. The man who is born to be a philosopher does not become one automatically and inevitably. The philosophical spirit is a tender plant and may easily be blighted in the bud.

Possibly Plato had in mind the particular situation and personalities of his time. Interpreters have suggested that he was thinking of men like Alcibiades, the brilliant and notorious student of Socrates, or Critias, another of Socrates' associates, who later led the oligarchical revolution and became chief of the Thirty Tyrants. However, Plato is not speaking of a few individuals; he is making a blanket statement about the majority of men born with a philosophical spirit. Corruption is the common plight of such men, he says, in the present state of society. A few are saved through accidental circumstances or some miracle.

Is this a likely story? Would a true philospher be so weak in character, so easily seduced from his vocation, or would he follow his special bent ascetically, unswerved by the ordinary lures of approval, pleasure, and power? Were those whose corruption Plato depicts so poignantly really philosophers to begin with, or were they merely "brilliant," intellectually talented men? Do social pressures and influences, then, merely separate the men from the boys, the real from the apparent philosophers?

Or does Plato's picture have the bite of reality as we look at the present situation in our comfortable, affluent society? Are those who are born with a philosophic spirit, and who demonstrate it in early life, seduced by the trappings of prestige and power, or do they go their own way, regardless of all lures? Do our social and academic institutions effectually foster or impede philosophically gifted men from becoming philosophers? Who gets our highest rewards—the Sophist (as Plato pictures him here) or the philosopher?

Is a man free to become what he is born to be? Or is he in part dependent on his immediate environment or divine grace?

The following questions are designed to help you test the thoroughness of your reading. Each question is to be answered by giving a page or pages of the reading assignment. Answers will be found on page 301 of this Reading Plan.

1 Why are the "punning riddles" like the objects of opinion?

2 What type of men do the greatest injury to philosophy?

3 What are the ordinary goods of life which distract the philosopher?

4 Who is comparable to "a bald little tinker" striving to rise above his place?

5 What are the various conditions which may save a man for philosophy?

6 What change does Socrates advocate in the way of teaching philosophy?

7 What does the metaphor of "circumcision" refer to in the allegory of the cave?

PLATO

The Republic

Vol. 7, pp. 386d-388a, 391b-401d

The problem of philosophical method has been a perennial subject of discussion throughout our tradition. What is the special way, if any, by which philosophical inquiry is pursued? Descartes devoted his most famous work to this question. (See the Ninth Reading.) One of the most fascinating, provocative, and elusive descriptions of the philosopher's way occurs in Plato's *Republic*, within the context of his discussion of the various stages of human apprehension and the various levels of objective reality.

The philosopher, according to Plato, possesses a mental power or skill, called "dialectic," whereby he apprehends the basic realities. Philosophy is thereby distinguished from all lesser modes of apprehension, including not only mere sense perception and opinion but also the model scientific discipline of mathematics. Where the mathematician proceeds by deductive logic from postulates which are accepted without further examination, the philosopher or dialectician goes beyond these assumptions to seek their ground in the first principles of reality.

Because its method is dialectic, philosophy is the cornerstone of mathematics and of all true sciences. Their very existence and value as knowledge depend on the method of a master science which transcends their special modes of inquiry. Philosophy, then, provides a comprehensive view of the whole of knowledge. It alone sees the unity of the sciences.

This view of philosophical method raises basic questions about the relation between philosophy and the sciences, and particularly about the relation between philosophy and mathematics—questions which are still critical today. It also sets the philosopher's special method and skill within the whole educational process, especially that "ascent from below" which, for Plato, marks the emergence of the true philosopher. This reading, then, discusses not only the method of philosophy but also the gradual steps in the philosopher's education, whereby he attains his special power and vision. Hence it provides one of the classical texts in the philosophy of education, the forerunner of a long line of distinguished discussions of education by the great philosophers.

Second Reading

I

The main theme of this reading is philosophical method. Plato deals here with the question of the special method of philosophy as contrasted with all other modes of knowledge, including that of the mathematical disciplines. He calls the philosopher's method "dialectic" and makes the attainment of dialectical skill the ultimate aim of his educational system.

To show us what philosophical method is, Plato presents the whole hierarchy of knowledge, which we have already considered in the First Reading. He makes use of the now-familiar distinctions between the sensible and intelligible realms, between becoming and being, and between opinion and knowledge. Now, however, a sharp distinction is made within the intelligible realm, between mathematical and philosophical knowledge, a distinction which serves to explain the special character of philosophical method.

Plato first specifies the peculiar method of philosophy in the famous "divided line" passage of Book VI, with which this reading begins. (See pp. 386d-388a.) What the parable of the cave presents in the form of myth, the divided line presents as a geometrical diagram. Like the blackboard aids used by the skillful classroom teacher, the divided line is a graphic device, intended to present clearly the various levels of human awareness, from unreflective imagination to pure philosophical knowledge. (See diagram, p. 22.)

The line is first divided into two unequal parts, representing the intelligible realm of ideas and the visible realm of material things. We may understand that the larger part represents the intelligible realm, and the smaller part the visible realm, so that the difference in quantity symbolizes a difference in quality:

The Divided Line

APPREHENSION OF
INTELLIGIBLE WORLD

KNOWLEDGE OF | FIRST PRINCIPLES

UNDERSTANDING OF | MATHEMATICAL OBJECTS

APPREHENSION OF
VISIBLE WORLD

BELIEF IN | VISIBLE OBJECTS

PERCEPTION OF | SHADOWS

the more, the higher; the less, the lower. Each of the two main
sections is again divided into subsections in the same ratio to
one another as that of the main sections; e.g., if the main sections are divided in a 2 to 1 ratio, the subsections within each
of the main parts are also divided in a 2 to 1 ratio. Thus the divided line represents a classical geometrical proportion. (See
p. 398a.)

The line and its four subsections, like the ascent from the
cave, represent graduated levels in the apprehension of reality, from the dimmest and most flickering to the clearest and
most certain. The lowest level is that of the perception of the
"shadows" or "reflections" of material things—that of mere
imagination or conjecture, which takes the copy for the real
thing. Just above this is the level of the natural and artificial
objects which are the material originals of the images of the
lower stage. This is the level of "belief" or "faith," in which particular things are apprehended but not the universal ideas of
which the particular things are imitations or approximations;
that is, the level in which horses, men, and vases are perceived
but not the ideas of "horse," "man," and "vase." Thus the relation between the two levels of the visible realm parallels that
between the visible and intelligible realms—"the copy is to the
original as the sphere of opinion is to the sphere of knowledge"
(p. 387a). The proportionate relation—qualitative as well as
quantitative—holds.

The intelligible world and its linear representation also
have a lower and an upper level. In examining them, we find
that the phrase just cited is misleading, for, precisely speaking,
there is an intermediate level between the two subsections of
"opinion" (corresponding to the visible world) and the top
level of pure knowledge. This intermediate level, between "belief" and "reason," is that of discursive thought or "understanding," and is best exemplified in the mathematical arts and sciences.

And the habit which is concerned with geometry and the cognate sciences I suppose that you would term understanding and not reason, as
being intermediate between opinion and reason. (p. 387d)

Plato points to two essential characteristics of mathematical
method which help us to understand what philosophical

method, in contrast, is. First, mathematics uses visible images—diagrams—to convey ideal forms and relations, e.g., triangles, circles, rectangles, lines. Secondly, mathematics proceeds from basic unexamined assumptions—"hypotheses"—such as the distinction between odd and even, to demonstrable conclusions. Mathematics, then, cannot be pure and perfect knowledge.

Although it deals with immaterial ideas, "which can only be seen with the eye of the mind" (p. 387c), mathematics is forced to make use of material forms and images in its demonstrations. And, although the mathematician proceeds from premises to conclusions with exemplary logical rigor, his premises are taken for granted and not examined with a view to discovering their foundations in the first principles of things. However clear and elegant its reasoning, mathematics is not grounded in the apprehension of ultimate reality. Looked at philosophically, its knowledge is precarious; for, to borrow a metaphor from Kierkegaard, the knot is not tied at the end of the thread.

On the highest level, the stage of "reason" or "intellect," represented by the top segment of the divided line, the knot is tied and knowledge is secure. The mind proceeds upward, from the hypotheses to the first principles which ground them, and then—and only then—it proceeds downward, through a careful step-by-step method, to demonstrative conclusions. The downward process is achieved without the aid of any sensible "crutches" (such as geometrical figures) and remains constantly in the realm of ideas.

And when I speak of the other division of the intelligible, you will understand me to speak of that other sort of knowledge which reason herself attains by the power of dialectic, using the hypotheses not as first principles, but only as hypotheses—that is to say, as steps and points of departure into a world which is above hypotheses, in order that she may soar beyond them to the first principle of the whole; and clinging to this and then to that which depends on this, by successive steps she descends again without the aid of any sensible object, from ideas, through ideas, and in ideas she ends. (p. 387c)

II

The key term in the above passage is "dialectic." It is through "the power of dialectic" that the mind apprehends ultimate reality or being. It is training in dialectic that constitutes the final stage in the education of the philosopher. What exactly does Plato mean by "dialectic"?

In its primary and most general sense, the term simply means "conversation." It was applied specifically to the kind of conversation in which Socrates discussed moral and philosophical questions. As "talk," dialectic involves the method of questions and answers to inquire into things. As mental awareness, it involves the apprehension of universal ideas through a careful process of logical discrimination and analysis. Through this dialectical procedure, the mind arrives at the synoptic vision of the unity behind the multiplicity of experience. Ultimately, then, dialectic becomes a conversation of the mind with itself.

For a vivid portrayal of dialectic, see the *Phaedrus*, where Socrates deals with "the comprehension of scattered particulars in one idea," and speaks of the dialectician as the "man who is able to see 'a One and Many.'" (See p. 134b-c.) For examples of the use of dialectic, see Plato's early dialogues which inquire into the nature of temperance, courage, piety, love, etc.

In the present reading, the meaning of dialectic is expounded within the context of the educational curriculum, which is intended to prepare the mind gradually for the synoptic vision of reality and the attainment of pure knowledge. (See pp. 391c-401d.) The preparatory studies comprise various branches of mathematics, to accustom the mind to withdraw from sensible particulars and to dwell among abstract ideas. The study of mathematics "converts" the mind and turns it away from the realm of becoming to the contemplation of being. The philosopher must first be a mathematician, "because he has to rise out of the sea of change and lay hold of true being" (p. 393c).

But mathematical studies are merely the prelude to "the hymn of dialectic." Only dialectic can attain the first principles, which provide the rational ground of knowledge and thereby provide the basis for the view of mathematics as a whole, and indeed for the grasp of the connections between all the sciences. Dialectic is the highest of all disciplines, "the coping-stone of the sciences" (p. 398c).

Then dialectic, and dialectic alone, goes directly to the first principle and is the only science which does away with hypotheses in order to make her ground secure; the eye of the soul, which is literally buried in an outlandish slough, is by her gentle aid lifted upwards; and she uses as handmaids and helpers in the work of conversion, the sciences which we have been discussing. (pp. 397d-398a)

Plato does not tell us directly what this wonderful power consists in. Indeed, Socrates tells his interlocutor, Glaucon, that what dialectic is can be communicated only to someone who is already proficient in the mathematical disciplines and hence has attained the power of dialectic which comes through such studies. But we are not left completely baffled, for Plato points out certain characteristics and results of this mysterious power, discipline, or science.

Dialectic, he says, is completely intellectual, without any admixture of sensible images, and proceeds by the light of pure reason alone. It is a methodical procedure for comprehending the "true existence," "nature," or "essence" of each thing. Through dialectic the thinker "arrives at the perception of the absolute good"—the basic idea at the root of all existence. (See pp. 397a-b, 397d, 398b.)

The result is a grounded and reasoned knowledge which can be defended under the crossfire of critical examination. The dialectician, in contrast to the mathematician, can "give and take a reason" (p. 397a). Dialectic involves "the greatest skill in asking and answering questions" (p. 398c). But this is not the tricky logic-chopping and "eristic" contention which was made notorious by the Sophists and is often displayed by callow youths eager to show off their argumentative skill (See pp. 400d, 401a.) Dialectic, we recall, is the road to the apprehension of being—what really is. Hence, the withstanding of the cross-examination demonstrates the possession of solid knowledge, based on proper procedures. For instance, as regards the idea of the good:

Until the person is able to abstract and define rationally the idea of good, and unless he can run the gauntlet of all objections, and is ready to disprove them, not by appeals to opinion, but to absolute truth, never faltering at any step of the argument—unless he can do all this, you would say that he knows neither the idea of good nor any other good; he apprehends only a shadow, if anything at all, which is given by opinion and not by science . . . (p. 398b)

See also the passage in the *Meno* (p. 177a) where Socrates distinguishes his cool, logical defense against a philosopher of the "eristic and antagonistic sort" from the gentle persuasion "in the dialectician's vein" which is proper among friends. (See also the *Theaetetus,* p. 526a-b.) The aim of dialectic is to know the truth and convert one's own soul or that of an interlocutor to the true vision of being—not to win an argument.

Finally, the distinguishing mark of the skillful dialectician is his capacity to comprehend all the sciences in their relation to one another and to being itself.

. . . the capacity for such knowledge is the great criterion of dialectical talent: the comprehensive mind is always the dialectical. (p. 399d)

III

If we glance again at Plato's suggested curriculum for the development of the philosopher, we get a clearer picture of what he considers the essential characteristics of true knowledge and the divergence of the various arts and sciences from this norm. In the first place, reiterating a constant theme of *The Republic,* he eliminates poetry and music, for they have psychological and ethical effects but provide no knowledge. Secondly, he rejects all useful studies, including not only the "degrading" technical skills but also the productive arts in general and the applied sciences. It is the useless, not the useful, purpose of mathematics that earns it a high place on the ladder of knowledge—unless by "useful" we mean what tends to the beautiful and the good. (See pp. 394c, 396d.) It is the "useless studies"—in the ordinary sense of "useless"—that "draw the soul from becoming to being" (p. 391c), not the disciplines that get things done and made.

. . . for the arts in general are concerned with the desires or opinions of men, or are cultivated with a view to production and construction, or for the preservation of such productions and constructions . . . (p. 397d)

Thirdly, true knowledge has for its object the immaterial, the invisible, the insensible—what is perceived by the mind, not what is seen by the eye. Hence, the motions of the heavenly bodies, although the most regular and harmonious of observable motions, are not the proper objects of knowledge and serve only to give a rough image of perfect motion. The particulars of sense experience are not, and cannot be, the subject matter of true science.

. . . that knowledge only which is of being and of the unseen can make the soul look upwards, and whether a man gapes at the heavens or blinks on the ground, seeking to learn some particular of sense, I would deny that he can learn, for nothing of that sort is matter of science; his soul is looking downwards, not upwards, whether his way to knowledge is by water or by land, whether he floats, or only lies on his back. (p. 395d)

The true astronomer in Plato's sense, concerned with perfect motions and speeds, could not possibly imagine that

. . . things that are material and visible can also be eternal and subject to no deviation—that would be absurd; and it is equally absurd to take so much pains in investigating their exact truth. (p. 396a)

Similarly, in the study of harmony, it is not what is heard by the ear that is essential but what is grasped by the mind. Hence Plato opposes not only the empirical harmonists, whom he pictures as wasting their time listening for "condensed" and "intermediate" notes and as "setting their ears before their understanding" (p. 396d), but also the Pythagorean philosophers, whose understanding of the harmonies is based on the limited range of human auditory experience.

. . . they investigate the numbers of the harmonies which are heard, but they never attain to problems—that is to say, they never reach the natural harmonies of number, or reflect why some numbers are harmonious and others not. (p. 396d)

It is such basic problems and the integral connectedness of their solutions that constitute true knowledge. Hence, in Plato's vision, astronomy, harmony, mathematics, and other traditional sciences, if conceived in this transcendental sense, and under the supreme direction of dialectic, would be organic parts of philosophical knowledge.

IV

Readers who are interested in further pursuing Plato's inquiry into the nature of knowledge and the way the mind attains it are invited to read the *Theaetetus*. (See pp. 512-550.) This dialogue provides an acute investigation of the problems

we have encountered in the first two readings. Unlike *The Republic*, which puts forth a positive doctrine of the nature and
objects of knowledge, the *Theaetetus* is a negative piece which
criticizes various inadequate theories of knowledge. It indicates
what knowledge may be by showing us what it is not, but
never tells us directly what its nature and objects are.

Among the various suggested theories which are challenged
are that knowledge is sense perception, that it is true opinion
(i.e., the belief that what is, is, without the knowledge of why
it is what it is), or that it is true opinion plus some "account"
(such as a breakdown into elements or essential characteristics). In discussing the first theory, Socrates skillfully refutes
Protagoras' doctrine that "man is the measure of all things";
that is, that the individual's sense perception is the measure of
objective reality.

An interesting aspect of the dialogue, from the viewpoint of
our present discussion, is that two of the interlocutors are famous mathematicians—Theodorus and Theaetetus—and some of
the illustrations are taken from mathematical concepts. Theaetetus is credited with discovering the basic principles of solid
geometry, which are expounded in Book XIII of Euclid's *Elements* and which Plato considers an essential part of the mathematical curriculum in *The Republic*. (See p. 395a-c.) It is this
great mathematician, shown in the dialogue as a promising
young man, whom Plato chose as Socrates' partner in the dialectical investigation of the nature of knowledge. Thus mathematics and philosophy are intimately engaged in a dialogue
which provides an excellent example of dialectic at work, and
on the very problem of knowledge itself.

V

*What kind of knowledge does the divided line com-
municate?*

In the divided line, Plato gives us what amounts to a geometrical diagram of human knowledge. Yet in his explanation of the line, he says that the use of such figures is a sign
of the inferior level of mathematics as compared with that of
pure knowledge. We see again that Plato does not hesitate to

use a form of presentation which he judges inferior in the apprehension of reality—just as he used poetic fiction in the parable of the cave—in order to communicate the deepest and most inexpressible truth.

The question naturally arises as to just how seriously Plato intends us to take this diagram. The mathematician's circles and squares supposedly approximate the absolute circle and the absolute square. Are we then to take the divided line as an accurate reflection of the stages of human knowledge and of the levels of reality with which they deal? Are there just these four basic levels and are they related in a geometrical proportion? Is reality so constituted that it, as well as the modes of apprehending it, must be expressible with mathematical regularity?

Or is the divided line just a teaching device, not intended as a faithful "likeness" of the levels of knowledge and reality, but intended to awaken awareness of the various gradations between the lowest and highest levels? Is it, for Plato himself, merely a bold hypothesis, a working sketch to stimulate and be modified by further inquiry? Is it the continuity or the segmentation of the line, or both, which is being emphasized?

Finally, we must consider how adequately diagrams can express philosophical truths. Is one picture worth a thousand words in helping us to grasp basic ideas? Which mode of expression do you find most communicative: the parable of the cave, the divided line, or the "straight" conversation between Socrates and his interlocutors? To which subsection of the line does poetic fiction belong?

What does Plato mean by "reason" or "intellect"?

At the top of the human modes of apprehension, Plato puts a faculty or state of mind called *nous* in the original Greek text. Its primary sense is simply "mind"; its secondary meanings are "purpose" and "meaning." Its sense in Plato's dialogues is subtle and complicated, to the point of being almost untranslatable. Our translator uses the terms "reason" and "intellect." Whatever the term used to approximate the meaning of *nous*, it is meant to convey the mental act or state by which the first principles of reality are grasped.

This supreme act or state is contrasted with the next higher stage of discursive understanding or thought, and is intimately associated with the dialectical process. Is *nous* (reason or intellect), then, intuitive vision? If so, of what is it a vision? Plato says it grasps "first principles" or "the first principle." Are these the same as the "ideas" dealt with in the First Reading? Is *the* first principle the same as "the idea of the good," the basic reality upon which all else is founded?

Nous may be the immediate grasp or vision of the first principles of reality. Nevertheless, as Plato presents it, it requires a long process of education, all the way into middle age. Fifteen years of training in mathematics and dialectics, plus another fifteen years of practical experience, precede the vision of the good in Plato's scheme of education. The key question in the present context is this—how is dialectic associated with *nous?*

How is dialectic associated with "reason" (nous)?

The immediate vision of first things is attained through the power of dialectic. It is the dialectician "who attains a conception of the essence of each thing" (p. 398b) and who arrives at the idea of the good. How does the dialectician go behind the hypotheses from which the mathematician starts but leaves unexamined? Is the dialectician's way inductive, as opposed to the deductive way of the mathematician? Does he meditate on obvious and commonly known ideas, raising his mind gradually to higher and higher levels of universal ideas, through some kind of inductive or intuitive process? What other ideas besides the good belong among the highest? Would the ideas of unity and of being belong there?

What kind of reasoning is involved in the "downward" process of dialectic from the first principles to the hypotheses? Is *nous* involved in the comprehensive, synoptic grasp attributed to dialectic, whereby it sees the various branches of knowledge as a whole? Is it plausible that we can go from the grasp of the highest level of abstraction (for instance, the idea of the one, of unity) to meaningful knowledge of the special sciences?

Fragments of the old Greek comedy ridicule the attempt of Plato's students and colleagues at the Academy to classify plants and animals. Would this be the proper pursuit for a dialectician, for a man who has *nous?* Where do biology and other natural sciences belong on the divided line? Where do the purified, abstract sciences of astronomy and harmony, envisioned by Plato, belong?

What is the relation between philosophy and mathematics?

Plato alternately praises mathematics as an essential discipline in preparing the mind to grasp transcendent reality and decries it as a species of ignorance and mere dreaming. (See p. 397d.) Indeed, most mathematicians, he says, are incapable of reasoning in the dialectical sense. (See p. 397a.)

There is no doubt that Plato had a high regard for mathematics and considered it the model discipline for philosophical inquiry, insofar as it dealt with ideal objects and did so with logical rigor. Measurement, proportion, and logical connection were for him essential qualities of knowledge, since they reflect the structure of reality. All accounts indicate that mathematics was central in the curriculum at Plato's Academy. (For the influence of the mathematical philosophy of the Pythagoreans on Plato's thought, see Aristotle's *Metaphysics*, Vol. 8, pp. 505a-506a.)

His criticism of mathematics as it existed in his own time was that it was all right as far as it went but that it did not go far enough. It failed to examine the basic assumptions on which its method was based. It indicated what systematic inquiry and logic could attain, but it was not systematic or logical enough. To achieve systematic perfection, dialectic, with its probing of first principles, is required; hence, Plato envisioned a reformed and purified mathematics, made possible by the work of the dialectician.

But a good deal of reciprocal influence is involved in Plato's presentation. Mathematics forms the dialectician and inspires him to search for the perfect science. It also furnishes the model for natural science, which Plato sees as a kind of mathematical physics. The physical science of astronomy becomes a pure geometry of the motions of bodies in space.

In showing the inadequacy of mathematics as compared

with dialectic, Plato seems to limit its mental procedure to deductive logic, proceeding from premises to conclusions. But does he not also suggest an intuitive grasp by the mathematician of such basic ideas as "greatness" and "smallness"? Are the basic mathematical ideas attainable by sense perception or deduction? Does geometry require an intuitive grasp of spatial forms and relations?

For some examples of the mathematician's apprehension of general ideas, see the discussion in the *Theaetetus,* p. 515a-c.

The following questions are designed to help you test the thoroughness of your reading. Each question is to be answered by giving a page or pages of the reading assignment. Answers will be found on page 301 of this Reading Plan.

1 What other use besides the philosophical does Plato admit for mathematics?

2 What are the two reasons why the mathematical sciences are so undeveloped?

3 What evils does the study of dialectic introduce?

4 At what age is the student of philosophy ready for the vision of the absolute good?

5 What mathematical operation is necessary in all the arts and sciences?

6 Why is gymnastic rejected as part of the philosopher's education?

7 What are the two kinds of objects of sense, in relation to thought?

ARISTOTLE

Metaphysics

Book I

Vol. 8, pp. 499-511

The very title of this work has provided the name for one of the main branches of philosophical inquiry— the study of the underlying principles of things. The book is itself one of the classical examples of such a study and has had an important and lasting influence on Western thought. Any serious inquirer into the realm of metaphysics must take it seriously, even when he feels compelled to reject its basic arguments.

Book I of this classical work is of interest to us for both historical and philosophical reasons. This introduction to the study of the principles—literally the "firsts" or "beginnings"—of things is also an introduction to the historical beginnings of Greek philosophy, and thereby of Western thought. Thus Book I launches us on two adventures—the quest for the first principles of things and the discovery of the thought of men whose writings have been almost lost to us. Names which have acquired a legendary, almost mythical character—Thales, Anaximander, Xenophanes, Heraclitus, Pythagoras, etc.—now take on substance as Aristotle follows the thought of these fathers of Western philosophy about the basic structure of the universe.

Also of interest to us in this reading is the dramatic encounter between Aristotle and Plato, as seen through Aristotle's eyes. Plato's greatest student here essays a description and criticism of the thought of his immortal master. The adequacy and justice of Aristotle's presentation of Plato's thought has been the subject of much debate in the millennia since it was first made. We have here a document of one of the first, and perhaps the most famous, of all the encounters between great philosophers of divergent views in the history of Western philosophy.

I

The ancient term "metaphysics" has taken on misleading connotations in our time. Many people identify it with the mystical or occult; indeed, works about the latter subjects are often to be found on shelves labeled "Metaphysics" in second-hand bookstores. The term has also taken on a pejorative sense—especially with persons who plume themselves on having a modern, scientific attitude—as denoting a bogus science, dealing with empty generalities and consisting of mere wind.

Actually, so far as we know, the term originated accidentally, as a convenient editorial designation. The editors who arranged Aristotle's writings after his death placed a number of treatises on basic philosophical themes—what Aristotle called "first philosophy"—immediately after the work on natural philosophy, entitled *Physics*. Hence these treatises were grouped under the classification *ta meta ta physika*, "the [writings] after the *Physics*," whence the title *Metaphysics*. At one time this work consisted of ten treatises or "books"; the addition of other treatises considered to belong with them brought the work to the fourteen books which it now comprises.

A glance at the table of contents, however, indicates that the transcendent meaning which the term "metaphysics" has taken on—whether with added laudatory or invidious connotations or not—is far from accidental. What may have originally been a mere term of convenience to aid editorial housekeeping has turned out to have a definite meaning. Since these treatises deal mainly with the reality which underlies all things —with "the study of being as such"—the term metaphysics has naturally assumed the sense of what is before or above the natural or physical realm. Aristotle even calls this science "theology" at one point. (See p. 548b.) Metaphysics, he says, is "the highest science"; it is "first philosophy."

The present reading, Book I, introduces us to the study of this science. It is labeled "Book A" in the Greek manuscript and obviously belongs first in this collection of treatises. We might entitle it "Aristotle's Introduction to Metaphysics." We might also call it "Aristotle's History of Early Greek Philosophy," for it provides one of the few ancient accounts of the pre-Socratic philosophers, as well as a critical interpretation of Plato's philosophy. If we do so, however, we should note that this is a philosophical history of philosophy, which assumes a certain view of what philosophy is and what the first principles of reality are. And Aristotle is not reticent about letting us know what his views on these things are almost from the beginning. The main purpose of his history is to compare the thought of previous thinkers about first principles with his own, and to show that his are the most complete and consistent.

II

Aristotle begins with a discussion of the nature, value, and origin of wisdom. (See Ch. 1-2.) He fits the highest and most abstract knowledge within the context of nature and of social development, preceding his philosophical history of philosophy with a natural and social history of philosophy. "All men by nature desire to know," he begins, and then points to our delight in sense perception and to the role of memory in learning—both among men and among the other animals. Beyond this primary stage comes "experience," an awareness derived from repeated instances of sense perception. And beyond "experience" come the specifically human activities of art and science. Thus human knowledge and skill are set in the context of other and lesser modes of apprehension among living organisms.

Art, for Aristotle, is one of the highest activities and virtues of man. It implies a kind of wisdom, for the artist acts on the basis of his knowledge of the general patterns of classes of things, of "universals," as opposed to the man of experience, who acts on the basis of his experience of particular instances without understanding the general patterns involved (e.g., the skilled physician as opposed to the practical healer).

Aristotle then goes on to show a gradual development in human history from the stage where the useful arts met the urgent life needs of men, to the stage where the non-useful arts fulfilled their needs for recreation and enjoyment, and finally to the stage where the abstract sciences, such as mathematics, emerged. He sees a gradual rise in value and wisdom from the most useful to the least useful pursuits. It is an essential characteristic of wisdom, in his view, that it is utterly disinterested, without any practical interest whatsoever, and pursued purely for itself. Hence, though the artist is held to be wiser than the mere empiric, the man of science is held to be wiser than the artist; for art is a productive activity, while science is a theoretical activity, and the latter is the higher. Wisdom in the full sense is defined as the theoretical knowledge of the first principles or causes of things.

At this point, Aristotle refers to common notions or opinions for support, as he often does in his writings. The above definition of wisdom, he says, corresponds with the common opinion of the nature of wisdom—that it is the knowledge of all things *in principle,* and the knowledge of what is most difficult to learn, most exact, most instructive, most desirable for its own sake, and most authoritative. Wisdom as he has defined it is all these things, he says, because first principles or causes are the basic, simplest, most abstract and most knowable objects of knowledge and include the ends of all things, including the supreme end or good.

Such knowledge, concerned with transcendent objects, may seem abstract and abstruse, but it originates in a simple human state and need—ignorance and the need to know—in a word, *wonder.*

For it is owing to their wonder that men both now begin and at first began to philosophize; they wondered originally at the obvious difficulties, then advanced little by little and stated difficulties about the greater matters, e.g. about the phenomena of the moon and those of the sun and of the stars, and about the genesis of the universe. And a man who is puzzled and wonders thinks himself ignorant (whence even the lover of myth is in a sense a lover of Wisdom, for the myth is composed of won-

ders); therefore since they philosophized in order to escape from ignorance, evidently they were pursuing science in order to know, and not for
any utilitarian end. (pp. 500d-501a)

Knowledge and understanding of the causes of things remove this state of ignorance—they abolish wonder.

For all men begin, as we said, by wondering that things are as they are,
as they do about self-moving marionettes, or about the solstices or the in-
commensurability of the diagonal of a square with the side; for it seems
wonderful to all who have not yet seen the reason, that there is a thing
which cannot be measured even by the smallest unit. But we must end in
the contrary and, according to the proverb, the better state, as is the case
in these instances too when men learn the cause; for there is nothing
which would surprise a geometer so much as if the diagonal turned out
to be commensurable. (p. 501b-c)

III

After the prologue on wisdom in Chapters 1-2, Aristotle
launches immediately into a discussion of the first principles or
causes of things, which are the objects of this highest form of
knowledge. The remainder of Book I (Ch. 3-10) is devoted to
this discussion, for the thought of early philosophers and the
criticism of their views is presented in terms of the first causes.

Aristotle begins by setting down his own view that there
are four "original causes," or four senses in which we say that
things are or come to be what they are: (1) the "substance" or
"essence" of a thing—the *formal* cause; (2) its material substratum—the *material* cause; (3) the source or agent whereby
it comes into being—the *efficient* cause; and (4) the purpose or
end for which it comes into being—the *final* cause.

We may take as the simplest example of the operation of
the four causes a piece of furniture, such as a bed or a chair.
The formal cause is its definition, what it is; the material cause
is the wood, metal, or other substance from which it is made;
the efficient cause is the craftsman or the craftsmanship by
which it is made; and the final cause is resting or sitting. The
first or formal cause, the definition, and the final cause, the purpose, obviously coincide in this case. Among natural objects,
the final cause is actually being what the definition states a certain class of things to be; the final cause of a man, a dog, or a

flower is simply being a man, a dog, or a flower, in all essential respects.

For more complex examples of the four causes, examine the passages in the *Physics* to which Aristotle refers. (See pp. 271a-c and 275a-c.)

Aristotle then invites us to check the correctness of his view of the causes of things with those of previous philosophers.

We have studied these causes sufficiently in our work on nature, but yet let us call to our aid those who have attacked the investigation of being and philosophized about reality before us. For obviously they too speak of certain principles and causes; to go over their views, then, will be of profit to the present inquiry, for we shall either find another kind of cause, or be more convinced of the correctness of those which we now maintain. (p. 501c-d)

First in this survey of Aristotle's predecessors come those early Greek philosophers who sought the basic principle of things in a material element, such as water, air, fire, or earth. Thales, for example, thought that water was the primal eternal substance from which all things arose and to which they returned; and Heraclitus thought it was fire; while Empedocles thought all four elements were the original causes of things. But all such views, according to Aristotle, only accounted for the material out of which things are made without telling us why or how they come into existence. The existence of a chair, for instance, is not explained by pointing to wood as the cause; for, while wood or some other material is necessary in the making of a chair, it does not by itself account for the working up of the material, for the productive change which transforms wood into a chair.

Realizing the inadequacy of explanation by material causes alone, thinkers sought for the efficient causes—"that from which comes the beginning of the movement" (p. 502c), that is, the principle which brings about the change. They saw that the goodness and beauty, as well as the existence, of things must be accounted for by mental rather than material principles. Anaxagoras, for example, saw an immanent reason (*logos*) present in all things, as the cause of the order of the world and of the movement and change of things. Empedocles, on the other hand, found two efficient causes, love (or friendship) and strife, in order to account for both the good and the evil in things. Such thinkers then sought to account for both "the matter and the source of the movement" (p. 503b), for both the material and the efficient causes, but in a rather confused and inconsistent way, in Aristotle's opinion.

The next philosophers in Aristotle's survey sought the basis of reality in far more abstract and abstruse principles than material or mental factors. The Pythagoreans, for example (called "the Italian school" because Pythagoras established his school in southern Italy), considered mathematical objects and relations—such as numbers and ratios—to be the first principles of things. They believed that all things—including justice and reason—can be expressed numerically. And they applied the mathematical relations and harmonies which they discovered in the musical scale to the heavenly bodies, seeking ratios and proportions in all things. (Some Pythagoreans also set up pairs of contraries as the first principles of things, such as odd and even, one and many, good and bad, etc.) Aristotle credits the Pythagoreans with discerning the material and the formal causes, since they "consider that number is the principle both as matter for things and as forming both their modifications and their permanent states . . ." (p. 504b). He thinks, however, that they were too simple-minded in treating of the formal cause and that they "defined superficially."

Another important group of ancient philosophers believed that the universe consists of a single unchanging substance. In denying the reality of change, becoming, and passing away, Aristotle notes, they avoided the need to discern the efficient cause of things. The most important of the "monistic" schools were the Eleatics, so called after Elea in Italy, where the school was centered. Parmenides, the greatest of the Eleatics (after whom Plato named one of his most difficult and important dialogues), held that only ultimate reality or being—the One—exists necessarily and that nothing else (that is, particular things) really exists. However, taking account of our actual experience of multiplicity, he qualified his original view to allow that what is one *by definition* is more than one *in our sense experience*. And he had recourse to two material principles—hot and cold or fire and earth—to account for existence and non-existence (unity and plurality) respectively. Aristotle believes then that Parmenides, in spite of his monistic doctrine, had some idea of an efficient cause. (See p. 502c.) For a recurrence of monism in modern times, see the Tenth Reading on Spinoza's *Ethics*.

Finally, Aristotle comes to the views of his teacher, the renowned Plato, the subject of our first two readings. Plato's philosophical influences, according to Aristotle, were Heraclitus, who held that sensible things are always changing and are hence unknowable; Socrates, who sought the universal concepts in the ethical rather than the physical realm; and the Pythagoreans. Heraclitus' picture of constant flux in sensible things and Socrates' search for "common definitions" led Plato to seek for universals in non-sensible things—in transcendent "ideas" or "forms."[1] In his view, it is through participation in the ideas or forms that the particular things of the sensible world exist. Thus, for Plato, the ideas or forms are the causes of things—corresponding to the formal causes in Aristotle's analysis.

As for the influence of the Pythagoreans, Aristotle thinks that what Plato calls "participation" is just another name for what the Pythagoreans called "imitation," when they said that things exist by imitating numbers. Plato agreed with the Pythagoreans that numbers are the causes of things. However, he put them in a realm intermediate between ideal and sensible things, and considered them as existing apart from sensible things, as opposed to the Pythagoreans, who considered numbers to be identical with sensible things. Aristotle attributes Plato's differences with the Pythagoreans to his training in dialectic and his search for common definitions. Nevertheless, says Aristotle, Plato also was able to account only for the material and the formal causes of things and had nothing to say about efficient and final causes.

[1] The terms "idea" and "form" are used interchangeably in Plato's dialogues and in Aristotle's account of his doctrine. "Idea" comes from the Greek term *idea*, meaning "nature," "kind," "sort." "Form" comes from the Greek term *eidos*, meaning "form," "shape," "figure," and also "kind," "sort." Either term refers to the objective essence or universal concept of a thing.

IV

Aristotle follows the survey of the views of his predecessors (Ch. 3-6) with a concluding judgment (Ch. 7) and a further criticism of the materialists, the Pythagoreans, and the Platonists (Ch. 8-9).

His concluding judgment is that preceding philosophers have discerned one or two of the four causes he has listed, and that none of them has indicated any cause beyond these four. "All evidently have some inkling of *them* [the four causes], though only vaguely" (p. 506b), he says rather patronizingly. Those who saw fire, earth, water, or air as causes recognized the material cause; those who viewed reason, love, or strife as a first principle recognized the efficient cause; and those who saw the ideas or forms as the basis of things recognized the formal cause. No one, however, says Aristotle, recognized the final cause—that for the sake of which things exist or come to be.

His main criticism of the materialists is that they can account only for perceptible and changing things, and that they fail to account adequately even for these, since they tend to ignore the efficient as well as the formal causes of things. An adequate view must account for both sensible and non-sensible, or intelligible, reality.

But these thinkers are, after all, at home only in arguments about generation and destruction and movement; for it is practically only of this sort of substance that they seek the principles and the causes. But those who extend their vision to all things that exist, and of existing things suppose some to be perceptible and others not perceptible, evidently study both classes, which is all the more reason why one should devote some time to seeing what is good in their views and what bad from the standpoint of the inquiry we have now before us. (pp. 507d-508a)

As for the Pythagoreans, they found their principles in nonsensible things and used them to account for physical events and phenomena. Yet, like the materialists, they identified reality with the physical, perceptible world. Actually, though, says Aristotle, their mathematical principles are better suited to account for imperceptible things—"the higher realms of reality"— than perceptible ones. Their principles do not really explain movement and change. Also it seems irrational to view numerical relations and properties as the basis of all reality and then to limit them to those numbers actually present in the world. Furthermore, it is not clear whether the numbers supposedly expressed in such abstractions as opinion, opportunity, injustice, etc., are the same as the numbers embodied in the material universe. Aristotle's observation that "mathematics has come to be identical with philosophy for modern thinkers" (p. 510c) is undoubtedly meant invidiously and was probably directed against contemporary Platonists or against Plato himself.

Finally, in Chapter 9, the longest chapter in Book I, Aristotle criticizes the views of Plato and the Platonists—"those who posit the Ideas as causes" (p. 508c). His main criticism of the theory of ideas is that it sets up two worlds which duplicate one another—the world of intelligible and the world of sensible objects.

For the Forms are practically equal to—or not fewer than—the things, in trying to explain which these thinkers proceeded from them to the Forms. For to each thing there answers an entity which has the same name and exists apart from the substances, and so also in the case of all other groups there is a one over many, whether the many are in this world or are eternal. (p. 508c-d)

Thus, for the Platonists, the universal idea of *man* exists apart from individual men. This, says Aristotle, is an unnecessary "doubling" of things, which seems to require a third entity to unify the ideal and empirical "doubles"—a "third man" to connect the idea of man and the individual man.

Another major objection to the Platonic ideas is that they fail to account for motion or change and do not contribute anything to our knowledge of sensible things. The reason for this, says Aristotle, is that they are purely transcendent and not at all immanent. If the ideas were in the particulars, as whiteness is in a white object, then we might say that the ideas are the causes of things. But this is not the case with the Platonic ideas.

Aristotle also objects strongly to the Platonic theory of "participation," which views the ideas as "patterns" or archetypes in which the particular things "share." This, says Aristotle testily, "is to use empty words and poetical metaphors" (p. 509c).

Where, he asks, is the efficient cause, the agent that uses the ideas as patterns or models for the individual things? There must be "something to originate movement" (p. 509d), so that things may come into being. And just look at all of the ideas or forms that would have to serve as patterns for a single object! For instance, in the case of man, the ideas of "animal" and "two-footed" as well as the idea of "man" would be needed. Furthermore, the ideas are both patterns and copies at the same time, for a form may be both the pattern for sensible things and at the same time a copy of a more general form; the species, for example, may be the pattern for the individual instances, and also the copy of the genus which includes it and other species.

All in all, Aristotle asserts, this is a confusing and unsatisfactory account of the causes of things. He lists some two dozen objections to the Platonic theory of ideas in Chapter 9. The interested reader may note them down, group them in various classifications, and judge which are the most important and cogent.

V

The reader is again cautioned that Aristotle's history of early Greek philosophy is intended to demonstrate that Aristotle's view of the first principles of reality is correct, or most adequate, and that previous views are fragmentary, preliminary approaches to it.

> It is evident, then, even from what we have said before, that all men seem to seek the causes named in the *Physics*, and that we cannot name any beyond these; but they seek these vaguely; and though in a sense they have all been described before, in a sense they have not been described at all. For the earliest philosophy is, on all subjects, like one who lisps, since it is young and in its beginnings. (p. 511c)

Many scholars who are versed in early Greek philosophy assert that Aristotle is often inaccurate and frequently unjust in his descriptions and judgments of the thought of his predecessors. Since the early philosophical writings are lacking in *Great Books of the Western World*, and in any case are so fragmentary that special skills are needed to interpret them adequately, we must reserve judgment on the correctness of Aristotle's survey of the pre-Socratic philosophers.

When he speaks of Plato's views, though, the case is quite

different. For Plato's writings are available to us, and we have already considered some essential aspects of Plato's thought. We should be able then to make some judgment, however tentative and uncertain, about the adequacy of Aristotle's description and criticism of Plato's views.

Before we do so, however, we may find some of the details in Aristotle's philosophical career interesting, even though they may seem more paradoxical than illuminating at times. The central fact of Aristotle's philosophical preparation is that he entered Plato's school, the Academy at Athens, when he was a young man and remained there for twenty years—which were also the last twenty years of Plato's life. Plato was his teacher and his friend, whom he held in high regard. (See the quotation from Aristotle's elegy on Plato cited in the Biographical Note, p. v.) Plato for his part praised Aristotle's mental attainments and applications, calling him "the intellect" and "the reader." There is also a story that Plato compared him to a colt that kicks its mother, indicating some tension. Still there seems to be no evidence that Aristotle's role at the Academy was that of a dissident and rebellious student.

It is quite likely that he began as a thoroughgoing Platonist, accepting the essential tenets of Plato's thought. Some indication of this is given by the fragments of early writings, attributed to Aristotle (written in dialogue form) which reflect Plato's views on a number of important points, including the belief in ideas as the first principles of things. As time went on, and particularly after Plato's death and the departure of Aristotle from the Academy, it is probable that the student developed views which differed considerably from those of his great teacher. Eventually Aristotle returned to Athens to found a school of his own, the Lycaeum, to become himself the master of gifted students and the head of a community of scholars.

On the one hand, then, Aristotle was Plato's student, and experienced with him that intimate contact which Plato considered essential for the teaching of the deepest things in philosophy. Aristotle never forgot this intimate relation and dialogue; indeed, he includes himself among the Platonists in the very writings in which he is criticizing salient Platonic views. See, for example, the curious and baffling use of "we" in the passage on p. 510b-c, which some translators translate as "we Platonists." See also the reference to "our belief in the Ideas" on p. 509a.

On the other hand, Aristotle undoubtedly had his own specific cast of mind, and particularly an appreciation of and interest in empirical events and objects. This grew increasingly stronger as he matured. His later period at the Lycaeum is marked by systematically organized research in natural and human history; and his whole philosophy, as is evident from the titles of the works included in Volumes 8-9, demonstrated an open and respectful attitude toward empirical phenomena as objects of knowledge. His basic tendency was to seek for general ideas or universals in the empirical world and to be repelled by the theory of a separate realm of ideas, above and apart from concrete actuality. And the process of change, especially the generation and passing away of things, was a central concern for him; he considered inadequate any philosophy that fails to account for this process satisfactorily. He never, however, lost the metaphysical emphasis he got from Plato, and thus could still consider himself a Platonist in his own way, one of the "we" in "we Platonists."

Thus we may say that Aristotle was Plato's student, the greatest of all, and that at the same time he was his own man. He himself put it somewhat differently in the *Nicomachean Ethics,* when he had to take issue with Plato's idea of the universal good.

. . . such an inquiry is made an uphill one by the fact that the Forms have been introduced by friends of our own. Yet it would perhaps be thought to be better, indeed to be our duty, for the sake of maintaining the truth even to destroy what touches us closely, especially as we are philosophers or lovers of wisdom; for, while both are dear, piety requires us to honour truth above our friends. (Vol. 9, p. 341b)

VI

Why is an analysis of causes important in understanding the world?

Ordinarily the term "cause" means for us either the agent or the agency which produces an effect—the *efficient* cause—or the purpose or end for which a thing or event comes into being—the *final* cause. Both of these answer the question "Why?" and the first also answers the modern scientific question, "How?" But it is difficult for us to understand the use of the term "cause" as regards matter and form. How can matter be said to be the "cause" of anything, when it lacks the efficient and purposive capacities which we commonly ascribe to causes? And how can the idea or form of anything be said to be its cause, except insofar as it is contained in the final cause as the end in view?

W. D. Ross, the noted British Aristotelian scholar, who edited the translation of Aristotle's works included in this set, has noted this modern difficulty as follows:

> It will be noted that of Aristotle's four causes only two, the efficient and the final, answer to the natural meaning of "cause" in English. We think of matter and form not as relative to an event which they cause but as static elements which analysis discovers in a complex thing. This is because we think of cause as that which is both necessary and sufficient to produce a certain effect. But for Aristotle none of the four causes is sufficient [by itself] to produce an event; and speaking generally we may say that in his view all four are necessary for the production of any effect. We have, then, to think of his "causes" as conditions necessary but not separately sufficient to account for the existence of a thing; and if we look at them in this way we shall cease to be surprised that matter and form are called causes. For certainly without them no natural thing can be or come into being.[2]

The term "principle" perhaps gives us more adequate sense than "cause" of what Aristotle is seeking—the basic factors which account for *what* things are or *that* they are. Looking at the events and objects apprehended in human experience, including the whole of nature, art, and human life, Aristotle finds four main kinds of basic principles or conditions for their being or coming into being—the formal, material, efficient, and final causes. For a thing to be and to be just what it is requires a certain kind of matter, a specific form, an act or actor that brings it into being, and an end or good which it serves by being and by being what it is. All these answer the question

[2] W. D. Ross, *Aristotle* (New York: Meridian Books, Inc., 1959), pp. 75-76.

"Why?" Understood in their totality, they afford a rational view of the universe.

Aristotle says in Book II, Chapter 7, of the *Physics* that the formal, efficient, and final causes often coincide in natural things, especially in the reproduction of organic species. Can we say, then, that "man" is the formal, efficient, and final causes of human reproduction? If so, in what sense do we use the word "man" in each case? And what is the material cause of human reproduction?

In the case of a statue, can we also say that the formal, efficient, and final causes are identical or "coincide"? We have seen how this can be said of the formal and final causes. How would the formal idea and final aim of the statue act as the impelling power in artistic creation?

Is it true that Plato has nothing to say about efficient and final causes?

Let us begin by looking at some selected passages from Plato's dialogues in Volume 7. Taking first the paragraph on page 124b-c in that volume (from the *Phaedrus*), we see that Plato ascribes the power of beginning motion in other things to the soul, which is self-moved and unbegotten. Turning next to the passage on creation in the *Timaeus* (pp. 447b-488a), we find that Plato states that all things that come into being must be created by something or someone outside it, an "artificer." In the case of the creation of the world, the divine artificer makes the world in the image of a perfect pattern, intending "that all things should be good" and to establish order in things. Again in the *Sophist* (pp. 577b-578b), Plato speaks of creation in its two modes, human and divine, defining as "creative" that power "which causes things to exist, not previously existing," which is a divine power in the case of natural things and a human power in the case of works of art. Nature is created by "a divine reason and knowledge," not from "some spontaneous and unintelligent cause." Finally in the *Philebus* we find the statement "that all percipient beings desire and hunt after good" (p. 614a), and also the suggestion that some things are means and other things are ends which the former serve. (See p. 632.)

Can you find in these passages any indication of efficient and final causes? If so which are the efficient and which the final causes? Does Plato's presentation of these causes accord with Aristotle's, or is there anything significantly different between the views of the two thinkers? For instance, would Aristotle accept a transcendent good, apart from and beyond particular beings, as their final cause? Would he accept the idea of a supernatural power or being as the efficient cause of things?

Let us turn back now to the selections from *The Republic,* which we considered in our first two readings. Do they contain any indication of efficient and final causes? If so, does Plato's view of them accord with or differ from Aristotle's?

Is Aristotle's criticism of Plato's theory of ideas a cogent one?

To criticize Aristotle's criticism of Plato seems a most presumptuous undertaking, even for a professional philosopher. It means challenging the opinion of one of the greatest thinkers of all time, who was also Plato's pupil for twenty years and was acquainted with Plato's thought at first hand. Yet we have noted certain important statements of Plato on the causes of things that seem to be ignored in Aristotle's criticism. And if we accept Aristotle's view as a faithful reflection of Plato's thought, apparently we must conclude that Plato, the father of Western philosophy, was a very simple-minded person who taught obvious nonsense. On the other hand, if we reject Aristotle's view as a mispresentation or caricature of Plato's thought, apparently we must conclude that Aristotle was not very bright himself and naïvely misunderstood a doctrine which he had been taught at first hand by its author, or that he deliberately misrepresented it in order to make his own views look better.

However, it may not be necessary to arrive at such invidious conclusions about thinkers of the intellectual stature and character of Plato and Aristotle. We may seek instead the fundamental differences in the thought of the two men and see how they are reflected in the critique in question. Again we must recall that Aristotle's history and criticism of early Greek philosophy is Aristotle's and that it is based on a very definite view of the nature of things.

In the first place, the idea or form of a thing is, for Aristotle, to be found only in the thing, and not in some transcendent realm of ideas, of which concrete existence is the reflection or imitation. "Treeness," for Aristotle, exists in particular trees, and only there; and so with animality, humanity, and other universals. The universal ideas are immanent in the concrete things, whence they are abstracted by our reason. He agrees with Plato that universals are objectively real and not merely mental products or fancies; but he disagrees that they exist beyond and apart from empirical things and that the latter participate in them as "copies."

We have already touched on the difficulties in Plato's theory of ideas in our First Reading. It was suggested there that Plato could not have believed in a realm of ideas *entirely* apart from the empirical world, for the whole doctrine of the ideal republic runs against that interpretation. Yet the connection between the sensible world and the archetypes which it embodies is quite obscure and leads easily to the charge of an unnecessary "doubling" of all things and a failure to account for concrete existence. Exactly how the process of "participation" of sensible things in the ideas takes place is not quite clear, and Plato himself acknowledged the difficulties in formulating this mysterious process and the inadequacies of his own presentation of it.

Undoubtedly, Aristotle's view of the relation between universals and particulars is more in agreement with the commonsense way of looking at things and is more easily stated and understood than Plato's view. It does not follow, however, that Aristotle's view is the truer one, or that Plato's view is necessarily without substance. The view that the sensible world of human experience is grounded in a transcendent, purely intelligible realm expresses one of the major possibilities for philosophical speculation about the structure of reality. As Plato presented it, this view is an attempt to account for both realms, for becoming as well as being, and it is only by "tying the knot" in the intelligible realm, according to Plato, that any explanation of the sensible world can be solidly grounded. Once this possibility is granted, we must grant the legitimacy of an alternative to Aristotle's account of the relation of universal ideas and particular existence. If we may hazard a very crude simplification, we may say that Aristotle is existence-centered and that Plato is idea-centered. But we must also remember that for both of them universals alone are the proper object of knowledge and that both of them are interested in accounting for the world of change and becoming.

Is it necessary to assume a realm of ideal perfection to account for concrete existence, a realm of universal ideas or forms from which existing things derive their reality? Does Aristotle's analysis of causes lack a metaphysical solidity that is provided in Plato's theory of ideas? For example, in the case of mathematical relations, must we assume a realm of perfect circles, which are imitated by the imperfect circles that we find in natural objects, or do we just find "circularity" in natural objects and abstract it, thereby, through our own rational activity, arriving at the idea of the perfect circle?

If the former is the case, just how are the ideal and empirical realms united, or, if they are completely separate, how do existing things imitate ideal perfection? If the latter is the case, how do we arrive at a rational ground for our mathematical ideas? In what sense can we talk of a perfect circle as existing and having certain properties? Is it merely a hypothetical construct to aid our understanding of the empirical world? If so, in what sense is it true?

Is it a cogent criticism of Plato's theory of ideas to say that it is inadequate because it does not account for movement and change? Does or does not the theory of ideas do this? Does it attempt to do this? If it does not, how else does Plato account for this aspect of reality?

Does Aristotle's inclusion of the supreme end or good among the things known through wisdom indicate an implicit agreement with Plato on the nature of final causes? What would be the essential criterion of agreement or disagreement in their views about the final cause?

For Plato's own discussion of the objections that may be raised against his theory of ideas, see the *Parmenides* (Vol. 7, pp. 486-511).

Is emancipation from wonder the final state of the philosopher?

Aristotle says that the philosophical quest begins in a state of bafflement or perplexity about things and ends in knowledge which abolishes the initial state. Men learn the causes of things, of which they were originally ignorant, and hence end in "the better state." Is this the only possible conclusion about the course of human thought and the response of man to the reality of which he is a part?

On the one hand, "wonder" connotes an intellectual curiosity about things and may lead to the process of rational appraisal and solution described so vividly by Aristotle. On the other hand, "wonder" connotes a sense of awe or admiration at the presence of things and involves an emotional as well as an intellectual response. Is it possible that wonder in the latter sense may be deepened rather than removed by reflection and spiritual development?

Can we say, then, that the philosopher might end in wonder, in a deepened sense, rather than merely begin in it and then drop it when he reaches a more developed state? Or does wonder in this sense mean that the philosopher has crossed the boundary between philosophy and religion and now views reality as a mystery to be marveled at rather than a problem to be solved?

Obviously, Aristotle rejects this view of things and would hardly consider it worthy of a philosopher. What do you think would be Plato's stand on this view of reality? Would his thought, aimed at the knowledge of all things, allow for the retention and deepening of wonder?

The following questions are designed to help you test the thoroughness of your reading. Each question is to be answered by giving a page or pages of the reading assignment. Answers will be found on page 301 of this Reading Plan.

1 Does sense perception give us authoritative knowledge about anything?

2 What are the arguments for calling wisdom a divine science?

3 What is wrong with Anaxagoras' argument that reason is the cause of things?

4 Why can we not ascribe the idea of a final cause to the thinkers who considered reason, friendship, the One, or the existent as causes and as goods or the good?

5 What impossible ideas follow from a literal adherence to Plato's theory of ideas?

6 Does Plato's theory of ideas account for artificial objects?

7 Do the Platonists prove that all things are one?

ARISTOTLE

Metaphysics

Book IV, Ch. 3-8

Vol. 8, pp. 524-532

We learn from sad experience, starting in early childhood, that we cannot have it both ways, that we cannot both have our cake and eat it too, that we cannot be in two places at the same time. It is the principle behind this simple mundane characteristic of our situation in the world—the so-called law of non-contradiction—that is selected by Aristotle as the ruling axiom of metaphysics. This principle at the heart of all reality is borne out, as Aristotle is quick to indicate, by ordinary experience and common sense.

Many eminent thinkers—notably Heraclitus and Hegel—have challenged the validity of this principle. Certain "fringe" areas and transitional stages have been discerned by modern philosophers which seem to indicate that the law of non-contradiction is not universally applicable. Nevertheless, that law has been the governing rule of ordinary discourse and of scientific communication for thousands of years. When someone says something, we expect him to mean something definite, and not something else—certainly not its opposite. However shifting and complex the matter may be with which he deals, or however inadequate and imprecise the terms he uses, we expect him to try to convey the order of things in the order of his thoughts and words. And we consider him lacking in intellectual honesty or in logical rigor if we detect him saying that something both is and is not, or both has and has not certain characteristics. It is impossible to agree or disagree with someone who contradicts himself and says "Yes" and "No" at the same time to the same question.

In Aristotle's view, these logical and linguistic requirements are necessary conditions of discourse because they are imbedded in the very structure of things. Nothing can both be and not be at the same time and in the same respect. Our very notions of truth and falsity follow from this impossibility of the coexistence of "is" and "is not," and all human knowledge depends on a rigorous observance of this condition.

Fourth Reading

I

This reading deals with the law of non-contradiction and its corollary law of the "excluded middle." Aristotle's discussion of this theme begins at about the middle of Chapter 3 and continues through the rest of Book IV. It is preceded by a discussion of the subject matter of the science of metaphysics, which we should bear in mind when we consider the law of non-contradiction.

Aristotle says that the subject of metaphysics is "being as such"; that is, being in general, the very fact of existence in all things. Hence the metaphysician studies the general characteristics and principles of reality, what characterizes and underlies all kinds of things, what accounts for their being and their being what they are. Here Aristotle introduces the term "substance" which is so important in his metaphysics. Being, he says, is possessed pre-eminently by substance (existing in individual things such as a man, a horse, or a chair), as distinguished from their various "affections" or "attributes" (e.g., two-legged, four-legged, small, or large). Being is possessed fully only by the ultimate, unchangeable substance, the primary reality which never comes into being or passes away but is always actual. This philosophical equivalent of God is the proper subject of metaphysics, which Aristotle sometimes calls "theology."

"Unity" (or "identity") is as important as substance in this view of reality. Whatever is, is one. It is just what it is and not something else, and this is true too of the kinds of things, which include things that are the same or similar. "The substance of each thing," says Aristotle, "is one in no merely accidental way, and similarly is from its very nature something that *is*" (p.

522d). However, contrariety as well as unity, otherness as well as sameness, must be studied in the science of being; for being, unity, etc., may be denied and their opposites affirmed about anything—a thing may not be at all or may not be in a certain way. "For all things are either contraries or composed of contraries, and unity and plurality are the starting-points of all contraries" (p. 524a). Hence, the "negations" and "privations" of substances must also be treated in the science of being as such.

It is also the task of this science to discover the axioms upon which our knowledge of being rests. It turns out that the axioms of the science of being are the same as the first principles of demonstration—"the principles of the syllogism"—consisting in the law of non-contradiction and its corollary, the law of excluded middle. Thus Aristotle places at the heart of the science of being axioms drawn from his formal logic. (See the discussion of the conditions of demonstration in Book I of the *Posterior Analytics*, pp. 97-99.)

"Contradiction" means simply saying the opposite of—or denying—what someone else affirms. The contradiction between affirmative and negative statements is demonstrated in the daily squabbles among children, in which the phrases "Is" and "Is not" are thrown back and forth *ad infinitum*.

We note that in this reading Aristotle uses both the term "contradictories" and the term "contraries." This usage involves a nice logical and linguistic distinction. "White" and "not-white" are *contradictory* terms. This means that both terms *cannot be* affirmed about the same subject at the same time. Yet one or the other *must be* affirmed. Something is either white or it is not white. "White" and "black," however, are *contrary* terms. This means that while both of them cannot be affirmed about the same subject at the same time, neither need be affirmed. Something may be neither white nor black. Hence both can be denied.

This distinction is usually shown in the relationship between "all," "none," and "some" propositions. "All of the houses are white" and "None of the houses is white" are *contrary* propositions. Both of them cannot be true at the same time, but both of them may be false. "All of the houses are white" and "Some of the houses are not white" are *contradictory* propositions. So also are the propositions "None of the houses is white" and "Some of the houses are white." Such pairs of propositions are contradictory, because if one is true, the other must be false; both of them cannot be true nor can both be false at the same time.

In the present reading, Aristotle is interested for the most part in contradictory terms and propositions, and is usually careful to distinguish between "contraries" and "contradictories." One apparent slip is the reference to gray, considered the intermediate between black and white, as an example of the intermediate between contradictories. (See p. 531c-d.)

II

The basic principle or axiom of metaphysics—of the science of being as such—is the law of non-contradiction (also called "the law of contradiction").

... the same attribute cannot at the same time belong and not belong to the same subject and in the same respect. . . . This, then, is the most certain of all principles. . . . For it is impossible for any one to believe the same thing to be and not to be. . . (p. 524d)

This is the master axiom on which the axioms of all the sciences rest. As expressed here, it applies both to objective reality and to the mind which apprehends it—to fact and to belief. It is impossible for reality to contradict itself—for a thing both to be and not to be at the same time and in a certain respect—for instance, for a thing to be in motion and at rest, or for a man to have both a pale and a dark complexion, simultaneously. It is also impossible for anyone really to think that reality contradicts itself, if he considers things carefully, whatever he may say, for then he or his mind would be in a state of self-contradiction, holding "contrary opinions at the same time."

Hence, Aristotle takes the rest of Book II (Ch. 4-8) to refute the arguments of those thinkers who "assert that it is possible for the same thing to be and not to be, and say that people can judge this to be the case," who assert that contradiction is possible in the world and in the mind that judges it. He does not oppose such thinkers with a positive demonstration of the law of non-contradiction, because he holds this to be one of those self-evident principles which are indemonstrable. Such an axiom, he maintains, is a "starting-point" upon which the whole process of reasoning rests, the basis of demonstration which cannot itself be demonstrated; otherwise we could never get started in our reasoning, but would be involved in a process of infinite regression. At some point we must rely on an intuitive judgment of first principles. (See pp. 525a-b, 530d.)

Hence, instead of providing a positive demonstration of this master axiom, Aristotle proposes to show that denial of the law of non-contradiction leads to absurdity, and thus to provide a negative, or indirect, demonstration of its validity. His suggested tactic is quite simple—merely to demand of the opponent of the law of non-contradiction that he say something, that he utter any word or term whatever that has a definite meaning. Without such definite meanings, says Aristotle, a man can say nothing and can discuss nothing—even with himself.

Let him say just one word, "man," for instance. Then he must mean by this a certain type of being with certain characteristics—"two-footed animal," "rational," etc. If he applies this term to anything and couples it with the significant term "is," he is saying that a certain object is a man, with definitely human characteristics, and he cannot possibly mean that the object is at the same time not a man. For reality is so constituted that it is impossible for a thing to be a man and not to be a man at the same time. Were it so constituted, all things would be one and have the same meaning, which amounts to their having no meaning, since there would be no distinctions among things. The world would be meaningless.

The law of non-contradiction implies that each thing has a "substance" or "essence" which make it what it is, and that with it go certain essential attributes, which are limited in number and always the same, such as "two-footed animal" in the case of man. The opponents of this basic axiom deny this and hold that all attributes are "accidental" and may be otherwise—for instance, "white" or "musical" in the case of man. Aristotle, however, maintains that whatever accidental attributes are predicated about anything (and they are potentially infinite), we must, in the last analysis, come back to the substance or essence of which they are an attribute, though an accidental one. Again the law of non-contradiction is established, for "contradictories cannot be predicated at the same time" about substance or essence (p. 527a).

If the opponents of the law of non-contradiction are right, we can say or deny anything, judging a man to be a ship (a "trireme"), for instance. But if everything is mixed together, then nothing, no definite thing, really exists. People who talk this way are talking about what is indeterminate, about non-being, about what is not actually real, for actual reality is always determinate—with a definite nature and definite characteristics. Logical analysis shows that ignoring the determinate character of things leads to utter absurdity. If we can say anything about anything, then it is even easier for us to say that a man is not a ship than that he is not a man; and since contradictory statements are possible in this view, we may say that he *is* a ship. And we may go beyond this absurdity to the "conclusion that it is not necessary either to assert or to deny" anything about anything (p. 527b). Not only will we be able to say that a man is not a man but also that he is neither a man nor not a man, and thus we end up in pure nonsense.

If we accept what the opponent of non-contradiction says, then we must conclude that he himself does not exist, and then he and his argument are alike done away with. If all statements may be judged true or false, then his too may be judged false, and he himself is asking us not to take them seriously. In any case, it is futile to argue with someone who says nothing—by saying "yes and no" or "neither yes nor no," but never definitely "yes" or "no."

This absurdity is also demonstrated pragmatically in our judgments of better and worse. Our conscious and deliberate actions show that we make decisions based on definite distinctions. We know that walking over a precipice is not either good *or* bad, depending on how a man feels or thinks. We know it is bad, and we try to avoid it. Our actions in everyday life demonstrate that we make definite judgments and choices. We go on a journey in preference to staying home, we judge one thing sweet and another not-sweet, we drink water instead of wine, and vice versa.

III

At this point (Ch. 5) Aristotle turns to the famous "relativist" argument of Protagoras that things are what they appear to be to anyone, that "Man (the individual man's perceptions) is the measure of all things." This doctrine, says Aristotle, is derived from and implies the rejection of the law of non-contradiction.

> . . . if all opinions and appearances are true, all statements must be at the same time true and false . . . so that the same thing must both be and not be. And on the other hand, if this is so, all opinions must be true . . . (p. 528c)

Aristotle expressly directs his discussion to those who take this view honestly, in response to their actual experience of the world (as distinguished from those who take this view perversely, merely for the sake of argument). They see that contrary phenomena occur in the same thing—growth and decline, life and death, rain and drought—and on the principle that nothing comes out of nothing, they conclude that the same thing must originally have had contrary attributes. This conclusion, says Aristotle, is partly right and partly wrong, for being may be either potential or actual, and "the same thing can be potentially at the same time two contraries, but it cannot actually" (p. 528d). For instance, a man may become either a hero or a coward, but he cannot actually be both at the same time. Furthermore, "there is also another kind of substance to which neither movement nor destruction nor generation at all belongs" (p. 528d), an ultimate reality which is always actual.

Another reason for believing that whatever appears to anyone really exists is the wide variety of sense impressions among men and even for the same man at different times. Truth in such matters, the honest relativists maintain, cannot be determined by taking an opinion poll and deciding, for instance, that what the majority thinks is sweet is sweet, and that what they think is bitter is bitter. It seems then that one sense impression is just as true as another; hence, "what appears to our senses must be true" (p. 529a).

Against this form of the relativist position, Aristotle argues that it is based on the identification of knowledge with sensation and of reality with the sensible world, which is pervaded by the indeterminacy involved in potential being and which is characterized by constant movement and change. The relativists conclude that nothing certain can be said about this realm. But Aristotle argues that to say that something is changing means that it is changing from an actually existing quality to a quality that is actually coming into being. Part of the old and part of the new coexist. Hence change is not mere indeterminacy but involves real distinctions. Furthermore, only a small part of the material universe is changing—the sublunary sphere —while the heavens move in set, unchanging patterns. And finally, as noted before, there is an ultimate reality or substance which is absolutely changeless.

Next Aristotle casts a critical eye on the claim, often made by the relativists, that sensation is infallible. Even if this is so, he argues, "appearance is not the same as sensation" (p. 530a), referring to optical illusions and other false impressions caused by distance and various physiological states. In practice, we do make distinctions between the truth of appearances in a waking and a dreaming state, to a skilled or an untrained observer, to a healthy or a diseased sense faculty. Furthermore, aside from the question of whether a particular sense impression is objectively true or not, it is always the impression of a certain quality and not at the same time of its opposite; for instance, that something is sweet or wet or heavy. Different persons may have different impressions about the sweetness or dryness of a certain wine, and the same person might have different impressions of it at different times, but a person never has the impression that it is both sweet and not-sweet at the same time. Putting this in terms of the senses,

. . . each of which senses never says at the same time of the same object that it simultaneously is 'so and not so'.—But not even at different times does one sense disagree about the quality, but only about that to which the quality belongs. (p. 530b-c)

A definite, unchanging quality of sweetness is assumed even when that quality is attributed wrongly to a certain object.

Sense impressions themselves obey the law of non-contradiction and do not assign contradictory predicates to the same subject.

Finally, granted that sense perception requires a perceiver, it does not follow that the existence of objects depends on their being perceived. The truth about things is determined by the things, not by the mind that apprehends—or misapprehends—them. The perceptions of man are not the measure of all things.

And, in general, if only the sensible exists, there would be nothing if animate things were not; for there would be no faculty of sense. Now the view that neither the sensible qualities nor the sensations would exist is doubtless true (for they are affections of the perceiver), but that the substrata which cause the sensation should not exist even apart from sensation is impossible. For sensation is surely not the sensation of itself, but there is something beyond the sensation, which must be prior to the sensation; for that which moves is prior in nature to that which is moved . . . (p. 530c)

Those who hold that all appearances are true must also hold that all things are relative—relative to the particular perception of a particular perceiver. Then they will say

. . . not that what appears exists, but that what appears exists *for him to whom* it appears, and *when,* and *to the sense to which,* and *under the conditions under which* it appears. (p. 531a)

But this is nothing more than a simple factual description that this is the way things appear to someone under certain specific conditions (e.g., that he saw pink elephants on his bedroom wall during a hangover). Stated in this way, and with these qualifications, this is a true statement about a particular experience. No judgment is involved one way or the other as to whether what appeared actually existed. All that the proponent of the truth of appearances can say is that what appears is true for this particular individual, not that it is true *per se.*

IV

Corollary with the law of non-contradiction is the law of excluded middle, which is stated by Aristotle in Chapter 7, as follows:

. . . there cannot be an intermediate between contradictories, but of one subject we must either affirm or deny any one predicate. (p. 531c)

If there were an intermediate, a "middle," term between contradictory terms, then we could make statements which are neither true nor false, but this is impossible. This is made clear by Aristotle's famous definition of truth and falsity.

To say of what is that it is not, or of what is not that it is, is false, while to say of what is that it is, and of what is not that it is not, is true; so that he who says of anything that it is, or that it is not, will say either what is true or what is false; but neither what is nor what is not is said to be or not to be. (p. 531c)

The denial of the distinction between truth and falsity leads to utter absurdity. It implies that all statements are true or that no statements are true. If all statements are true, then the contrary statement that all statements are false is true; while if all statements are false, then the statement that all statements are false must be false. These statements "destroy themselves." Against such absurdity, we must have recourse to definite meanings that reflect the distinctions among things.

But against all such views we must postulate, as we said above, not that something is or is not, but that something has a meaning, so that we must argue from a definition, viz. by assuming what falsity or truth means. If that which it is true to affirm is nothing other than that which it is false to deny, it is impossible that all statements should be false; for one side of the contradiction must be true. Again, if it is necessary with regard to everything either to assert or to deny it, it is impossible that both should be false; for it is *one* side of the contradiction that is false. (p. 532c)

V

Are there any aspects of reality to which the principles of non-contradiction and excluded middle seem inapplicable?

In our ordinary experience and expression, we obviously cannot say that something both is and is not, or that it does and does not bear certain characteristics. Wherever we can make clear distinctions between things and qualities, we do so; and we judge the meaningfulness of each other's statements by our success in doing so. But there are certain aspects of the world as we experience it that seem too mixed to require a definite either/or statement (an "is" or "is-not") or to preclude a both/and statement ("is" and "is-not").

For instance, in the transitional stage between childhood and adulthood it is difficult to say whether the young person is a child (boy or girl) or an adult (man or woman). He or she sometimes seems to be in a queer in-between state, to which neither of the contraries (childhood and adulthood) applies, and sometimes in an odd double state to which both of the contraries apply. Such a transitional phase seems to stand outside the necessary application of the principles of non-contradiction and the excluded middle, which obviously apply to a clearly childish or adult stage.

Another example is the transition from life to death. Given a clear and distinctive definition of life, it seems obvious that one cannot say of any organism that it is simultaneously alive and dead. "Living" and "dead" are apparently polar extremes that cannot possibly coincide. Yet, as many modern thinkers have pointed out, dying is a process which takes time, no matter how "instantaneous" death may seem, so that there is an interval between the time when an organism is fully alive and the time when it is quite dead. It is impossible to say of it in this interval that it is living or dead, or one may even say that it is partly alive and partly dead.

Now, the protagonist of the law of non-contradiction might reply that the law still holds, insofar as it may be affirmed or denied that the intermediate state—i.e., adolescence or dying— is in fact the case, and that we cannot both affirm and deny it. Such a contention, however, raises two critical questions. First, is it possible in any continuous process, such as the one that the life cycle entails, ever to say precisely where one stage ends and another begins? Will there not always be an intermediary, ambiguous "fringe" area, between stages, no matter how precisely we differentiate them? Secondly, would Aristotle countenance such a mixed, in-between state as the subject of affirmation or denial? See his discussion of "the intermediate between contradictories" in his discussion of the excluded middle (pp. 531c-532a). But see also his remarks on change of quality, involving an interval where something of the old quality and something of the new quality coexist (p. 529d).

Is the principle of non-contradiction merely a logical "rule" or does it also express something about the structure of reality?

It is possible to accept the law of non-contradiction, categorically or with qualification, as merely one of the rules set up for meaningful discourse among men. So regarded, it offers us a handy measure whereby we may test the consistency of our statements and judgments and regulate communication with others; but it says nothing about the ultimate structure of things. The law of non-contradiction, then, might be seen as one of the rules of the game of thought and one of the rules for the use of language.

Aristotle obviously does not present the principles of non-contradiction and of excluded middle from any such "conventional" or linguistic standpoint. He presents them as basic principles of metaphysics—of the science of being as such. Non-contradiction is for him a rule for our assertions and our thoughts because it is a principle of reality. It is not merely that we are not permitted to speak or think contradictorily; it is that reality itself is not contradictory and that is why we cannot legitimately think or speak contradictorily. For Aristotle, logic reflects reality; words reflect things.

In this view, actual reality is *determinate*. That is why it does not contradict itself and why we should not contradict ourselves when we talk about it. What really exists, he says, is something definite with specific characteristics. The world we live in is made up of distinct things and attributes, of distinct kinds of things and qualities. What is indeterminate is not real, or not fully real, or not yet real. To come into being—to emerge from potentiality into actuality—means to become determinate. Only completely potential being can be wholly indeterminate.

Hence to talk sensibly about things, to express adequately the way they are or what they are, we must make clear distinctions and say either "yes" or "no," either "is" or "is-not." In actual reality, something exists or does not exist, it either has or has not certain qualities, and we cannot think (whatever we may say) that it both exists and does not exist or that it both has and has not certain qualities. Only as regards potential being, only about what has not yet happened or come to be, can we assert both the affirmative and negative or leave things indeterminate.

Would a different view of reality, a different metaphysics, from Aristotle's result in a different logic? What would such a logic be like? One of the famous alternatives had already been stated long before Aristotle by Heraclitus, the great pre-Socratic philosopher, and his thought is alluded to more than once in this reading. For Heraclitus, it is not permanence but change—the constant "flux" of things—that is the ultimate reality. He propounds the unity, not the separation, of opposites, or, rather, he teaches that unity and harmony are produced by the conflict of opposites.

"Opposition unites," he says. "From what draws apart results the most beautiful harmony. . . . All things come into being by a conflict of opposites, and the sum of things flows like a stream." Physical nature is a twofold process, comprising an "upward" and a "downward" movement. The "upward" movement consists in the change from solid to liquid to vaporous states, while the "downward" movement reverses the process. But the two movements are going on simultaneously, otherwise the balance and harmony of the universe could not be maintained. The two movements are parts of one universal process; hence, says Heraclitus, "upward, downward, the way is one and the same." In a musical instrument, harmony is maintained by the opposing strengths of strings and frame, or by the forward and backward movements of the bow across the strings. Reality itself is a balance of being and non-being in the unified process of becoming.[1]

Georg F. W. Hegel, one of the great modern philosophers, returned to this ancient insight of Heraclitus and made it the basic principle of his metaphysics and logic. For Hegel, the actual world is constituted of opposites, and the law of non-contradiction is valid only in the realm of abstract understand-

[1] See Milton C. Nahm (ed.), *Selections from Early Greek Philosophy*, 3rd ed. (New York: F. S. Crofts & Co., 1947), pp. 84-97.

ing. "Everything is opposite," he maintains. "Neither in heaven nor in earth, neither in the world of mind nor of nature, is there anywhere such an abstract 'Either—or' as the understanding maintains. Whatever exists is concrete, with difference and opposition in itself."[2] Organic and inorganic, human and non-human, nature and mind, acid and base—each member of the pairs exists in an essential relation to the other. ". . . the acid is implicitly at the same time the base: in other words, its only being consists in its relation to its other. . . . Contradiction is the very moving principle of the world: and it is ridiculous to say that contradiction is unthinkable. The only thing correct in that statement is that contradiction is not the end of the matter, but cancels itself."[3]

Here Hegel refers to what he calls the "dialectical" movement of things from a positive stage of coming into being (thesis), to a negative stage of passing out of being (antithesis), to a third stage which combines and transcends the first two stages (synthesis). But the process of change does not end there, for the synthesis becomes the first stage or thesis for a new series of developments. Hence, we can say of nothing that it is or is not, but only that it is becoming, which means that it both is and is not at the same time. We cannot assert either being or non-being separately, but only both of them together—as becoming.

Would Aristotle agree that the world is constituted of contraries, If so, where does the essential difference between his and Hegel's view of the order of things lie? Would Aristotle say that Hegel is talking only of potential and not actual being? Why does Aristotle make permanence rather than change the characteristic of ultimate reality?

[2] *The Logic of Hegel*, trans. William Wallace, 2nd ed. (London: Oxford University Press, 1892 [reprinted 1904], p. 223.
[3] *Ibid.*

The following questions are designed to help you test the thoroughness of your reading. Each question is to be answered by giving a page or pages of the reading assignment. Answers will be found on page 301 of this Reading Plan.

1 How does philosophy differ from "sophistic" and from "dialectic"?

2 What makes the philosopher superior to the natural scientist?

3 If a term has several meanings, but they are limited in number, can it be used in meaningful human discourse?

4 What would be the consequences if all attributes were accidental?

5 Who said that you cannot step into the same river even once?

6 How do the doctrines of Heraclitus and Anaxagoras affect the notions of truth and falsity?

7 If things may be more or less "so and not so," what does this imply about objective truth?

LUCRETIUS

On the Nature of Things

Books I-II

Vol. 12, pp. 1-30

T his work is the only philosophical writing in the *Great Books of the Western World* written in verse. It sets forth a speculative account of the nature of things in the traditional verse pattern of epic poetry. It is both the most instructive document which we possess of Epicurean philosophy and also a magnificent, glowing, passionate poem.

The philosophy which inspires this great didactic poem is materialistic or naturalistic. The basic idea of the work is the atomistic structure of matter, an idea borrowed from early Greek physics. According to this, everything that exists is composed of invisible, indivisible particles—the "first-Beginnings" of things. Life, sensation, and thought are derived from the arrangement, motion, and collisions of these ultimate entities.

Lucretius celebrates the basic structure of things, thus envisioned, with moral fervor and poetic beauty. He does not merely present a cool, theoretical account of the way things are, but voices a wholehearted acceptance, though tinged with melancholy. Moreover, he presents his purely materialistic or naturalistic explanation of the world as a cogent refutation of all supernatural or metaphysical explanations.

"Earth is enough" for Lucretius, as for any modern materialist or naturalist. The causes of things are to be found in the things themselves, ". . . in such wise things will light the torch for other things" (p. 14d). No ultimate ends of purposes, no final causes, are involved or need be involved. Things are what they are, and behave as they do, without supernatural guidance or intervention, without subordination to a metaphysical highest good. Realization and acceptance of the materialistic explanation of things, Lucretius promises, will bring freedom from fear of the gods, of death, and of a future life. He announces at the beginning that this salutary practical result is his main motivation for writing this work on the nature of things.

Fifth Reading

I

Lucretius' work, *On the Nature of Things*, is a prime example of the fact that the greatness of a book need not depend on the originality of its thought. Its very title is borrowed from previous works by Empedocles and Epicurus, its style and form are shaped by the didactic poems of Empedocles and Ennius (the greatest of the early Roman poets), and its content is taken over, sometimes verbatim, from the philosophical doctrines of Epicurus. Nevertheless, Lucretius' vivifying poetic power, his felicitous use of words and images, his clear and lucid reasoning, and, above all, his conviction of the truth and beneficent value of Epicurus' thought, combine to make this passionate philosophical poem one of the greatest works in ancient Latin literature and one of the gems of philosophical writing. Moreover, due to the fragmentary state of the extant writings of Epicurus, Lucretius' work has provided succeeding ages with the fullest account of the Epicurean philosophy.

Materialism—that philosophy which sees matter as the basic reality—goes back to the origins of early Greek thought, as we have already seen in our reading of Book I of Aristotle's *Metaphysics*. The particular form of materialism celebrated by Lucretius' poem is *atomism*, the doctrine that the world is constituted of indivisible particles of matter plus the "void," or empty space, through which they move. The origins of atoms may be traced as far back as Empedocles (*c*.490-430 B.C.), but it was first systematically developed by Leucippus of Miletus and his disciple Democritus of Abdera (*c*.460-*c*.370 B.C.). According to them, the world is constituted of an infinite number of invisible, indivisible particles which vary in size and shape but are otherwise the same—solid and impenetrable.

75

They move through the void—which is real though incorporeal—where they collide and become entangled with one another. Through these atomic collisions and entanglements, the visible things of the world are formed. From the tiny atoms, universes grow.

This theory of Leucippus and Democritus provided an explanation of all natural phenomena—of psychological as well as physical processes—with a few basic principles. The soul too, in this view, is composed of atoms, though of a much finer and swifter sort than those of the body. Life and death were explained in terms of the aggregation and dispersion of these rarefied and speedy atoms.

This theory explained things mechanically, in terms of the motions of material particles, apart from any transcendent cause or purpose. "Mechanism as to motion, atomism as to structure, materialism as to substance, that is the whole system of Democritus," says George Santayana.[1] Furthermore, the motions take place necessarily and unavoidably, so that this system was deterministic as well as mechanical.

It was to this system, in the form in which it was presented by Democritus, that Epicurus (341-270 B.C.) turned when he sought a physical theory which would support his ethical doctrine. His aim was to point out the way in which man may achieve contentment. Among the obstacles to tranquility, in his opinion, were the fear of the gods and the fear of death. The system of Democritus was tailor-made for the purpose of showing that all things are determined by physical forces, and hence, that we need not fear nor depend on the action of whatever gods there be (who, in Epicurus' view, though existing, remain apart from and unconcerned with the world and man). And since death is a matter of the dispersion of atoms, involving the annihilation of sensation, there need be no fear of death or what comes after it.

However, Epicurus made one important change in Democritus' theory. A wholly regular, mechanical, and necessary order of things leaves no room for human freedom, which Epi-

---

[1] George Santayana, *Three Philosophical Poets: Lucretius, Dante, and Goethe* (Cambridge, Mass.: Harvard University Press, 1944), p. 27.

curus wanted to maintain, nor for the collision of the atoms, which brings about their entanglement and thus the formation of things. Epicurus, in distinction from the early atomists, attributed weight to the atoms. Their weight, he said, causes them to fall down through the void, but not in straight, parallel lines; otherwise they would never collide. Epicurus solved this problem by postulating "an inherent declination"—a spontaneous, unpredictable, oblique movement whereby the atoms swerve from their straight and narrow course. Thus chance and unpredictability lie at the very heart of things, and human spontaneity and free will are rooted in natural structures.

Two hundred years later, Lucretius (*c*.98-*c*.55 B.C.) found in Epicurus' thought the cure for what he saw as the spiritual malaise of his time. Men were living in mental anguish, fear, and superstition, dreading death or what comes after it and apprehensively trying to propitiate ominous supernatural powers. Lucretius believed that the serene, tranquilizing teachings of Epicurus about the nature of things and the conduct of life provided potent medicine for the ills of his contemporaries. Hence he proclaimed Epicurus a divine savior, one of the great benefactors of mankind, and proceeded to put his therapeutic thought in the beguiling form of poetry.

The work he wrote is notable in the history of philosophy as the first systematic account of Greek thought in the Latin tongue. It is also notable in the history of literature as the only important poem written in epic verse (dactylic hexameter) which has come down to us from the period of the Roman Republic. Undoubtedly, the work is a remarkable poetic and intellectual achievement, which not only succeeds in expressing a philosophical doctrine in a form designed for imaginative literature but does so with memorable impact and power and with argumentative cogency.

Here is Lucretius' own eloquent explanation of how he came to write a philosophical work in poetic verse.

... because on a dark subject I pen such lucid verses o'erlaying all with the Muses' charm. For that too would seem to be not without good grounds: just as physicians when they purpose to give nauseous wormwood to children, first smear the rim round the bowl with the sweet yellow juice of honey, that the unthinking age of children may be fooled as far as the lips, and meanwhile drink up the bitter draught of worm-wood and though beguiled yet not be betrayed, but rather by such means recover health and strength; so I now, since this doctrine seems generally somewhat bitter to those by whom it has not been handled, and the multitude shrinks back from it in dismay, have resolved to set forth to you our doctrine in sweet-toned Pierian verse and o'erlay it as it were with the pleasant honey of the Muses, if haply by such means I might engage your mind on my verses, till you clearly perceive the whole nature of things, its shape and frame. (p. 12c-d)

I I

On the Nature of Things is divided into six "books." Books I and II deal with the atomistic view of the structure of things. Book III shows how the soul, too, is composed of atoms and disintegrates at death. Book IV deals with the processes of sense perception, thought, and reproduction, and denounces sexual love. Book V describes the origin of the world and of human civilization. Book VI deals with various natural phenomena and closes with a vivid portrait, based on Thucydides' description, of the plague at Athens in the fifth century B.C. This reading comprises Books I and II, treating Epicurus' atomic theory.

The poem opens with an invocation to "increase-giving Venus," through whose fructifying power all living things come into being, to bestow on Lucretius the creative capacity to write these verses on the nature of things—for the enlightenment of his friend Gaius Memmius, the Roman poet and orator. Lucretius prays to the "lady" also to bring peace to his time of war and civil strife, so that the unharassed mind may take in what he has to say. He then states his theme:

For I will essay to discourse to you of the most high system of heaven and the gods and will open up the first beginnings of things, out of which nature gives birth to all things and increase and nourishment, and into which nature likewise dissolves them back after their destruction. (p. 1d)

This knowledge of the nature of things, he says, will save men from the crushing fear inculcated in them by religion. The great example of the victory of scientific knowledge over superstitious dread was provided by Epicurus, "the first to burst the fast bars of nature's portals" (p. 2a). Lucretius paints this inspiring picture of the philosopher as a conquering hero:

. . . on he passed far beyond the flaming walls of the world and traversed throughout in mind and spirit the immeasurable universe; whence he returns a conqueror to tell us what can, what cannot come into being; in short on what principle each thing has its powers defined, its deepset boundary mark. (p. 2a)

For Lucretius, as for Epicurus, speculative knowledge has a practical purpose. The knowledge of nature's laws and patterns will dispel superstitious terror. Such knowledge rests on the basic principle that all that exists is a form of previously existing material and comes into being through purely natural processes. *Nothing ever comes from nothing through an act of divine creation.*

This terror then and darkness of mind must be dispelled not by the rays of the sun and glittering shafts of day, but by the aspect and the law of nature; the warp of whose design we shall begin with this first principle, nothing is ever gotten out of nothing by divine power. Fear in sooth holds so in check all mortals, because they see many operations go on in earth and heaven, the causes of which they can in no way understand, believing them therefore to be done by power divine. For these reasons when we shall have seen that nothing can be produced from nothing, we shall then more correctly ascertain that which we are seeking, both the elements out of which every thing can be produced and the manner in which all things are done without the hand of the gods. (pp. 2d–3a)

There must be "fixed seeds" or "first-beginnings" of things, then, to account for the generation of the objects we know and for the particular forms they take: ". . . an unchanging matter has been assigned for begetting things and what can arise out of this matter is fixed" (p. 3c). Otherwise, anything could come out of anything, men from horses, oranges from apple trees. Fixed conditions, seasons, and cycles of growth are also required for the birth and development of living things.

A corollary of the principle that nothing comes from nothing is the principle that *nothing is totally destroyed.* "Moreover nature dissolves every thing back into its first bodies and does not annihilate things" (p. 3d). Since all things consist of an "imperishable seed" or "everlasting matter," none of them can be utterly destroyed. The connection between these "first bodies" may be destroyed and they may be dispersed, resulting in the death or destruction of the particular concrete thing, but the elemental bodies which constitute them are imperishable. "A thing therefore never returns to nothing, but all things after disruption go back into the first bodies of matter" (p. 4b). In the total economy of nature nothing is utterly lost and destruction is constantly balanced by new birth. (See also pp. 18d-19a, 22b.)

That nothing comes from nothing and that nothing is ever completely destroyed—these are the two fundamental principles of Lucretius' view of the nature of things. Therefore, he reasons, there must be primary physical elements—*the atoms*—which he calls variously "first-beginnings," "fixed seeds," or "first bodies." These must be absolutely solid, indivisible, and indestructible, for they are the basic material elements out of which all existing things are made and to which they return. Because they are absolutely solid, they cannot be penetrated or broken into pieces; hence, they are indestructible and everlasting. If they were not, then everything would have long since been reduced to nothing, and there would be nothing from which new things could arise. These solid and indestructible "fixed seeds" or "first bodies" are the basis of natural genesis and of the eternality of the physical world.

Lucretius has admittedly arrived at this conclusion through speculation, not observation. While the atoms are material, they are so minute that they are invisible and imperceptible *in their solitary singleness*. Nevertheless, Lucretius insists, their material existence is indirectly demonstrated by the larger bodies, the perceptible, tangible, visible things of our experience, which are made up of these minute "unseen bodies." He argues, on the analogy of invisible winds, odors, and temperatures, and of the invisible processes involved in the drying of clothes, the erosions of rocks, and organic growth, that the invisibility of atoms is no indication that they do not exist.

One other factor besides the atoms is required to account for the nature of things—*the void*. There must be empty space through which the atoms move and which separates them from one another. Without it there could be no motion and no new things, for everything would be packed together solidly, without room in which to move. That things are not so constituted is shown not only by the fact of motion but by various phenomena which indicate that things are porous and penetrable: the oozing of water through rocks, the movement of food through the body, the processes of growth in plants, and the passing of voices through walls. The fact that large objects may be lighter than small objects indicates that some things have more void in them (and fewer atoms) than others. "Therefore that which we are seeking with keen reason exists sure enough, mixed up in things; and we call it void" (p. 5c).

The atoms and the void—these are the two ultimate constituents of all existing things. All natural phenomena are essential properties or "accidents" of these two basic factors. No third factor is required to account for the nature of things. Hence, Lucretius concludes, none exists, and we will never arrive at one, through either our senses or our reason.

Upon these two basic constituents of things, Lucretius builds the whole universe. This must be infinite, Lucretius argues, because there can be nothing outside the whole of things, and whatever is bounded (finite) must have something outside it. Moreover, there could be no motion or change in a finite universe—all matter, through the natural downward force of its weight, would collect together at the bottom ("at the lowest point") in a stagnant heap, and the rest of the universe would be empty. But the actual universe is one of constant motion, implying an infinite void and infinite matter to balance it in the constitution of things (and it has no bottom, top, or sides).

All things are ever going on in ceaseless motion on all sides and bodies of matter stirred to action are supplied from beneath out of infinite space. (p. 13b)

III

In Book II Lucretius takes up the details of the constant process of motion and change, of perpetual perishing and becoming, in which the sum of things remains the same. This is not only a matter of the obvious motion of visible objects but even more importantly of the speedy, turbulent motions of the invisible atoms through infinite space, out of whose collisions and entanglements visible bodies are formed. This basic process of the formation of things depends on the slight "swerve" of the atoms from straight lines of descent as they fall downward through the void.

> . . . when bodies are borne downwards sheer through void by their own weights, at quite uncertain times and uncertain spots they push themselves a little from their course: you just and only just can call it a *change of inclination*. If they were not used to swerve, they would all fall down, like drops of rain, through the deep void, and no clashing would have been begotten nor blow produced among the first-beginnings: thus nature never would have produced aught. (p. 17d, italics added)

Lucretius makes this slight deviation of the atoms from the straight and narrow path of descent the natural basis for his affirmation of the freedom of the will. In a remarkable passage, he describes this freedom as

> . . . the power by which we go forward whither the will leads each, by which likewise we change the direction of our motions neither at a fixed time nor fixed place; but when and where the mind itself has prompted. . . . For beyond a doubt in these things his own will makes for each a beginning and from this beginning motions are welled through the limbs. (p. 18b)

A purely mechanical system of causes in physical nature, without swerving motions, would leave such a power inexplicable, an unbelievable anomaly. The sheer force of external causes alone does not account for the actions of men or of atoms. In man, the will resists ("this something chooses") and checks or redirects physical movements. Among atoms, the "change of inclination" attests to an inner cause of action. Man's power of free action has been derived from this inner capacity of the "first bodies."

> . . . that the mind itself does not feel an internal necessity in all its actions and is not as it were overmastered and compelled to bear and put up with this, is caused by a minute swerving of first-beginnings at no fixed part of space and no fixed time. (p. 18d)

Lucretius then proceeds to show how the variations in shape, size, fineness, and smoothness among the atoms account for the variety of things and for our sensual experience of them. Things composed of smooth and round atoms have a pleasant effect on our senses, those composed of hooked or jagged atoms have an unpleasant effect. "For touch, touch, ye holy divinities of the gods, the body's feeling . . ." bears witness to the variation in shapes and qualities among the atoms. (See p. 20c.) Dense, hard substances are composed mostly of hooked atoms, closely entangled with one another, while fluid substances are composed mostly of smooth, round elements without mutual cohesion.

There is *a limited number of shapes and sizes among the atoms,* for there is a fixed limit to the forms and qualities of things. Matter, which itself is infinite, has a finite number of shapes. However, there is *no limit to the number of atoms with a particular shape.* The species or kinds of atoms are limited, but the number of individuals within each species is not; otherwise the material universe could not be infinite. Lucretius' first point, then, is this:

. . . the first-beginnings of things have different shapes, but the number of shapes is finite. (p. 21a)

His second point, however, is this:

. . . the first-beginnings of things which have a like shape one with the other, are infinite in number. (p. 21c)

Natural laws and patterns regulate the union of the various kinds of atoms so that, among living things each species reproduces after its kind, and this is the rule too among non-living things.

. . . we see that all things produced from fixed seeds and a fixed mother can in growing preserve the marks of their kind. This you are to know must take place after a fixed law. . . . But lest you haply suppose that living things alone are bound by these conditions, such a law keeps all things within their limits. (p. 24a)

But to balance this limitation by natural law, Lucretius points to the multitude of possible worlds there must be. Granted the assumption of an infinite universe and of an unlimited number of atoms, other earths, other heavens, and other races of men and animals must exist. Nothing in nature exists alone in its kind but is always a member of a class of species. The same applies to our earth and heaven—they are not unique. Lucretius proclaims this theory of other worlds beyond ours as a great new truth which by its very novelty will create in-credulity at first (See p. 28a-d.)

IV

Lucretius' materialistic view of the nature of things is brought out with special force in his account of the atomistic basis of sensation. It is directed against the "pathetic fallacy" that the material substratum of feeling and emotion itself has feelings and emotions.

. . . whatever things we perceive to have sense, you must admit to be all composed of senseless first-beginnings. . . (p. 26a)

Living things are begotten from non-living things, and the senses of living things out of non-sensible things. Life and the sensation that goes with it are caused by a certain arrangement of the atoms and their mutual motions and positions. The nutritive process is an evident example of how material elements are the basis of life and sensation. The breaking up of the union of atoms is the cause of death and with it of the ceasing of mental functions and sensation. Pain comes from a disordering of the atoms, and pleasure from the return to their normal arrangement. But the atoms themselves suffer no pain and enjoy no pleasure; they do not think and they do not feel anything. The larger bodies which they constitute, however, feel and think, as a result of their connections and disconnections, their shapes, sizes, textures, etc.

But if . . . a man may laugh though not made of laughing things, and think and reason in learned language though not formed of thoughtful and eloquent seeds, why cannot the things which we see to have sense, just as well be made up of a mixture of things altogether devoid of sense? (p. 27c)

The theological implications of this view of the universe are expressed most forcefully in Lucretius' denial of an overarching design, intelligence, or guidance in the universe.

For verily not by design did the first-beginnings of things station themselves each in its right place guided by keen intelligence. . . (p. 13c)

All occurs through their chance and spontaneous collisions and interminglings. Nothing occurs through divine providence, which is the refuge sought by the ignorant to explain the why and wherefore of things. The obvious imperfection of the natural world clearly refutes this, says Lucretius.

But some in opposition to this, ignorant of matter, believe that nature cannot without the providence of the gods in such nice conformity to the ways of men vary the seasons of the year and bring forth crops, ay and all the other things, which divine pleasure the guide of life prompts men to approach, escorting them in person and enticing them by her fondlings to continue their races through the arts of Venus, that mankind may not come to an end. Now when they suppose that the gods designed all things for the sake of men, they seem to me in all respects to have strayed most widely from true reason. For even if I did not know what first-beginnings are, yet this, judging by the very arrangements of heaven, I would venture to affirm, and led by many other circumstances to maintain, that the nature of the world has by no means been made for us by divine power: so great are the defects with which it stands encumbered. (p. 17a-b)

With this rejection of the notion of divine providence goes what seems to people brought up in the Judaeo-Christian tradition a curious view of the divine nature and power. Lucretius does not deny that there are gods; he simply denies that they have any concern with human affairs or that they have the power to control the infinite universe. They cannot be moved by human prayers, and they cannot change the course of things.

For the nature of gods must ever in itself of necessity enjoy immortality together with supreme . . . repose, far removed and withdrawn from our concerns; since exempt from every pain, exempt from all dangers, strong in its own resources, not wanting aught of us, it is neither gained by favours nor moved by anger. (p. 23b)

If you well apprehend and keep in mind these things, nature free at once and rid of her haughty lords is seen to do all things spontaneously of herself without the meddling of the gods. For I appeal to the holy breasts of the gods who in tranquil peace pass a calm time and an unruffled existence, who can rule the sum, who hold in his hand with controlling force the strong reins, of the immeasurable deep? Who can at once make all the different heavens to roll and warm with ethereal fires all the fruitful earths, or be present in all places at all times, to bring darkness with clouds and shake with noise the heaven's serene expanse, to hurl lightnings and often throw down his own temples, and withdrawing into the deserts there to spend his rage in practising his bolt which

often passes the guilty by and strikes dead the innocent and unoffend-
ing? (p. 29a)

In a curious way this passage somewhat resembles the question addressed by God to Job in the Old Testament, but it implies the opposite answer. It is not some mysterious divine
power which controls "the immeasurable deep" and the rest of
nature, says Lucretius. Things just happen as they happen without supernatural directions.

This view culminates in the magnificent conclusion to Book
II, which sings the inevitable cycle of generation and decay
which characterizes everything that exists. This world, too, will
come to an end. Indeed, the age in which Lucretius lives manifests all the signs of enfeeblement and decay. The end of the
world is coming, he says. His message resembles that of the
New Testament evangelists, but, unlike them, he calls not for
repentance in order to enter a new order of things but for acceptance of the inevitable and uniform cyclical pattern of things,
which will continue forever and ever. "No golden chain let
down to earth from heaven" will save us from the inexorable
advent of decay.

In this way then the walls too of the great world around shall be
stormed and fall to decay and crumbling ruin. Yes and even now the age
is enfeebled and the earth exhausted by bearing scarce produces little
living creatures, she who produced all races and gave birth to the huge
bodies of wild beasts. For methinks no golden chain let down to earth
from heaven above the races of mortal beings, nor did the sea and waves
which lash the rocks produce them, but the same earth bare them which
now feeds them out of herself. Moreover she first spontaneously of herself produced for mortals goodly corn-crops and joyous vineyards; of herself gave sweet fruits and glad pastures; which now-a-days scarce attain
any size when furthered by our labour: we exhaust the oxen and the
strength of the husband-men; we wear out our iron, scarcely fed after all
by the tilled fields; so niggardly are they of their produce and after so
much labour do they let it grow. And now the aged ploughman shakes
his head and sighs again and again to think that the labours of his hands
have come to nothing; and when he compares present times with times
past, he often praises the fortunes of his sire and harps on the theme,
how the men of old rich in piety comfortably supported life on a scanty
plot of ground, since the allotment of land to each man was far less of
yore than now. The sorrowful planter too of the exhausted and shrivelled
vine impeaches the march of time and wearies heaven, and comprehends

not that all things are gradually wasting away and passing to the grave, quite forspent by age and length of days. (pp. 29d-30c)

V

Does the practical motivation of this work detract from its philosophical validity?

George Santayana, a modern naturalistic philosopher, criticizes Epicurus for choosing a materialist account of things "on the same irrelevant moral grounds on which it has usually been rejected."[2] Is this criticism applicable also to Lucretius? Are moral grounds entirely irrelevant in philosophical speculation and scientific knowledge? Do they enter into the non-materialist philosophies of Plato and Aristotle? Should we distinguish between mere bias or personal preference, which may distort our findings of the way things are, and an intellectual taking into account of the moral order as part of the nature of things? Do you think Lucretius wants to have things the way he says they are, or that he finds that things are a certain way, and therefore accepts and celebrates this arrangement?

Santayana says that Lucretius, through his antireligious bias, presented a distorted view of the religious sentiment in man, not doing justice to the aesthetic and imaginative values of religious belief. A fully mature materialism or naturalism, he says, would be openly aware and appreciative of the very natural emotions and feelings involved in religious experience. Do you agree with this criticism of Lucretius' account of religion? Are the emotions described by him the only emotions involved in religious faith? Do they sufficiently account for its existence? Or is such a question a subjective distraction from the objective point made by Lucretius that nature is not governed by divine power?

Are Lucretius' arguments valid scientifically?

There is no doubt about Lucretius' keen powers of observation of the world of ordinary experience. Almost every passage of our selection reveals this. Yet the basic elements referred to in his account of nature are invisible and not directly a matter

[2] *Ibid.*, p. 29.

of ordinary experience. His description of the atoms and their behavior is arrived at through reason and imagination—indeed, a good deal of imagination—and supported by arguments from analogy with ordinary experience.

Are such arguments from analogy valid? Do our observations of visible things enable us to infer anything about invisible things? Does observation of experienceable appearances provide the basis for knowledge of underlying realities? For instance, does the argument from invisible winds, erosion, drying, etc., prove that there are invisible atoms? Actually, all the processes mentioned are tangible or visible, at least in their effects. We see the wind rustling the leaves or feel it on our cheek; we witness the various stages of erosion or the drying of clothes. Does the fact that the underlying causes of these processes are unknown or not directly experienceable prove that there are primary, indivisible bodies at the core of things? Are any alternative explanations of natural processes equally credible?

As for the void, are empty spaces in things the only possible explanation of the oozing of water through rocks, the movement of food through the body, and the process of plant growth, as well as the lightness of some bodies as compared with others? And are we to take seriously the ascription of our feelings of pleasure and pain to the smooth and jagged arrangements of atoms, respectively, which constitute the things we experience?

Are such analogies simply naïve, charming, simple-minded but erroneous speculations which have nothing to do with the real nature of things? Or are they the vestibule of scientific inquiry, from which we must all start in our first explorations of things? Many commentators have observed how astonishingly "modern" the scientific theories of Democritus, Epicurus, and Lucretius are, despite their errors, crudity, and naïveté. The basic concepts of a mechanistic, atomistic, materialistic view of things—similar to those of modern physics—were already present in the minds of these ancient pioneers of thought. Is the loss of the naïveté and simplicity which went with this acute intuition something to be regretted or something about which we may feel smugly superior in our more sophisticated scientific age?

Is the material universe infinite or finite in Lucretius' view?

On the one hand, Lucretius tells us plainly that the store of matter and the void that contains it are infinite. Moreover, he says that, although there is a limited number of *types* of atoms, there is an infinite number of individual atoms. Yet he also assures us that the sum of things awlays remains the same in a universe where nothing is created from nothing and nothing is completely destroyed, in a balanced cosmic economy of coming into being and passing away.

Do we have a real ambiguity here or an ambiguity in the meaning of the term "infinite"? (1) On the one hand, as Lucretius uses the term, it means "boundless." As applied to the natural world, it means that it is not bounded by anything outside it, that there are no fences hemming in the material universe. (2) On the other hand, in this reading the term also means "unlimited in number," as applied to the individual atoms or the quantity of matter.

Lucretius, however, says that "the store of matter" is unchangeable, "for nothing is either added to its bulk or lost to it." (See p. 18d.) He states both the fixity and the boundlessness of the universe in a single sentence, thus:

And no force can change the sum of things; for there is nothing outside, either into which any kind of matter can escape out of the universe or out of which a new supply can arise and burst into the universe and change all the nature of things and alter their motions. (pp. 18d-19a)

Speaking of the types of atoms, he says that "a fixed limit has been assigned to things which bounds their sum on each side," but then, speaking of the individual atoms, he says that they must be infinite in number within each type, "or the sum of matter will be finite" (p. 21c-d).

Is Lucretius' universe infinite, finite, or both in different respects? Does the fixity of the sum of matter imply a finite universe? Can there be an infinite number of individual atoms if the sum of matter is fixed?

Does the "swerve" in the motions of the atoms account for free will in man?

According to the atomistic view, men, like other things, are constituted of atoms, and their mental acts are to be explained by the movements of the atoms. Hence Lucretius, following his master Epicurus, thought that the freedom of the will which he found present in man must be rooted in some basic spontaneity of action in the atoms—otherwise mechanical necessity would rule human behavior. To assert that man has free will while nature is ruled by necessary causes would imply a "break" in nature, in contradiction to the materialist assumption of a basic continuity among things.

In what respects are the atomic "swerve" and free will the same? For one thing, they are both *inner causes* of action, as contrasted with external forces. For another thing, they are *unpredictable,* "neither at a fixed time or a fixed place." This implies that in both atomic motions and human actions things *could have taken place otherwise* than they have.

But are the atomic "swerve" and man's free will in all respects the same? Lucretius speaks of the will resisting physical impulses and redirecting movements, according to an act of *choice* ("this something chooses"). He does not, however, use this kind of language when speaking of atomic motion, which he presents more in terms of *chance* than of choice. After all, the atoms neither think nor feel. Obviously, then, they lack consciousness and purpose.

Are consciousness and purpose necessary for the kind of freedom involved in free will? Or are spontaneity and unpredictability essential characteristics of a more universal type of freedom, which includes both the spontaneity of action found in unconscious things and the freedom of the will present in conscious, rational beings? Is the level of consciousness and rationality continuous with the rest of nature, or does it signify a radical discontinuity, a "jump," an unbridgeable gap among things? Assuming such a "gap," are the two kinds of freedom—atomic swerve and free will—still analogous to and correspondent with one another?

The following questions are designed to help you test the thoroughness of your reading. Each question is to be answered by giving a page or pages of the reading assignment. Answers will be found on page 301 of this Reading Plan.

1 Why is it difficult for Lucretius to express Greek thought in Latin verses?

2 Why are the causes and events of the Trojan War "accidents"?

3 Which of the early Greek philosophers is famous for his obscurity?

4 What does Anaxagoras mean by the term "homoeomeria"?

5 What way of life is required by nature?

6 Are the primary elements of matter colored?

7 What is the analogy between the material atoms and the elements of Lucretius' verse?

AQUINAS

Summa Theologica

Part I-I, QQ. XVI-XVII

Vol. 19, pp. 94-104

One of the most basic of all philosophical problems is the meaning of truth. On the answer to the time-old question "What is truth?" depends our view of the nature and the very possibility of human knowledge. Is truth something in the mind, or in things, or in both? Does sense experience give us truth? What is the test of truth?

Thomas Aquinas, the great medieval theologian, building on the foundation of Aristotle's theory of the mind and its functions, gives a classic, clear, and balanced answer to this set of questions. Truth and falsity, he says, are attributes of our thoughts about things. These terms refer essentially to the rightness or wrongness of the intellectual act of judgment. Whether a judgment is true or false is decided by the way things really are.

In this analysis, truth involves two factors: a judging mind and existing things. Are truth and falsity then to be attributed only to judgments and the verbal statements which express them? Is there not a sense in which things and persons are true or false? Must we not distinguish between truth and falsity in sense perception too?

In the present reading, Aquinas discusses these and other questions having to do with knowledge and truth. He proceeds in systematic fashion, carefully qualifying his answers, in order to give due weight to the various aspects of the process of human knowledge and to the subtle distinctions involved in the meaning of truth. At the same time, while dealing with a basic philosophical question, he makes it clear that his answers rest on a Christian notion of the origin and end of things.

Sixth Reading

I

The *Summa Theologica,* as its title indicates, is a systematic exposition of Christian theology. It presupposes a special act of divine revelation bestowed on a certain people and on particular persons. Its basic aim is to set forth so far as possible the rational grounds for believing, or at least for not disbelieving, in the Christian faith. These characteristics of the work would for many people deprive it of philosophical worth, in contrast with the "free," non-dogmatic basis of the great philosophical works written in ancient and modern times.

However, a cursory glance at the table of contents of the *Summa Theologica* reveals that it deals with themes that have been the object of philosophical inquiry all through the ages: with the nature of man and the human mind, with good and evil in human conduct, with the way in which man comes to know things, and with the nature of truth. Moreover, a reading of the various treatises discloses that even theological questions are approached within the frame of rational discourse—with arguments and counter-arguments—and with due account being taken of the thought of the non-Christian philosophers. Indeed, the *Summa* is essentially an attempt to reconcile the truths derived from natural human reason with those which, according to the Christian faith, are bestowed by divine revelation.

Aquinas, like most eminent medieval thinkers, was both a philosopher and a theologian. He accepted, with some modifications, Aristotle's basic views of the nature of man and of the universe. His treatment of the problems of human knowledge and of truth presupposes close study and general acceptance of what Aristotle has to say on these subjects in the *Metaphysics* and *On the Soul*. He continually refers to Aristotle in the *Summa Theologica* as "the Philosopher," and undoubtedly Aristotle was *the* philosopher for him. However, Aquinas was no mere slavish imitator of an ancient master. Rather he used Aristotle's basic philosophical doctrines creatively in setting forth his own views of the major themes. Like most great thinkers, he built on the thought of the past but constructed an edifice that was the product of his own vision as well as of the materials and tools bequeathed to him.

As we read through this brief selection, we will note that Aquinas cites previous thinkers not merely to appeal to great names for support or to criticize the doctrines of the past but to show the various viewpoints from which basic philosophical questions must be approached to do justice to the various aspects of things. Although neo-Platonic thinkers like Augustine are usually cited in the objections which Aquinas refutes in his replies, their position is often approved of as stating one aspect of truth.

Nevertheless, there is no doubt that Aquinas sides with Aristotle's and against Plato's version of how men grasp the truth about things. Man is for Aquinas a unity of mind and body, dependent on sense experience for his knowledge of the world and grasping universal concepts in his encounter with the concrete things in which they are present. And it is the concrete things, the existing things, that he comes to know through the universals, not mere abstract forms or ideas in a realm transcending the world of human experience.

At the time he was writing the *Summa Theologica*, Aquinas was engaged in an intellectual struggle with the various neo-Platonic schools of Christian philosophy which held a leading place in medieval thought. Among the decisive questions on which this battle was waged were those concerning the nature of knowledge and the meaning of truth. For the ancient origin of this dispute, the reader is referred to the selections from Plato and Aristotle in earlier readings. See also Aristotle's discussion of truth and falsity at the end of Book V of the *Metaphysics* (Vol. 8, pp. 546c-547a), and of the process of knowledge and judgment in Book III of *On the Soul* (Vol. 8, pp. 656-668).

For Aquinas' discussion of how man knows things, see the "Treatise on Man" in the *Summa Theologica* (Part I-I, QQ. LXXXIV-LXXXIX; Vol. 19, pp. 440-480).

The *Summa Theologica* is presented in a special form developed during medieval times. Each topic is set forth under a title question and a series of subquestions, or "articles." For instance Question XVI, "Of Truth," consists of eight articles or "points of inquiry," each of which is headed by the particular point in the form of a question. Thus Article 1 of Question XVI is entitled, "Whether Truth Is Only in the Intellect?" The first paragraph of each article contains the position that Aquinas will criticize and oppose, flatly or with qualification. The statement of the position to be criticized is always preceded by "It seems that. . ."

Thereupon follow various arguments for the position, entitled "objections" (i.e., to the position Aquinas holds) and numbered consecutively. After giving due notice to these viewpoints, Aquinas proceeds to state his own position, beginning with a short statement, usually citing an authority such as "the Philosopher," and preceded by the words *"On the contrary."* Then comes his full statement beginning with the words *"I answer that. . ."* After this statement he gives his "replies" to the "objections," listed in the same numerical order as the points to which they respond.

In reading Aquinas' full answer and his replies to objections, we should note that he does not always criticize his opponents' positions as being false, but usually as being one-sided and affording only a partial apprehension of the truth about the things disputed.

II

The essential thesis in Aquinas' doctrine of truth is that truth or falsity can primarily be attributed only to an act of the mind (and hence to its "enunciations" in speech). We can in some sense speak of things and persons as being "true," but these are special and derivative uses of the term. Truth primarily refers to an act of the intellect—*judgment.*

Aquinas distinguishes this act ("the intellect composing and dividing") from another basic act of the intellect, whereby it apprehends the universal essences or forms of things ("knowing what a thing is"). In his view, the human mind is so constituted that in its normal state it always grasps correctly the universal forms (man, tree, stone, round, white, etc.). The question of truth and falsity arises only when we try to combine or separate these concepts in making judgments about particular existing things, when we attribute a certain predicate to a certain sub-ject—that *this particular thing* "is" a tree, a stone, a man, a house, round, white, square, or what-not. If what we judge to be the case is actually the case, our judgment is true; otherwise it is false.

Thus truth essentially is the result of an act of the intellect, but whether that act has arrived at the truth is decided by the actual state of things outside the mind: "truth is defined by the conformity of intellect and thing" (p. 96a). Or, more ex-actly, truth is the conformity of what the intellect judges things to be and what they actually are.

When, however, it judges that a thing corresponds to the form which it apprehends about that thing, then first it knows and expresses truth. This it does by composing and dividing, for in every proposition it either applies to, or removes from the thing signified by the subject, some form signified by the predicate . . . (p. 96a)

But though sense experience is an essential element in hu-man knowledge, according to Aquinas, yet this definition of truth clearly implies that the senses cannot know the truth. Only the intellect can make the comparison between things and concepts which is involved in judgment. Although the senses perceive things, and although sense perception is neces-sary for the mind's grasp of universal concepts, the senses themselves cannot grasp the universals nor compare them with things.

Aquinas concludes in Question XVI, Article 2, that the senses cannot know the truth—that "truth is not in the senses." However, in Question XVII, Article 2, Aquinas somewhat mod-ifies this conclusion. Common experience tells us that the senses sometimes mislead or deceive us. They often give us a false report of the way things are. Hence, since truth and falsity are contraries and thus attributable to the same things (see Q. XVII, Art. 4), we may say that truth is in the senses—"in so far as they apprehend sensible things truly . . . and this takes place through the senses apprehending things as they are . . ." (p. 102a-b). Similarly "falsity exists in the senses through their apprehending or judging things to be otherwise than they really are" (p. 102b).

Yet, despite this language about the senses "apprehending or judging" things truly or falsely, Aquinas' Reply to Objection 3 in this article makes it clear that he still maintains that the senses cannot make judgments, cannot compare things and concepts, cannot "compose and divide," and hence cannot *know* the true and false. They cannot know the "conformity of intellect and thing," and by definition "to know this conformity is to know truth." (See p. 96a.) All that the senses can do is to convey impressions or images of things, accurately or not. If they do so inaccurately, then we will be deceived about things —through defective sense perception, not through an error in intellectual judgment.

By definition, then, truth or falsity is something that may be attributed only to an intellectual act—to judgment. But also by definition, it is the actual state of things which determines whether our judgments are true or not. Can we then speak of a true state of things or of things being either true or false? Yes, answers Aquinas, to a certain extent and with certain qualifications we can speak of a truth in things.

. . . since the true is in the intellect in so far as it is conformed to the thing understood, the aspect of the true must pass from the intellect to the thing understood, so that also the thing understood is said to be true in so far as it has some relation to the intellect. (p. 94d)

"In so far as it has some relation to the intellect" is the key term and the decisive qualification here. Truth is primarily in the intellect and only secondarily does it "pass from the intellect to the thing understood."

Aquinas distinguishes between two types of truth in things, as related to the intellect: (1) absolute or essential, and (2) relative or accidental. The first type refers to things in relation to the intellect which *originated* them—that of the artist or craftsman in the case of man-made objects or that of the divine creator in the case of natural objects. A thing is true absolutely when it perfectly expresses the form in its creator's mind. Thus we may speak of a "true house" and a "true vase," or of a "true stone" or a "true tree"—of the truth of things insofar as they are dependent on the intellect of their creator for their existence.

The second type refers to things in relation to the intellect which *knows* them, to the true likeness or reflection of things in the intellect. What this "accidental" or "relative" truth consists in is explained in the discussion of falsity in things (see Q. XVII, Art. 1). The answer to the question presented there provides a clear distinction between absolute and accidental falsity in things. Falsity in the absolute sense—as regards the *being* of things—occurs when they do not conform with the idea in their maker's mind. Although this is a common occurrence among the works of fallible mortals, it does not occur among natural objects, which are the work of God—except for such creatures as man, who have the power to resist God's will.

Falsity in the accidental sense—as regards the mind's *knowledge* of things—occurs in two ways: (1) through the use of a wrong word or thought for the thing (a falsity of "sign"), and (2) through external appearances or likenesses (a falsity of "cause"). An instance of the first, taken from Aristotle's *Metaphysics,* is thinking "that the diagonal of a square is commensurate with the side." (See Vol. 8, p. 546c.) Such a diagonal is a false diagonal. There is no such thing. An instance of the second—false likeness—is gall that looks like honey, or tin that appears to be silver.

In the case of false likenesses, are we really justified in talking about a falsity *in things?* Are we not rather confronted with a case of false representation or false opinion on our part—of falsity *in the mind?* Aquinas answers that a thing is false in this sense only when it *always and naturally* produces a false opinion. This corresponds with the remark previously cited from Aristotle that things are called false " 'that are naturally apt to appear such as they are not, or what they are not' " (p. 101c). All the plants which naturally appear to be other than they are would fall under this heading, such as false anemone, false dandelion, false lily of the valley, etc.

Can we also speak of truth and falsity among human beings? We have already noticed that man, uniquely among natural things, may be false, may refuse to be what God has ordained him to be, and thus may fall into sin—which is called "untruth" or "lying" in the Bible. Can we then speak of men being true or false? Is there an existential or "life" truth among men, as well as an intellectual truth?

Aquinas deals with this subject in the context of his discussion of the relation between the true and the good (Q. XVI, Art. 4, Reply Obj. 3):

The virtue which is called truth is not truth in general, but a certain kind of truth according to which man shows himself in deed and word as he really is. But truth as applied to life is used in a particular sense, in so far as a man fulfils in his life that to which he is ordained by the divine intellect, as it has been said that truth exists in other things . . . (p. 97c)

III

Our concern so far has been to understand Aquinas' theory of truth insofar as truth is an attribute of human knowledge. However, in the exposition of his doctrine, Aquinas raises certain metaphysical questions, such as the relation of truth and being, of the good and the true, and of the eternality and immutability of truth. These questions are discussed in Question XVI, Articles 3-8. A careful reading of these articles may aid in understanding the basic view of human knowledge which has been summarized above.

For example, the "convertibility" of truth and being, discussed in Article 3, is relevant to the discussion of truth in things. Truth has to do with the mind's apprehension and judgment of what is—of whatever is—for, in Aquinas' view, all things that are, are knowable. Hence, what is known truly may be said to be in the mind, as thought. Aquinas cites with approval Aristotle's saying that "the soul is in some manner all things." Hence we may say that the true is "convertible" with being, where there is a perfect correspondence between thought and thing.

The whole basis of the truth of our judgments, as we saw in Aristotle's *Metaphysics,* is that a thing is what it is and is not something else, and cannot be both at the same time. Thought reflects actuality, hence "the true" and "being" are interchangeable terms: "being when understood is true" (p. 96d). At the same time it is an existing mind that understands the truth about things, so that we may speak of the being of the intellect as well as of things. Again we have a "convertibility" of terms.

The true resides in things and in the intellect, as said before (A. 1). But the true that is in things is convertible with being as to substance, while the true that is in the intellect is convertible with being as that which manifests with what is manifested; for this belongs to the nature of truth, as has been said already. . . . It may, however, be said that being also is in things and in the intellect, as is the true; although truth is primarily in the intellect, while being is primarily in things; and this is so because truth and being differ in idea. (p. 96c)

What about the relation of the true and the good? We have already seen that there is a kind of existential or moral "life" truth in man—when he shows himself forth as he really is and fulfills his divinely ordained vocation. Which comes first? Which depends on the other—truth or good?

Aquinas answers that *logically*—in the order of thought—the true comes before the good. The true, as we have seen, is closely related to being, in itself, "absolutely and immediately." This is the relation of the intellect to being insofar as it is *knowable*. The good, on the other hand, is related to being insofar as it is perfect. This is the relation of the appetite or will to what is *desirable*. Since "knowledge naturally precedes appetite," it follows that the true must be prior logically to the good.

This is so logically, "in the order of intelligible things." But "in the order of things desirable," the good precedes the true, which is then one among many goods (such as beauty). As far as logical priority is concerned, Aquinas sets up this hierarchy among being, the true, and the good.

A thing is prior logically in so far as it is prior to the intellect. Now the intellect apprehends primarily being itself; secondly, it apprehends that it understands being; and thirdly, it apprehends that it desires being. Hence the idea of being is first, that of truth second, and the idea of good third, though good is in things. (p. 97c)

Much has been made of Aquinas' supreme confidence in the capacity of the human mind to know the truth about things.

But we must remember that human imperfection, in intellectual as in moral matters, is taken for granted by this Christian thinker and is always measured against the divine perfection. Truth, in the mind or in things, says Aquinas, is to be found perfectly only in God. Indeed God is rightly said to be the truth, and the supreme measure of all truth. (See Q. XVI, Art. 5.)

But the created intellect, specifically the human intellect, attains no such truth. There is no one truth in the human mind, but many truths. These many truths, indeed, reflect the "one primary truth" that underlies all things and which is in the divine intellect. But although this one primary truth is "reflected in the soul, as in a mirror, by reason of the first principles of the understanding" (p. 98d), and is indirectly the basis of human knowledge, it is not present directly in the human mind, in which truth is always many and not one. (See Q. XVI, Art. 6.)

Similarly the truth of our intellect is not eternal. Only an eternal intellect, that is, God's, can know eternal truth. Truth, humanly speaking, according to Aquinas' precise definition, has to do with the comparative judgments that we make and the propositions that we state, with what had a beginning in time and hence is not eternal. Aquinas makes this point cogently in his Reply Objection 4 in Question XVI, Article 7:

Because our intellect is not eternal, neither is the truth of enunciable propositions which are formed by us eternal, but it had a beginning in time. Now before such truth existed, it was not true to say that such a truth did exist, except by reason of the divine intellect, in which alone truth is eternal. But it is true now to say that that truth did not then exist, and this is true only by reason of the truth that is now in our intellect, and not by reason of any truth in the things. For this is truth concerning non-being, and non-being has no truth of itself, but only so far as our intellect apprehends it. Hence it is true to say that truth did not exist, in so far as we apprehend its non-being as preceding its being. (p. 99c-d)

Not only does human truth have a beginning in time, but it is changeable. Only in an intellect with perfect knowledge and unchangeable opinions can there be immutable truth. Such immutability is to be found in the divine, not in the human intellect. As for the change from true to false opinions among men, this occurs in two ways: either (1) the opinion changes while the thing remains the same, or (2) the thing changes while the opinion remains the same. Clearly, what we think or say about changeable things must correspond with the changes in the things. Hence the truth of propositions changes, and in this respect truth is certainly mutable. For instance, it is true to say that it is raining at one time, but it may not be true an hour or so later.

IV

Is there truth and falsity in sense perception?

Aquinas talks of the senses "apprehending things as they are" and "apprehending or judging things to be otherwise than they are." Is this not in line with the "correspondence" or "conformity" theory of truth which Aquinas espouses? If I see what I take to be a man at a distance, and it turns out on closer inspection to be a statue, a scarecrow, or a stone formation, then I have "seen" what is not actually there and hence have seen falsely. Also myopia, astigmatism, or an hallucination like Macbeth's about the dagger before his eyes may produce false images. If my senses "deceive" me, that is, lie to me, does this not imply that they can tell the truth about things?

Aquinas would reply that truth and falsity are a matter of the correct application of concepts to the particular case. Only the intellect can abstract the general concepts of man, tree, stone, round, etc., and compare them with the particular things of sense experience. Although the senses provide the images or "phantasms" of material things, knowledge is conceptual and essentially an intellectual product. We know the world by means of concepts—through the intellect.

Moreover, the mind not only knows things through intellectual operations, but it knows that it knows and may reflect upon the act of knowing. This reflective act of consciousness is, of course, impossible for the senses, which just mirror the material particulars and events.

For although sight has the likeness of a visible thing, yet it does not know the comparison which exists between the thing seen and that which itself apprehends concerning it. But the intellect can know its own conformity with the intelligible thing. . . . (p. 96a)

Aquinas talks of the senses *"apprehending or judging"* things. Are these two distinct operations of the senses? Do the senses *judge* things? Can we then speak of the truth or falsity of perceptual judgments?

Suppose I say that an object is a man and it turns out to be a tree or some other natural object. Is the proposition "X is a man" an error in intellectual judgment—in "the intellect composing or dividing"—or an error in the senses "apprehending or judging"? How would I determine that my statement is false—through the senses, the intellect, or both?

How do we distinguish between falsity in the senses and false likenesses in things?

There are some cases where the difference between correct and incorrect judgment of a situation may mean the difference between life and death, or wholeness and injury. Driving at night or in a dense fog along the open highway presents many such occasions. For instance, suppose I see a vehicle with a single headlight coming toward me and I judge it to be a motorcycle, but it turns out to be a car with one headlight burned out—does the error lie in the senses or the thing? Suppose I am driving in a dark night or a thick fog, and I misjudge the distance between my car and the one ahead because it has no lights on—where does the cause of my "misjudgment" lie?

Suppose I partly submerge a perfectly straight stick in water and the submerged part looks bent—does the falsity lie in my senses or in the thing? Suppose I look down a railroad track and the parallel rails appear to come together in the distance—is this a case of false sense perception or of "false likenesses" in things? How would you classify the cases where a statue, a scarecrow, or a group of stones is mistaken for a man?

Is there any alternative to the "correspondence" theory of truth?

One of the most famous alternatives to the "correspondence" theory of truth—that truth is a matter of the conformity of our judgments with external things—is the "coherence" theory of truth. According to the latter, truth essentially has to do with the whole of our thought about the world, not with particular judgments and propositions. Single judgments or propositions are considered true or false only within the whole of thought which adequately reflects the whole of reality. The kind of mind that would be able to acquire such total knowledge has been sketched in Plato's portrait of the dialectician in *The Republic*. The first notable presentation of the coherence theory of truth occurs in Spinoza's *Ethics*, which we consider in the Tenth Reading.

Does this theory only shift the test of truth from conformity of a single proposition with a single state of things to conformity of a thinker's total thought with the state of the whole of things? What determines whether a coherent, organic whole of interrelated propositions is true? If it is the systematic coherence itself that is the criterion of truth, how do we distinguish between coherent fictions, such as those presented in great epic poems and novels, and actual facts? Even if we grant that these great works of the imagination reflect the actual state of things how do we arrive at this conclusion—merely through noting the perfect coherence of parts or through referring to our experience and understanding of the actual world?

Does the coherence theory imply that the world is a systematic unity of things and events which may be seen all at once in the synoptic vision of the philosopher? But if truth lies in coherence, then we may attribute truth to the world of the mind without distinction, rather than to the correspondence of the mind's thought with the actual world. Does the coherence theory do away with the fundamental distinction between the judging mind and the external reality which it judges?

Aquinas, the great proponent of the correspondence theory, is obviously opposed to the type of thought that underlies the coherence theory. However, does the present reading indicate any possible points of agreement between him and the advocates of the coherence theory? Does his affirmation that the mind is, in some sense, all things provide any support to that theory? Also, the coherence theorists emphasize the partial truth of various alternative and opposing views, and their adequacy when connected with other partial views within the whole of thought. Is Aquinas' attempt to reconcile various views, to indicate their truth under certain aspects, and to work them into a synthetic, more adequate view an analogous enterprise?

Would Aquinas agree that man, through natural reason, can arrive at a coherent view of the whole of reality?

The following questions are designed to help you test the thoroughness of your reading. Each question is to be answered by giving a page or pages of the reading assignment. Answers will be found on page 301 of this Reading Plan.

1 Why does Augustine oppose the view that "that is true which is seen"?

2 How does Aquinas apply the analogy of the character of health and the power of medicine to truth in intellect and in things?

3 In what way are the will and the intellect mutually inclusive?

4 If conformity with things decides the truth of our intellect, what decides the truth of things?

5 How does Aquinas answer Augustine's point that the nature of a circle is a truth that is both created and eternal?

6 Are there many truths "univocally" or "analogically" speaking?

7 What type of falsity is involved in the sentence cited from Augustine: "The true tragedian is a false Hector"?

MONTAIGNE

The Essays

"Apology for Raimond de Sebonde"

Vol. 25, pp. 208-294

> They said "You have a blue guitar.
> You do not play things as they are."
>
> The man replied "Things as they are
> Are changed upon the blue guitar."
>
> Wallace Stevens, "The Man with the
> Blue Guitar"[1]

It would be hard to represent the difference between medieval and Renaissance ways of thought more dramatically than to consider the writings of Michel de Montaigne immediately after those of Thomas Aquinas. What a contrast we are offered between a unified scheme of thought, based on a supernatural origin and end of things and expressed in carefully articulated systematic form, and the multifarious world of Montaigne's essays, centered on the natural and the human world, appealing to the evidence of personal experience and expressed in the loosest, most informal manner possible! We also notice a remarkable change from

---

[1] Wallace Stephens, *The Collected Poems of Wallace Stephens* (New York: Alfred A. Knopf, Inc., 1954), p. 165.

Aquinas' firm conviction that the human mind can attain the truth about things, within certain limits, to a questioning of whether man can reach certain knowledge about anything.

"What do I know?" is Montaigne's favorite expression, not only at the beginning but also at the end of his investigation of all the varieties of human experience, opinions, and customs. He sets as his intellectual model a balanced, open attitude toward the varieties of appearances and opinions, an attitude which neither definitely affirms nor denies propositions. He sets as his practical model conformity to the trodden path of custom, habit, and tradition—the conservative middle way between extremes.

No one has presented more eloquently the subjective and historical influences on man's judgment of things. Between things as they are and man's mental grasp of them, says Montaigne, stand personal makeups, dispositions, interests, and conditioning, as well as the customs, traditions, and attitudes of a particular place and time. Granted the operation of all these influences on the mind of man, how can we ever be sure, he asks, that we ever do see things as they are? This kind of question is, of course, quite familiar to us at the present time, when theories about the psychological and sociological influences on intellectual judgments are so common.

The "Apology for Raimond de Sebonde" is ideally suited to present these various aspects of Montaigne's view of the problem of knowledge, and it is, like all his pieces, delightful reading. What could be a dry and abstruse subject becomes in Montaigne's hands the topic of a lively and genial conversation. As in his other essays, Montaigne frequently appeals to his own personal experience, thought, and character for evidence, since they are the material with which he is most familiar.

Seventh Reading

I

Montaigne's *Essays* are the work of a gentleman scholar, who retired from public life at the age of thirty-eight, "weary of the servitude of law courts and public offices," to take up residence on his country estate. He held aloof from the religious and dynastic struggles that were splitting his country into fiercely warring camps. He devoted himself to a life of study and meditation on whatever subjects interested him, reading as he pleased through his voluminous library, and writing his thoughts on various topics and authors in the essays that have made him famous.

The "Apology for Raimond de Sebonde" is unique among these essays in many respects. George Saintsbury, the eminent British critic of French literature, called it a "curious" essay, and even questioned whether it should be called an essay at all. For one thing, it is by far the longest of Montaigne's essays, taking up as much space as the first twenty-eight essays in this volume. For another, it comprises an extraordinarily tenacious and consistent concentration on a single topic—the uncertainty of human knowledge—as compared with most of the essays, which follow so many lines of interest that it is sometimes difficult to tell what their subjects are.

Nevertheless, it retains many of the distinctive characteristics of the other essays. First, it is written in the same warm, conversational style as they are. Despite the seriousness of its subject, this essay is no academic treatise. It is the talk of one human being with his fellows about a topic of common concern. Second, it contains many references to Montaigne's own personal experience and character. "I . . . have my eyes continually bent upon myself," he confesses, "like one that has no great

112

business elsewhere to do" (p. 274a). Third, it is packed with copious citations from the great writings of the past, particularly from the ancient Greek and Latin authors. Far from being an idle attempt to fill space, these citations serve to show a multiplicity of points of view or to reinforce a particular point which Montaigne is making. In an essay such as this, which is intended to demonstrate the astonishing variety of opinions among learned men, this device becomes especially important.

The occasion for writing this essay came about, characteristically for Montaigne, in an accidental way. He had translated a work entitled *Theologia naturalis; sive Liber creaturarum magistri Raimondi de Sebonde (Natural Theology; or the Book of Creatures,* by Master Raimond de Sebonde) to please his father. The latter had received the work from a friend, who hoped it might counteract "the novel doctrines of Martin Luther," which he believed were undermining traditional religious beliefs by subjecting them to the individual judgment of the believer. Montaigne's father had put the work aside for a number of years and only found it by accident shortly before his death, whereupon he requested his son to put it into French for him. "Having by chance, at that time, little else to do," says Montaigne, he proceeded to the difficult task of translation, doing the best he could, and won his father's approbation when he had finished.

Montaigne himself thought that the author (of whom all he knew was that he was a Spaniard and professor of medicine at Toulouse two centuries before)[2] had done an excellent job of grounding the articles of Christian faith on "human and natural reasons" and thus refuting "the atheists." However, he found that readers of the book had two main objections to it: (1) that it is impious to try to prove through human reason a faith which can come to man only through divine revelation, and (2)

[2] Sebonde was professor of medicine, theology, and philosophy at Toulouse about 1430. His book on natural theology, published in 1484, was put on the Church's Index of Prohibited Books in 1558. The book was taken off the Index in 1564, but its Preface was still prohibited reading. The reason for the prohibition was that the book, and especially the Preface, claimed far too much power for unaided human reason in theological matters.

that Sebonde's arguments are too weak and may easily be refuted. Dealing with these objections provided him with the occasion to write this essay and to expound his views of the weakness of human reason.

II

Montaigne does not deny the first objection to Sebonde's work. While praising its attempt to use human reason to support Christian beliefs, he holds that the human mind is incapable of coming to them without divine grace and revelation. Thus far he seems to agree with the objection from those whom he regards as religious zealots, but there is an important difference between him and them.

It is true, he says, that insofar as we have the Christian faith by merely human means, we do not have it properly, yet, he adds, "I am afraid we only have it by this way" (p. 209c). In proof of this startling assertion, he cites the inconstancy of religious belief, which is altered by various human influences and considerations, and he points to the actions of professed Christians. If men were Christians through divine initiative, he argues, they would act like Christians, but this is obviously not the case. Montaigne's prime example of this practical contradiction is the religious war going on in France in his time, in which religion provided the excuse for the worst kind of actions. Men simply do not act as if they really believed in an infinitely good and powerful God.

Montaigne concludes that professed Christians are such only because they were born in a certain place and time. If they were born in another place and time, they would be adherents of the prevailing religion there and then. "We are Christians by the same title that we are Perigordins or Germans" (p. 211c). Respect for tradition and authority and the expectation of rewards and punishments in the afterlife also influence religious belief, but these are all matters of human concern and self-interest, not of divine inspiration.

We must note parenthetically, however, that Montaigne insists frequently in this essay that the Christian faith comes through God's power alone, and not at all through human means. "Our faith is not of our own acquiring, 'tis purely the gift of another's bounty," he says (p. 239c). Only the divine initiative, God's gracious revelation, can account for such an extraordinary belief. It becomes somewhat of a problem to reconcile this constant refrain with the statement in the present context that "we only receive our religion after our own fashion, by our own hands, and no otherwise than other religions are received" (p. 211b).

As for the second objection, that Sebonde's arguments are too weak to prove his point and may easily be refuted, Montaigne terms it "more dangerous and malicious than the first," because it opens the way to atheism and religious disbelief. To challenge and overcome this dangerous presumption, he avows, he will now proceed to show how miserable and weak man and all his faculties are.

> The means that I use, and that I think most proper, to subdue this frenzy, is to crush and spurn under foot pride and human arrogance; to make them sensible of the inanity, vanity, and nothingness of man; to wrest the wretched arms of their reason out of their hands; to make them bow down and bite the ground, under the authority and reverence of the divine majesty. (p. 213a)

Montaigne grants that Sebonde's arguments are weak and may be challenged, but he insists that they are the best that can be produced by the human reason, which is far too frail and petty to understand divine things. Hence he holds it presumptuous of man to try to do this, and even more arrogant to try to question the existence of God. Montaigne does not stop here, however. He goes on to question the capacity of man to understand *any* level of reality—the natural as well as the supernatural.

> We must do more than this, and make them know that, to convict the weakness of their reason, there is no necessity of culling out rare examples: and that it is so defective and so blind, that there is no so clear facility clear enough for it: that to it the easy and the hard is all one; that all subjects equally, and nature in general, disclaims its authority, and rejects its mediation. (p. 213c)

Thus he announces the main theme of this essay: radical doubt as to the capacity of human reason to attain certain knowledge about anything.

III

Montaigne begins his attack on the power of reason by arguing (1) that man shares this capacity with the rest of nature, particularly the animals, and (2) that insofar as human reason is unique, it brings him misery rather than happiness. He ridicules man's presumptuousness in claiming for himself what is common to all creatures and what in his case is a burden rather than a blessing.

Presumption is our natural and original disease. The most wretched and frail of all creatures is man, and withal the proudest. He feels and sees himself lodged here in the dirt and filth of the world, nailed and rivetted to the worst and deadest part of the universe, in the lowest story of the house, and most remote from the heavenly arch, with animals of the worst condition of the three, and yet in his imagination will be placing himself above the circle of the moon, and bringing heaven under his feet. 'Tis by the vanity of the same imagination that he equals himself to God, attributes to himself divine qualities, withdraws and separates himself from the crowd of other creatures, cuts out the shares of animals his fellows and companions, and distributes to them portions of faculties and force as himself thinks fit. (p. 215a-b)

All this I have said to prove the resemblance there is in human things and to bring us back and join us to the crowd: we are neither above or below the rest. All that is under heaven, says the wise man, runs one law and one fortune . . .

. . . .

There is indeed some difference; there are orders and degrees; but 'tis under the aspect of one same nature . . .

. . . .

Man must be compelled and restrained within the bounds of this polity. Wretched being, he is really not in a condition to step over the rail; he is fettered and circumscribed, he is subjected to a co-ordinate obligation with the other creatures of his class, and of a very humble condition, without any prerogative or preëminence true and real; that which he attributes to himself, by vain fancy and opinion, has neither body nor taste. (p. 218c-d)

Montaigne goes into a lengthy description of those characteristics of animal behavior which, he holds, indicate that animals have somewhat the same intellectual capacities as man, and even surpass him in many respects. Indeed, the animals, he says, equal and sometimes exceed us in the moral virtues. He compares their state of "peace, repose, security, innocence and health," with the human lot of "inconstancy, irresolution, incertitude, sorrow, superstitition, . . . ambition, avarice, jealousy, envy, irregular, frantic and untamable appetites, war, lying, disloyalty, detraction, and curiosity" (pp. 231d, 232b). He ascribes this wretched state to man's capacity to judge and know, and regards it as a bad advertisement for the benefits of reason.

The above is a pragmatic line of argument which is relevant to the practical advantages or disadvantages of human reason rather than to its power to attain certain knowledge. It enables Montaigne to take up and develop a theme broached at the beginning of the essay: that learning does not make us wise, happy, and virtuous. The truth is, he says, that ignorance is bliss and knowledge is hell. Not only are philosophy and learning incapable of diminishing pain, but they lead to the painful dread of possibilities, from which animals and unlearned, insensitive men are free.

However, it is not a brutish lack of intelligence and sensitivity that Montaigne holds up as a model, but the acknowledgment of the limitations of our knowledge. He cites that ancient sage Socrates as his paradigm of the ignorant man. Socrates disclaimed the possession of knowledge and claimed that he only knew that he was ignorant. His method of teaching was not to present knowledge or make statements about things but always to keep on questioning, "never determining, never satisfying," constantly inquiring rather than instructing.

The acknowledgment of ignorance is the ultimate result of man's long quest for knowledge. After all the accumulation of "knowledge" through the centuries, men find themselves in a state of complete uncertainty, with "nothing massive and firm, nothing but vanity." The result is only an acuter sense of their ignorance and of the shaky state of whatever knowledge they think they have. "We have only by long study confirmed and verified the natural ignorance we were in before" (p. 239d).

IV

These considerations lead Montaigne to examine "whether it be in the power of man to find out that which he seeks" (p. 239c) and to consider what the philosophers have had to say about this subject. He finds three main schools of thought: the dogmatists, the absolute skeptics, and the "epichists."

The dogmatists believe that they have attained certain knowledge. The absolute skeptics believe that it is impossible for man to discover the truth. The "epichists" (coined from a Greek word which means "to keep in, hold back, check, stop, wait"), believe it is equally unwarranted to say that one has attained certain knowledge or that it is impossible for man to attain it.

This third type of thought, also called "Pyrrhonism" (after its originator, Pyrrho of Elis, a Greek philosopher of the 4th century B.C.), advocates a complete suspension of judgment—neither affirming nor denying knowledge. In a sense, this is a more extreme form of skepticism than the absolute skepticism which denies that we can know anything, for the latter is a dogmatic assertion, which claims "great and extreme knowledge." The Pyrrhonians are much more consistent—they will not assert anything.

. . . the profession of the Pyrrhonians is to waver, doubt, and inquire, not to make themselves sure of or responsible to themselves for anything. (p. 240d)

Montaigne acclaims "this extremity of doubt, which jostles itself" (p. 241b). It leads to the peace of mind, the calm and balanced inner state which is the goal of so many schools of philosophy. The avoidance of any kind of fixation of belief frees the mind from sectarian dogmas and from the requirement either to affirm or to deny statements about things of which one is ignorant.

Is it not of some advantage to be disengaged from the necessity that curbs others? is it not better to remain in suspense than to entangle one's self in the innumerable errors that human fancy has produced? is it not much better to suspend one's persuasion than to intermeddle with these wrangling and seditious divisions? What shall I choose? "What you please, provided you do choose." A very foolish answer, but one, nevertheless, to which all the dogmatists seem to point; by which we are not permitted to be ignorant of that of which we are ignorant. (p. 241c)

The Pyrrhonians refuse to affirm anything, because things may equally be one way or the other. The effect of this attitude

. . . is a pure, entire, perfect, and absolute suspension of the judgment: they make use of their reason to inquire and debate, but not to fix and determine. Whoever shall imagine a perpetual confession of ignorance, a judgment without bias or inclination, upon any occasion whatever, conceives a true idea of Pyrrhonism. (p. 242a)

But what is the result of suspension of judgment on action, which must be either one thing or another? Why, this is no problem to the Pyrrhonians, says Montaigne. They do what comes naturally, conveniently, easily, avoiding the disturbance that comes from trying to live according to some abstract notion of the nature of things. They provide a model of docility, both in politics and religion, following the common, traveled road. Suspension of judgment goes with a practical conservatism.

But, granted that Pyrrhonism results in peace of mind and ease in action, does it not make philosophy's quest for "truth, knowledge, and certainty" futile? Why keep on pursuing philosophy, if, as Empedocles says, " 'there is not one thing of which we can positively say it is' " (p. 244d)? In answering this question, Montaigne gives his view of what philosophy is or should be.

First of all, he says, there is sheer pleasure in philosophical inquiry, aside from any results or lack of results that it may have. There is an element of play in "the studious passion," and we should not take what philosophers say any more seriously than they do themselves. They are not above tossing out fictional inventions, such as "Atoms, Ideas, and Numbers," as actual entities, or above favoring practically beneficial untruths above harmful truths. They indulge in such fanciful speculations not to establish "any certain truth, but merely for exercise" (p. 246a).

Indeed, philosophy is a kind of poetry—"a sophisticated

poesy"—which tries to present a plausible account of things of which no man can have certain knowledge, in order to give us, as Plato said, a likely story. (See *Timaeus*, Vol. 7, p. 447b.-d.)

. . . philosophy presents us, not that which really is or what she really believes, but what she has contrived with the most plausible likelihood and the fairest aspect. (p. 259a)

These observances are made in the context of a long passage which holds up to ridicule the opinions of philosophers on such important subjects as God, the soul, and immortality. We are struck, says Montaigne, by the extreme diversity of opinions, the contradictions of the various points of view, the tendency to see everything from the human standpoint and in the human image, and the general unworthiness and ridiculousness of philosophers' arguments. The best part of wisdom for all these heavy thinkers would have been to admit that they were ignorant about things which are unknowable by human reason and inexpressible in human speech. They are unable even to understand human reason and human nature. Who are they, then, to presume to say what God may or may not be and what He may or may not do, and to mouth such inanities about the soul and immortality?

Of philosophy, Montaigne says,

. . . she has so many faces, so much variety, and has said so many things, that all our dreams and fantasies are there to be found; human imagination can conceive nothing, good or bad, that is not there . . . And I am the more willing to expose my own whimsies to the public, forasmuch as though they are spun out of myself and without any pattern, I know they will be found related to some ancient humour, and there will be no want of some one to say, "That's whence he took it." My manners are natural; I have not called in the assistance of any discipline to frame them: but weak as they are, when it came into my head to lay them open to the world's view, and that, to expose them to the light in a little more decent garb, I went about to help them with reasons and examples: it was a wonder to myself incidentally to find them conformable to so many philosophical discourses and examples. I never knew what regimen my life was of till after it was near worn out and spent: a new figure, an unpremediate and accidental philosopher. (pp. 263d-264a)

The true words of wisdom are simply these: "What do I know?" Montaigne tells us that he bears these words "in the emblem of a balance" (p. 254a). The implication is that one is always uncertain what one knows or if one knows, especially about such deep and basic things as God, the soul, and immortality.

The remedy against the foolishness of the philosophers is to question their authority and to examine their assumptions. And we should go further and also question what is handed down by tradition and commonly believed, and so to examine all assumptions. The reason so much nonsense is accepted is that men take ancient beliefs "by authority and upon trust." What is commonly held comes to be "an accepted jargon," so that merely "assumed truth" comes to be "received belief," and is held to be as sacred as the dictates of law and religion.

The reason that man do not doubt of so few things is that they never examine common impressions; they do not dig to the root where the faults and weakness lie; they only debate about the branches: they do not ask whether such and such a thing be true, but if it has been so and so understood; it is not inquired whether Galen said anything to purpose, but whether he said this or that. (p. 260b)

Do not grant the philosophers any of their assumptions, warns Montaigne. Once you do this, you have to follow where they lead you. "Whoever is believed upon his presuppositions is our master and our god" (p. 260d). Do not let them get away with the specious ploys " 'that there is no disputing with persons who deny principles' " (p. 260d). It is just the principles, that is the presuppositions, of a science that are to be questioned if we are to examine them critically at all. The philosophers' assumptions are of human, not divine, origin; hence, they are all to be questioned, all "to be put in to the balance." And do not let them get away with appealing to common sense experience; it is they who have made reason the ultimate arbiter. Let them, in all consistency, prove whatever they say to our reason.

They must not tell us, "it is true, for you see and feel it to be so": they must tell me whether I really feel what I think I feel; and if I do feel it, they must then tell me why I feel it, and how, and what; let them tell me the name, origin, parts and junctures of heat and cold; the qualities of agent and patient; or let them give up their profession, which is not to admit or approve of anything but by the way of reason; that is their test in all sorts of essays: but certainly, 'tis a test full of falsity, error, weakness, and defect. (p. 261b-c)

Yet after this appeal to examine all statements critically, Montaigne advises us to follow the middle way, avoiding extremes in thought as in action.

Keep yourselves in the common road; it is not good to be so subtle and cunning . . . I advise you, in all your opinions and meditations, as well as in your manners and all other things, to keep yourself moderate and reserved, and to avoid all novelty and strangeness . . . (p. 270b-c)

Freedom of thought is a dangerous thing, save for a few hardy souls. The mind has to be restricted by laws, customs, and other fetters in order to keep man from going amuck.

. . . therefore it will be much better for you to keep yourself in the beaten path, let it be what it will, than to fly out at a venture with this unbridled liberty. (p. 270d)

He notes wryly, however, that in his own day the liberty of thought of the ancient philosophers has been replaced by a single opinion, laid down "by civil authority and decrees," to which all men conform uncritically. Whatever is current "coin" in the intellectual interchange between men is accepted as legal tender without question.

. . . the alloy is not disputed, but how much it is current for. . . . all things pass for current pay, without scruple or contradiction. (p. 271a-b)

V

In what sense is Montaigne a skeptic?

There are many senses in which persons are called skeptics. A very common one refers to those who doubt the truth or the divine origin of a religious faith, such as Christianity. Is Montaigne a skeptic in this sense? He explicitly disavows and opposes this kind of skepticism in this essay. Yet Pascal considered him an insidious enemy of the Christian faith, and directed many of the arguments in his *Pensées* against Montaigne. The great nineteenth-century French literary critic Sainte-Beuve also believed this about Montaigne and based his judgment especially on the "Apology for Raimond de Sebonde." Is there anything in this essay which would give rise to such a judgment? Does the piece lead to skepticism about religious beliefs in general, about Christianity in particular, about the Roman Catholic faith, or about the claims of natural theology to attain religious truths through human reason?

Another sense in which the term skeptic is used is to refer to persons who hold that it is impossible to attain certain knowledge about anything. This absolutely dogmatic skepticism is difficult to maintain consistently, since it implies a certain knowledge about the limits of human knowledge, and thus seems to contradict itself. A more moderate form of this type of skepticism is that which expresses doubt about the power of the human mind to attain the truth in certain spheres of reality, such as the metaphysical or supernatural. Is Montaigne a skeptic about the capacity of human reason in either the absolute or the qualified sense?

Another sense of the term skeptic, which has fallen into disuse, refers to the critical attitude of mind suggested by its etymological origin in a Greek word which means to "look about, look carefully at, view, examine, consider." Skepticism in this sense, then, is an attitude of critical examination—as regards judgments and opinions and the various claims to knowledge. Many philosophers—Socrates, for instance—might be regarded as skeptics in this sense. Was Montaigne this kind of skeptic?

T. S. Eliot, commenting on Pascal's fascination by Montaigne and even his imitation of his opponent on certain points, has this to say about Montaigne as a skeptic:

But what makes Montaigne a very great figure is that he succeeded, God knows how . . . in giving expression to the scepticism of *every* human being. For every man who thinks and lives by thought must have his own scepticism, that which stops at the question, that which ends in denial, or that which leads to faith and which is somehow integrated into the faith which transcends it.[3]

What does Montaigne's argument about animal reason prove?

One of the oddest parts of a strange "apology," or defense, which actually opposes the main principles of thought it is sup-

[3] T. S. Eliot, *Selected Essays*, new ed. (New York: Harcourt, Brace & Co., Inc., 1950), p. 363.

posedly defending, is the comparison of human with animal reason. For one thing, the main ground for Montaigne's equating of human and animal reason is the correctness of judgment which he sees manifested in animal behavior. This seems to argue for the capacity of human reason to know the true state of things, against which his whole essay is apparently directed.

Montaigne then abandons this line of reasoning, to grant a certain uniqueness about human reason, and attribute to it the miserable state of man in comparison with the animals. The animals are superior to man in not possessing this uniquely human power of reason, he says. But here Montaigne is attributing to human reason not only inherent incapacity to know the truth but certain undesirable practical consequences. We seem to have departed from the main line of argument.

Why has Montaigne proceeded in this way? Does his argument for the likeness of human and animal reason add a certain weight to his doubt or denial that human reason by itself can attain religious truth? Does his argument for the misery caused by human reason insofar as it is unique have any relevance to the question of its power to know things?

Throughout this essay Montaigne consistently couples the theoretical and the practical, the intellectual and emotional advantages of the suspended judgment, of the neither/nor attitude. The Pyrrhonian balance of judgment leads to a balanced inner state of mind, he says. Is this inner peace irrelevant to his main argument or not? Does he offer it as a proof of the validity of this type of skepticism or as an essential bonus that goes with the proper attitude of intellect?

Are theoretical skepticism and practical conservatism naturally allied or opposed?

Commonly we tend to associate skepticism about established views with radicalism. Philosophers since Plato have pondered on the disturbing effect of critical inquiry upon social institutions. John Dewey puts this common view thus:

Let us admit the case of the conservative: if we once start thinking no one can guarantee where we shall come out, except that many objects, ends and institutions are doomed. Every thinker puts some portion of an apparently stable world in peril and no one can wholly predict what will emerge in its place.[4]

Yet historically skepticism of the Pyrrhonian type is associated, as Montaigne points out, with practical and social conservatism. Pyrrho's aim was to achieve peace of mind and to avoid all disturbances. A balanced skepticism which neither affirmed nor denied anything provided the theoretical part of his cure. A conservatism in practical affairs, following the path of custom and tradition and not starting any trouble, formed the practical part.

As Montaigne looked around him and saw his countrymen killing, wounding, and torturing one another in disputes about religious truth, he must have felt that it is convinced belief rather than doubt that leads to radical change and turmoil. Although one might expect Montaigne to be sympathetic with some of the strains of Reformation thought, on the contrary, throughout the essay, he inveighs against the destruction and upheaval caused by innovators in religious matters. For the Reformers were no skeptics. They were firm believers who held that they possessed the true faith. It is the "true believers"—on both sides—who cause all the trouble, not the skeptics, Montaigne seems to be saying.

The three great revolutions of modern times are the American, French, and Russian revolutions. Is any of them associated with an absolute skepticism or a suspension of judgment? Which of them is closest in spirit to Montaigne's skeptical attitude toward human nature and its capacities?

As you look around you nowadays, do you associate radicalism with skepticism or some type of faith? Can you name any contemporary spokesmen for conservatism who are skeptical about man's powers to know and to act?

Does the type of skepticism favored by Montaigne lead to a friendly attitude toward modern science?

We would expect skepticism toward claims to knowledge in the metaphysical and supernatural realm to lead to an em-

[4] Joseph Ratner (ed.), *Intelligence in the Modern World: John Dewey's Philosophy* (New York: The Modern Library, 1939), epigraph.

phasis on knowledge in the natural realm, especially to the kind of knowledge that can be obtained and verified by observation through the senses or scientific instruments. Yet Montaigne, who lived in a time of scientific revolution, shows no friendliness in this essay toward the new science. Indeed, he is suspicious of all innovations in scientific theory. His reaction to the new Copernican theory that the earth revolves around the sun is that we need not take it seriously. It too may be supplanted by another theory in a thousand years. Since scientific theories supplant one another, he argues, why go to the bother of changing the old ones? We cannot be sure of which one is true, anyway. What is newer is not necessarily truer. Why take a chance on new doctrines?

Interestingly, he appeals to our common, ordinary experience as against the rational and mathematical conclusions of the new science. When someone says that sailors who navigated their ships successfully, though following an erroneous theory of the motions of the winds, did so by chance and not by knowledge, he responds that he "had rather follow effects than reason" (p. 277b). And he appeals to the truth of common experience against the supposedly "inevitable demonstrations" of geometry, for instance, that two straight lines will never meet. He even turns against his favorite skeptics, the Pyrrhonians, for using their arguments "to ruin the appearance of experience," and declares that the new science "has followed them in this design of controverting the evidence of effects." The Copernican theory would have been regarded as perverse Pyrrhonian reasoning in ancient times.

Thus, Montaigne's skepticism seems to be inimical to natural science as well as to metaphysical speculation. It seems to lead to a crotchety, conservative antagonism toward what has come to be known as "the advancement of science." It may be that Montaigne lacked a due appreciation for the new science simply because he lived before the great advances in knowledge made by such scientific geniuses as Galileo and Newton. Or it may be that a fundamental view of the nature of reality and the capacity of the mind to fathom it was involved, which would not have been swayed by the discoveries of the seventeenth-century "age of genius."

The Danish historian of philosophy Harald Höffding says that it is Montaigne's concept of nature as an open, infinite, multifarious reality that is his last word—not his skepticism. It is Mother Nature that is the matrix and norm, before which man-made, arbitrary concepts and laws are found wanting. There is a cosmic way or nature of things, just as there is a particular way or nature in each individual, and universal nature in her boundless generosity allows for an infinite number of individual ways. Infinity and individuality are the main keynotes of nature. Human thought and convention are to be opposed where they blind us to the fullness of nature and the varieties of the forms of existence.

Yet Montaigne sees in particular customs and ways of life an expression of nature. He implies, says Höffding, "that Nature reveals herself through that which has become use and wont, and thus his conservatism is a part of his faith in Nature, although, according to Montaigne's own view, the new must be every bit as 'natural' as the old."[5] Höffding concludes his defense of Montaigne against the charge of mere skepticism thus:

His scepticism—which is really an assertion of the right to think—induced him to transcend artificial barriers; and his rich experience and learning taught him what was to be found on the other side of these limits, *i.e.* new individual forms, by means of which one and the same single infinite nature finds expression.[6]

Would Montaigne's line of thought lead to an acceptance of the possibility of probable rather than certain knowledge?

At one point, Montaigne seems clearly to reject the alternative of probability and to hold out for certainty in matters of knowledge. "Either we can absolutely judge, or absolutely we cannot" he asserts (p. 272b.) Hence he espouses the Pyrrhonian balance of judgment against the Academics' (dogmatic skeptics) willingness to acknowledge that some things are more likely than others. Yet at another point he pictures philosophy as the telling of likely stories, and cites approvingly Plato's

[5] Harald Höffding, *A History of Modern Philosophy* (New York: Dover Publications, Inc., 1955), Vol. I, p. 30.
[6] *Ibid.*, p. 33.

statement that " 'what I have said is the most likely to be true of anything I could say' " (p. 259a). True, what he emphasizes in this passage is the mythical, fictional nature of philosophical concepts, but he seems also to be voicing an appreciation of the hypothetical, tentative quality of philosophical thought which grasps, however vaguely and inadequately, something of the nature of things, and provides the likeliest, most probable account possible. Also the emphasis on custom and tradition—"the swing of the world" (p. 242c)—seems to admit, at least in practice, some approximation to a knowledge of the way of things.

Does this advocate of common sense, of the middle way in all things, admit or reject the possibility of probable knowledge? Does he see only two alternatives—complete ignorance as against certain knowledge—or does he recognize a third way between the two extremes, which is available to unaided human reason? If the latter is the case, how are we to reconcile it with his rejection of the Academic "probabilists' " inclination to the more likely judgment? Does he assume this negative position merely to maintain his rhetorical stance in his theoretical argument against those who claim human reason can attain certain knowledge?

The following questions are designed to help you test the thoroughness of your reading. Each question is to be answered by giving a page or pages of the reading assignment. Answers will be found on page 301 of this Reading Plan.

1 What part did Peter Bunel play in the writing of this essay?

2 What is wrong with Plato's arguments against atheism?

3 What nonverbal means of communication do men use?

4 What are the examples of mutual aid among animals?

5 Is reason or obedience the way to virtue for man?

6 Are the incredible and irrational concordant with the conditions of Christian belief?

7 What does the obscurity of the philosophers indicate?

BACON

Advancement of Learning

Book II, Ch. 5-24

Vol. 30, pp. 39-95

T he writings of Francis Bacon mark one of the turning points in Western thought. They call on philosophy to become the midwife of social change, and they make fruitfulness in practical operations the test of philosophy's value. For Bacon, it is not contemplation but productive activity which is the highest aim of philosophical thought.

The modern tone of this doctrine is unmistakable. It had a revolutionary effect on philosophy, education, and the organization of scientific research in England. A generation after his death Bacon was hailed as a "new Aristotle," the "restorer of physics," and the "secretary of nature." The main principles of this new thought of the seventeenth century are still very much with us as we approach the twenty-first. We may trace Bacon's influence down from John Locke to John Dewey, and to modern utilitarians, materialists, pragmatists, and expounders of the social uses of science.

Bacon first expressed this doctrine in the *Advancement of Learning*, which comprises an extraordinarily ambitious proposal to revolutionize the whole system of education and scientific research in England and provides what is probably the handiest presentation of the new doctrine. Designed to persuade and convince, it became for the generation after Bacon an inspiring manifesto, calling for the transformation of England's educational and scientific institutions.

The work covers the whole of natural human knowledge—divided into history, poetry, and philosophy—as well as divine revealed truth. The present selection, which deals with philosophy, provides an excellent opportunity to grasp the main principles of Bacon's thought.

Eighth Reading

I

Francis Bacon was convinced that the sciences of his day were blind and futile. It was his announced purpose to restore the "original commerce" between man and the world, that is, man's knowledge of things, and hence his rule over nature. The great project of Bacon's life was to complete a voluminous masterwork which would set forth all that had to be done to achieve a restoration, or "instauration" as he called it, of the sciences. As it turned out, he completed only the first two of the projected six parts of the work, entitled *The Great Instauration* —Part I, on the division of the sciences, and Part II, on the new "organon" (instrument, method, or logic) for the interpretation of nature.

The *Advancement of Learning*, published in 1605, provided a preparatory sketch of the principal ideas of *The Great Instauration*. Indeed, when the latter was published in 1620, Bacon had finished only the second part, the *Novum Organum*, and he suggested that Book II of the *Advancement of Learning* might serve as a substitute for the first part, until he got around to writing it. In the end, however, Bacon simply adapted and considerably expanded the early work, translated it into Latin, and published it in 1623 as the missing first part of *The Great Instauration*.

In the *Advancement of Learning*, then, we have Bacon's original version of the first step in the proposed renovation of the sciences. Unlike all the rest of his philosophical writings, which were written in Latin, this work was written in English and in Bacon's most elegant and felicitous prose style. It was addressed to James I who had recently ascended the throne of England. Bacon addressed him because James had the supreme

133

power to change English institutions and was himself a man of learning, or considered himself such. Bacon, a master in the art of flattery, refers frequently to the king's learning in this work. For instance, he has this to say in the words of dedication in Book I:

. . . there hath not been since Christ's time any king or temporal monarch, which hath been so learned in all literature and erudition, divine and human. (p. 2a)

And there is much more in this vein in the dedicatory section of Book I. He suggests that once the king understands the real situation of the sciences, he himself will make his own proposals for the advancement of knowledge. And he notes that the head of the state is the proper authority for what has to be done "by public designation," not "by private endeavors."

Following this double plan of attack and persuasion, Bacon deals in Book I with the present discredit to learning and the dignity of learning in the past. Learning is now discredited because of the opposition of churchmen and politicians and the futile practices of the learned. As for the dignity of learning, he cites the biblical eulogies of wisdom and learning and the healthy effect that learning has had on civic virtue and sound government. Book II, after some preliminary remarks criticizing the universities as the repositories of dead learning, proceeds to give an account of the whole of learning, both human and divine, that is, both that acquired through natural reason and that attained through divine revelation.

II

Bacon divides human learning into history, poetry, and philosophy, corresponding with the faculties of memory, imagination, and reason. The historical disciplines, including natural history, describe actual events which men have perceived and remembered. The poetic arts construct a "feigned history," in which things happen as it pleases us, not as they actually occur. Philosophical studies rely on reason alone to disclose the underlying nature of things, though they are indebted to the historical disciplines for the materials they provide for consideration, and to poetry for its deep and vivid revelation of human passions and manners.

It must be noted that although Bacon presents a very detailed and explicit division of the sciences, he also insists on their organic unity. Thus he cautions:

And generally let this be a rule, that all partitions of knowledges be accepted rather for lines and veins than for sections and separations; and that the continuance and entireness of knowledge be preserved. (p. 49a)

He divides philosophy into three branches according to its objects—God, the world, and man—but then he immediately points out that there is a single, primary philosophy which is the root or trunk from which all the branches grow. He calls for the development of this primary philosophy (*philosophia prima*, "summary philosophy," or "original or universal philosophy") through a discovery of the common axioms or patterns of things—"the same footsteps of nature, treading or printing upon several subjects or matters" (p. 41a).

Bacon thereupon deals with his tripartite division of human learning—with "divine philosophy" or "natural theology" (see Ch. 6), with "natural philosophy" (see Ch. 7-8), and with "human philosophy" (see Ch. 9-23).

Natural theology comprises the knowledge of God which is attainable through the contemplation of nature and the use of human reason, as distinct from the knowledge attainable through divine revelation. Bacon claims for this science only that it will refute atheism and afford some knowledge of the nature and attributes of God, not that it will offer evidence to support the specific doctrines of revealed religion.

Natural philosophy, the study of the physical world, is divided into "natural science" and "natural prudence." The first is a theoretical inquiry into the causes and principles of things. The second is a practical discipline which applies the knowledge acquired in natural science to the achievement of certain desired effects ("operations" or "works").

Natural science or theory is itself divided into two parts: physics and metaphysics. Physics investigates the variable, transitory, and relative aspects of things; metaphysics, their fixed and constant aspects. The core of natural science, and thus of natural philosophy, is the discernment of the essential "forms" or patterns of things.

> . . . the invention of forms is of all other parts of knowledge the worthiest to be sought, if it be possible to be found. (p. 43d)

This would seem to make metaphysics the master science, as it was of old. But Bacon hastens to point out that for him, and contrary to Aristotle's view, "first philosophy" and metaphysics are two different things. First or summary philosophy is the basic knowledge underlying all other knowledge, including divine, natural, and human philosophy; whereas metaphysics is that branch of natural philosophy which seeks the "essential forms" of material substances. Plato went wrong, says Bacon, "by considering of forms as absolutely abstracted from matter, and not confined and determined by matter" (p. 44a). What Bacon means by "forms" is indicated by the following list:

> . . . to inquire the forms of sense, of voluntary motion, of vegetation, of colours, of gravity and levity, of density, of tenuity, of heat, of cold, and all other natures and qualities, which, like an alphabet, are not many, and of which the essences (upheld by matter) of all creatures do consist . . . (p. 44b)

In contrasting physics and metaphysics, however, Bacon makes at least verbal use of Aristotle's distinction between the four causes. Physics, he says, deals with the material and efficient causes of things; metaphysics, with their formal and final causes. Thus physics may seem to explain a form, such as whiteness in snow or froth, but all it does is to explain the material process—e.g., "that the subtile intermixture of air and water is the cause." But this is not the form of whiteness, which only metaphysics can discover.

Discernment of the forms provides the simplification of things which is necessary for both theoretical knowledge and productive operations. In the first place, it makes it possible for us to grasp "the infinity of individual experience" with a few simple forms of principles. Such an "abridgement" of the multiplicity and variety of things is the ultimate aim of all knowledge. Hence Bacon sketches a "pyramid" of knowledge, from the most to the least various. In natural philosophy this consists of natural history as the base, physics as the middle stage, and metaphysics as the peak.

In the second place, knowledge of the essential forms opens up the widest field for obtaining desired effects. The light it sheds on the nature of things gives us freedom and power to work on nature. Here it far surpasses the application of physical knowledge, which can light us only to the repetition of what has occurred before, "in a like case."

For physical causes give light to new invention in *simili materia*. But whosoever knoweth any form, knoweth the utmost possibility of super inducing that nature upon any variety of matter; and so is less restrained in operation, either to the basis of the matter, or the condition of the efficient . . . (p. 45a)

Final causes, as well as formal causes, are the subject matter of metaphysics. In this work, Bacon does not reject the inquiry into final causes as a sterile pursuit, as he does in other works. He says only that to bring final causes into physical inquiries will produce confusion and arrest discovery, for final causes are properly pursued only in metaphysical inquiry. Both material and final causes are true and compatible explanations of things, each in its own sphere.

Bacon includes mathematics under metaphysics, on the ground that "quantity determined or proportionable [is] one of the essential forms of things as that that is causative in nature of a number of effects," and also that "figure" is "the most abstracted and separable from matter, and therefore most proper to metaphysic" (p. 46a). Mathematics is either pure or mixed with the axioms and principles of natural philosophy. Pure mathematics serves to train the mind and keep it intellectually acute.

After this discussion of "natural science or theory," Bacon turns to "natural prudence, or the part operative of natural philosophy." He divides the latter into three parts: experiment, philosophy, and magic, corresponding to natural history, physics, and metaphysics in the pyramid of knowledge. "Experiment" means broadly what it does nowadays; however, it refers to operations discovered both through accidental and through contrived experiences. "Philosophy" refers to the knowledge of physical causes. "Natural magic" refers to the operations made possible by knowledge of the metaphysical forms or natures of things.

Bacon looks to natural magic for "radical or fundamental alterations and innovations in nature" (p. 46d). He recommends setting up a "kalendar" (inventory) of the inventions already made, together with a list of those not yet discovered or held impossible, "to the end that by these optatives and potentials man's inquiry may be the more awake in deducing direction of works from the speculation of causes" (p. 47c). He also advocates intense concentration on experiments which will give rise to the contrivance of further experiments, thus leading to the most basic knowledge and hence to the most basic inventions. Basic research, as well as "immediate and present use," is to be emphasized; the magnetic compass, for instance, resting on basic scientific knowledge, is as important for navigation as the sail, which is the product of common experience and necessity.

Bacon also suggests two more "kalendars" to aid inquiry generally in natural philosophy. The first is a list of doubts as to beliefs that are not proved (*non liquets*), which is salutary both for the prevention of error and also for the direction of inquiry into the paths that need to be opened. Bacon warns against the tendency to take such lists as permanent, thus making them bars to further inquiry.

. . . when a doubt is once received. men labour rather how to keep it a doubt still, than how to solve it; and accordingly bend their wits. Of this we see the familiar example in lawyers and scholars, both which, if they have once admitted a doubt, it goeth ever after authorized for a doubt. But that use of wit and knowledge is to be allowed, which laboureth to make doubtful things certain, and not those which labour to make certain things doubtful. (p. 48a)

The second inventory is "a kalendar of popular errors," a list of common beliefs which pass uncriticized through common speech and custom.

Lists of doubts or "problems" have the great virtue of displaying the various ways in which thinkers have approached the basic questions about nature, and "it may be every one in some one point hath seen clearer than his fellows." Hence, we should collect their views and get "all the possible light which remaineth to us of them" (p. 48c).

III

Having discussed natural theology and natural philosophy, Bacon now turns to human philosophy, where man himself is the subject of inquiry. From the viewpoint of man, this study is "the end and term of natural philosophy," while from the standpoint of nature, it is "but a portion of natural philosophy" (p. 49a). It is divided into two parts: the study of individual man and the study of man in society.

Individual man is a unity of body and mind. A few studies, such as physiognomy, dream interpretation, and a certain branch of medicine deal with the mutual effects of body and mind on one another. However, the main division in this branch of human philosophy is that between the sciences that deal with man's body and those that deal with his mind.

There are four studies dealing with the body, corresponding with four physical goods: medicine for health, "cosmetic" for beauty, "athletic" for strength, and "voluptuary art" for pleasure. Bacon deals at some length with medicine, because he considers it a science which has been "more professed than laboured, and yet more laboured than advanced" (p. 51d). He calls for an exact knowledge of the basic causes and cures of disease, careful case histories, a more advanced study of anatomy, and a developed pharmaceutical science. Furthermore, he holds that one of the aims of medicine should be to ease pain, and advises physicians to use their skill to procure a good death ("euthanasia") for their mortally sick patients.

The studies dealing with the mind fall into two parts, one dealing with its nature and the other with its faculties. As for the first, says Bacon, we may improve our natural knowledge of the nature of the mind, but ultimately we must rely on divine revelation. He contents himself here with dealing with "two appendices" to such knowledge—"divination" (the art or science of prediction) and "fascination" (the action of the mind on bodies outside it).

Bacon, however, discusses at length the sciences dealing

with the faculties of the mind. These fall into two main groups, one dealing with the understanding or reason, the other dealing with the will or appetite. He has already, he tells us, dealt in another work with the imagination, the "messenger" between the reason and the will.

"Rational knowledge," the study of the human understanding or reason, is the most important part of human philosophy. It is the master science, "the art of arts," the key to all the other arts and sciences. It includes four basic intellectual arts—invention, judgment, custody, and delivery. These comprise the human skills in the discovery, demonstration, retention, and communication of knowledge.

The art of "invention" is of two kinds: the discovery of the arts and sciences and the discovery of speech and arguments. Bacon provides an incisive critique of the way in which the arts have been discovered in the past, by chance or necessity—"it is no other method than that which brute beasts are capable of" (p. 57a). He also provides a critique of crude empiricism and inductive reasoning. Induction from the infinite particulars of sense experience, as previously practiced, is too gross and uncertain a procedure to reach the "middle propositions" (between the concrete particulars and abstract generalities) which are the core of all the arts and sciences.

For to conclude upon an enumeration of particulars, without instance contradictory, is no conclusion, but a conjecture; for who can assure (in many subjects) upon those particulars which appear of a side, that there are not other on the contrary side which appear not? (p. 57c)

But even if "some principles or axioms were rightly induced," we would not be able to deduce the necessary middle propositions from them. Nature and the operations based on it are too subtle to be penetrated by deductive reasoning (via the syllogism). All such arguments rest ultimately on words, which "are but the current tokens or popular notions of things" and are often nothing but vague and crude generalizations. However, Bacon refuses to give way to despair about man's ability to attain certain and precise knowledge about the world, and counsels us to seek the solution of our difficulties in the proper method.

This I speak, not to disable the mind of man, but to stir it up to seek help: for no man, be he never so cunning or practised, can make a straight line or perfect circle by steadiness of hand, which may be easily done by help of a ruler or compass. (p. 58b)

Bacon finally sums up the invention of the sciences under two headings: "learned experience" and "interpretation of nature." (The latter, a refined development of the former, is discussed in the *Novum Organum*.)

The invention of speech and arguments is directed to the proper organization and use of the fund of knowledge that has already been discovered. One of its most valuable functions is to collect acquired knowledge and raise specific issues for further inquiry under certain "topics." Raising the right questions "is half of knowledge," says Bacon, for we have to know in some sense what we are seeking in order to arrive at the right answer.

"Judgment," the second intellectual art, comprises the arts of proof and demonstration—inductive and deductive. It proceeds by two methods—"direction" and "caution." The first, traditionally called "analytics," sets up a normative analysis of propositions whereby to judge the proper connection of terms. The second deals with sophistical arguments and subtle fallacies of thought, called *elenches*. It strives to avoid ambiguity of terms and to divide things into their proper classes or categories.

The method of "caution" also deals with the much more important and profound kind of fallacies "which spring from the impressions of the imaginations," which Bacon calls elsewhere "the idols of the mind." These are of three main types: those "imposed upon us by the general nature of the human mind," those "imposed upon us by every man's own individual nature and custom," and those "imposed upon us by words." Later in the *Novum Organum*, Bacon added a fourth "idol," arising from accepted systems of philosophy and science. (See the *Novum Organum*, Book I, 41-44, pp. 109c-110b, and the ensuing discussion.)

"Custody" comprises the arts which help us to retain what we have learned—through writing or memory. "Common-place books"—collections of key passages or arguments—are a useful device for the retention of knowledge. As for memory, no useful "art of memory" is available at the time Bacon writes.

The fourth basic intellectual art, "tradition" or "delivery," comprises all the arts by which we communicate among ourselves—through gestures, speech, and writing. These arts include hieroglyphics, grammar, prosody, ciphering, logic (as a method of presenting knowledge), and rhetoric.

Having disposed of the four intellectual arts which constitute "rational knowledge," Bacon now proceeds to discuss "moral knowledge," the study of human will and desires. It is the discipline and cultivation of the latter that makes ethics a useful science. Hence Bacon divides moral knowledge into two parts, one dealing with the nature of good, and the other telling us how to attain it, that is, "how to frame and subdue the will of man to become true and conformable to" the pursuit of good (p. 69d).

As for the nature of good, it is of two kinds: private and social. Private good consists in self-preservation, self-perfection, or self-expansion (through works and acts). Dynamic activity is a greater good than passive conservation or than peace of mind. Social good is higher than private good because it is the greater, general good, and because it is fulfilled in the individual's acts and duties towards others. Passivity and contemplation, which are individual goods, have no place in social life, which is essentially active.

As for the cultivation of good, it is necessary that we have a solid knowledge of men's dispositions, "tempers," and emotions, for their disorder results in vice. It is the poets and the historians, and not the moral philosophers, who "are the best doctors of this knowledge." While human dispositions and emotions are "given" natural things that cannot be changed by us, we can influence them to direct conduct ("manners") toward the good. We can do this through such factors as habit, education, example, praise, blame, and studies. Bacon offers a few practical "precepts of the wise ordering and exercises of the mind" through custom and habit.

Private good having been considered, Bacon now turns to social good, which is the subject of "civil knowledge" (political or social philosophy). This science is divided into three parts, corresponding with the three essential social functions—"conversation, negotiation, and government"—and the three social goods—"comfort, use, and protection." The subject of civil knowledge, says Bacon, "of all others is most immersed in matter, and hardliest reduced to axiom" (p. 81d). He proceeds therefore by citations from biblical and classical writings, and practical advice on the conduct of life, business, and politics, to fill the whole of a long chapter (23). We must recall that Bacon was lord chancellor of England as well as the architect of the great new interpretation of nature.

I V

This completes Bacon's survey of human philosophy, and thereby of philosophy as a whole. With his task completed, Bacon turns back to consider what he has written thus far, and reacts with a note of humility about his own efforts and with a flourish of pride in the new age in which he lives. This work, he says, is nothing but a tuning of "the instruments of the Muses, that they may play that have better hands" (p. 95b). And the cultural situation of his time warrants his assurance that others will master the "instruments" which he has been tuning.

Among the new cultural factors are the printing press, the voyages of discovery, the general release of men from public business, a peaceful atmosphere, and an end of the religious controversies which formerly diverted men from scientific inquiry. Above all, there is the general factor of "the inseparable propriety [property] of time, which is ever more and more to disclose truth" (p. 95c). He regards his own time, the third era of learning in Western history, as potentially the greatest of all, on condition that men use their powers and opportunities rightly.

. . . this third period of time will far surpass that of the Grecian and Roman learning: only if men will know their own strength, and their own weakness both; and take, one from the other, light of invention, and not fire of contradiction; and esteem of the inquisition of truth as of an enterprise, and not as of a quality or ornament; and employ wit and magnificence to things of worth and excellency, and not to things vulgar and of popular estimation. (p. 95c-d)

V

Now that we have completed a summary view of this wide and detailed survey of philosophical knowledge, with its many divisions and subdivisions, we should note some of the main themes and principles expressed here.

1. First, there is the constant stress upon use, action, and production as the end of knowledge. More exactly, there is an emphasis on the mutual influence of theory and practice or production on one another. On the one hand, theory is the means to practice and operations. On the other hand, productive operations and practical activity provide a solid ground for theoretical knowledge. Theory and practice work together to illuminate and guide one another. The new "interpretation of nature" is a development out of "learned experience." It rests on observation and experience, not on book learning and speculative reasoning.

2. Related to this major stress is Bacon's emphasis on the social use of knowledge. Granted that contemplation is a great private good, the social good is greater than the private. The social good involves not only ethical acts and duties but also the whole enterprise of science and technology. Bacon refers frequently in this selection to the importance of inventions, of new techniques and instruments, such as the magnetic compass, in the advancement of mankind. In this regard, Bacon is an original thinker, opening up a line of thought that was to be developed in later centuries.

3. Third, there is the emphasis on a new method of inquiry to achieve the new interpretation of nature and socially useful operations. Mere experience, highly developed reasoning powers, or the recent "excellence and vivacity of wits" are not enough. Only a carefully worked-out method, based on past experience and modifiable by future experience, will arrive at the correct interpretation of nature and at the techniques that follow from it. Hence Bacon's emphasis on the careful compilation of lists of topics, problems, and errors, on the collection of already acquired knowledge in convenient form, and other useful household hints for the scientific inquirer. And, above all,

there is the recommendation to find the simplest ideas and patterns of things and to go on from them to the more complex phenomena, through a new kind of inductive reasoning.

4. Bacon advocates a cautious critical attitude toward the picture of things which we get through our senses and our minds. He denies that immediate sense perception by itself correctly reflects objective reality, yet he holds that "the senses are very sufficient to certify and report truth," provided that they are aided by instruments and operations which disclose what is not apparent to the naked senses. Similarly, he sees the mind as "like an enchanted glass, full of superstition and imposture," if it is not corrected by various precautions. As the ruler or compass helps a man to draw a straight line or a perfect circle, so instruments aid the senses to perceive correctly; likewise, an awareness of the illusionary proclivities, or "idols," of the mind leads us to discount erroneous interpretations and thereby points the way to the true ones.

V I

Is Bacon's "new method" at variance with the method actually employed by modern science?

Bacon is often criticized for having advocated a method of inquiry which missed some of the essential features of that actually used by the great figures, such as Galileo, Bacon's contemporary, who inaugurated modern science. While his emphasis on the importance of the collection of particular facts is recognized as a praiseworthy departure from medieval methods of inquiry, he is criticized for neglecting the intellectual role of judgment and selection in the interpretation of facts. He is particularly criticized for his neglect of the role of hypothesis in guiding scientific inquiry and of deductive reasoning in demonstrating its results. His aversion to mathematics is also contrasted with the method of the new science, which was preeminently mathematical, emphasizing measurement and the mathematical expression of natural laws.

On the basis of your reading of this selection, would you agree that all of these criticisms are true? Does Bacon advocate a piling up of facts regardless of particular lines of inquiry?

Does he have any understanding of the use of tentative hypotheses as directive stimuli to scientific investigation? What role does he assign mathematics in discovering and demonstrating the nature of things? Is deductive reasoning of any importance in his scheme for the advancement of knowledge?

Would the accumulative, empirical method attributed to Bacon by his critics be more applicable to the historical and social sciences than to the physical sciences? Or must each department of science have essentially the same kind of method in order to maintain the unity of science proclaimed by Bacon? Does he advocate the same basic method for each science or group of sciences?

What does Bacon mean by "forms"?

Bacon tells us that he prefers to use traditional terms rather than to coin new ones, and he contrasts his own outward respect for philosophical tradition with Aristotle's adverse criticism of his predecessors. However, it is not always clear just how far Bacon uses traditional terms in the same sense as previous thinkers and wherein he gives them a new connotation. The term "forms" provides an excellent example of this.

Are Bacon's forms the same as Plato's forms or ideas? Bacon pays his respects to Plato for having seen that the forms were the true objects of knowledge but then, as we have seen, says that Plato was mistaken in abstracting them from matter. Are Bacon's forms then the same as Aristotle's formal causes, the essences or natures of things, which are expressed in their definitions? Such expressions as "the forms of substances" seem to indicate this. But as the discussion proceeds, the forms seem to comprise physical forces or principles, whose laws we must master in order to produce the effects we desire.

So, on the one hand, Bacon's "forms" are the most general, simplest qualities of things—heat, light, weight, colors, etc. And, on the other hand, they are the principles or laws by which these qualities come to be or are produced. Is Bacon, in his theory of forms, on the verge of the modern scientific view of dynamic causal laws? Consider these excerpts from the *Novum Organum:*

It is best to consider matter, its conformation, and the changes of that conformation, its own action, and the law of this action or motion; for forms are a mere fiction of the human mind, unless you will call the laws of action by that name. (p. 111c)

. . . forms, or the true differences of things (which are in fact the laws of simple action) . . . (p. 118c)

For although nothing exists in nature except individual bodies, exhibiting clear individual effects according to particular laws, yet in each branch of learning, that very law, its investigation, discovery, and development, are the foundation both of theory and practice. This law, therefore, and its parallel in each science, is what we understand by the term form, adopting that word because it has grown into common use, and is of familiar occurrence. (p. 137b-c)

Nor again, would we be thought to mean (even when treating of simple natures) any abstract forms or ideas, either undefined or badly defined in matter. For when we speak of forms, we mean nothing else than those laws and regulations of simple action which arrange and constitute any simple nature, such as heat, light, weight, in every species of matter, and in a susceptible subject. The form of heat or form of light, therefore, means no more than the law of heat or the law of light. (p. 149c)

Yet how can we harmonize this view of the forms with the distinction between the metaphysical form of whiteness and the explanation of the physical process by which whiteness occurs in snow or froth? (See above, p. 136.)

Does Bacon's theory of the "idols" of the mind lead to skepticism about the mind's capacity to view things as they are?

Spinoza considered it one of Bacon's basic errors that

. . . he supposes that, besides the deception of the senses, the human intellect is fallible by its very nature, and imagines everything after the analogy of its own nature, and not after the analogy of the universe, so that it is like an uneven mirror [turned] to the rays of things, which mingles its own nature with the nature of the things, etc.[1]

For Spinoza, who held that the mind can attain certain truth, acting through its own nature (by deduction from clear and

[1] A. Wolf (ed.), *The Correspondence of Spinoza* (London: George Allen & Unwin, Ltd., 1928), pp. 76-77.

simple ideas), to accept Bacon's view would be to put all human knowledge in doubt. Spinoza's remark does raise a real difficulty; for, although Bacon offers many practical hints and "cautions" on how to counteract the natural tendency of the human mind to deception, the question still remains as to how we know when we are being led astray and when we are on course. The whole point of Bacon's inductive method is to lead the mind to conform itself to the objective state of things, but if we cannot trust the mind to do this naturally—indeed, according to Bacon, the human mind is disposed by its generic and individual nature to err—how are we to know when we have avoided these basic errors? How are we to know that we are seeing things as they are in themselves and not as we are subjectively disposed to see them?

Will experience demonstrate our errors? Can all the levels and aspects of the real world be demonstrated experimentally? Will productive operations demonstrate wherein we have been misled by subjective disposition? Will they do so in regard to all types of knowledge about nature?

In any case, is it experience or productive operations, or our interpretation of experience and operations made through some act of the intellect, that demonstrates our fallacies?

How would Bacon answer these questions? Does he indicate how the mind is to be purified of its inherent tendencies to see things subjectively, in the human image? Does he say how we can be sure that we have eliminated these errors and are viewing the objective world and not our false images of it?

Do you recognize these "natural," inherent tendencies to err in yourself? If so, how did you become aware of them? Was there anything in your mind itself to warn you that you were going wrong, apart from any cautionary experiences? Did the repeated hard lessons of experience teach you this? Or was it reading Bacon's warnings in this selection that first made you clearly aware of these inherent tendencies to err? Have you been able to cope with and counteract these tendencies? If so, how?

*Is it appropriate to associate philosophy so closely
with technology and social use?*

It is Bacon's avowed purpose to take philosophy out of the heavens, where he claims the ancient philosophers wrongly put it, and to return it to its rightful place on earth as the intellectual overseer of human progress. Do you think he is right or wrong in taking this position?

Should philosophy be entirely removed from scientific, technological, and social activities, or should its role and purpose be determined by such activities? Or is it possible for philosophy to be detached from technical and social use in certain aspects, while intimately involved as regards to other aspects? How would Plato, Aristotle, and Lucretius have answered these questions?

Where do you think philosophy should be placed in the university curriculum—with the social sciences, the humanities, theology, mathematics, or in some other area of inquiry?

The following questions are designed to help you test the thoroughness of your reading. Each question is to be answered by giving a page or pages of the reading assignment. Answers will be found on page 301 of this Reading Plan.

1 What are the three parts of physics?

2 Why did Democritus give a more reliable account of physical causes than Plato and Aristotle?

3 Why is it hard to tell whether a physician is a master of his art or not?

4 What faculty of the mind has one face turned toward reason, the other toward action?

5 What is the fallacy of "the cave"?

6 Do thoughts have to be expressed only in words?

7 In what respect is rhetoric inferior, in what respect superior, to wisdom?

DESCARTES

Discourse on the Method
of Rightly Conducting the Reason

Parts I-IV

Vol. 31, pp. 41-54

"I *think, therefore I am"*—these words uttered over
three hundred years ago mark a historic moment in
Western thought. René Descartes, the man who pro-
nounced these words, is generally credited with being
the father of modern philosophy; and the *Discourse on
Method,* the work in which they appeared, is regarded
as one of the great beacon lights in the history of philosophy.

Starting with Descartes, Western thinkers centered
their attention on the structure of the mind rather than
of things, on the subject of knowledge rather than its
object. With Descartes' new stress on self-consciousness as the only immediately certain knowledge, the
question of how we know external reality became a
knotty and disturbing question for philosophical
thought. This new interest is obvious in our subsequent readings in Locke, Berkeley, Hume, and Kant.

This subjective, "idealistic" tendency in Descartes' thought, however, was derived from his exigent concern for the attainment of absolutely certain knowledge and was directed toward providing a solid, unquestionable foundation for such knowledge. He started with himself and his own consciousness, but his ultimate aim was to devise a reliable, exact method of knowledge and, through following it, to establish a unified, organic system of the sciences. Starting with one universal human reason, and following one universal method, he hoped to arrive at one universal science—a systematic knowledge of all the things knowable by man.

One of the main charms of the *Discourse on Method* —and it is one of the most charming and delightful works in the history of Western philosophy—is this combination of a subjective interest and starting point with a concern for exact method and certain knowledge. As Descartes himself notes, what might well have been presented as a formal treatise has instead been presented in the form of a biography—a "history" or "fable" (a story with a moral). He intends, he says, "to set forth my life as in a picture," so that we may see how and why he came to devise his new method.

Thus we have here a very rare and rich form of literature—the philosophical confession. In such a piece, the writer says in effect, "This is the story of my intellectual life. This is how I came to think the way I do. This is how I discovered the ultimate basis of knowledge." It is just such a story that Descartes tells us here—humbly, modestly, frankly, and highlighted by that moment, in a stove-heated room in winter quarters in Germany, when a young man of twenty-three had the moment of insight that made him the "father" of modern thought.

Ninth Reading

I

It is no mere happy accident that Descartes' *Discourse on Method* comes in this reading plan just after the selections from Montaigne and Bacon. With them, he stands in contrast to the traditional cast of Greek and medieval thought, which culminated in the magnificent synthesis of Thomas Aquinas. He shares with Montaigne the stress on immediate experience, on the variety of human customs and opinions, and on the dubiousness of human knowledge. And he shares with Bacon the zeal to construct a new scientific method, both for the betterment of human life and for the advancement of knowledge.

The contrast between him and these two fellow thinkers of modern times is, however, even more instructive than the similarity. Unlike Montaigne, he is convinced that man can attain certain knowledge, and the obvious inadequacy of previous knowledge is only the spur to attain adequate knowledge. Doubt for him is a method, a preliminary stage on the way to certainty, not an ideal state of mind.

Not that indeed I imitated the sceptics, who only doubt for the sake of doubting, and pretend to be always uncertain; for, on the contrary, my design was only to provide myself with good ground for assurance, and to reject the quicksand and mud in order to find the rock or clay. (p. 50c)

The variety of customs and opinions is simply a warning as to the unreliability of custom and convention as a guide to truth. As for private, personal experience, it is to be plumbed to its depths to discover the immediately graspable truth upon which all certain knowledge may be built.

The differences between Descartes and Bacon, who also sought a new method for the advancement of knowledge, are also significant. For certain knowledge, Descartes looks to human reason and specifically to a mathematical type of reasoning, not to an adjustment of the mind to the external world through a methodically developed arrangement of data. He trusts the natural powers and operations of the mind, properly applied, to grasp the truth about things. His method assumes a distinctively human faculty of "good sense," which is by nature present in all men—"the power of forming a good judgment and of distinguishing the true from the false" (p. 41b). Moreover Descartes looks within and summons the testimony of his inner states in a way that Bacon never would. Where Bacon directs the mind to things rather than to itself, Descartes makes self-consciousness central and considers the mind more knowable than its objects. Certainty for him starts and ends in states of mind.

The *Discourse on Method* was written to introduce the elementary principles of Descartes' thought to the general public. As he indicates in that work, his basic ideas were already well known in intellectual circles and were even being taught in some universities. He had already written for his own clarification, but had not published, the *Rules for the Direction of the Mind,* setting forth the principles of his method. (See pp. 1-40.) He planned first his work on the physical universe, called *The World,* in which he held that all material things are governed by mechanical laws. However, the Inquisition's censure of Galileo, for his use of the Copernican hypothesis that the earth revolves around the sun, caused Descartes to postpone, or rather suppress, publication of his treatise on physics, since it too was based on Copernicus' theory. (See pp. 54d, 60d-61a.)

Bitterly disappointed, but determined to make his views known without antagonizing the authorities, he decided to publish three long scientific essays, showing how his new method had proved fruitful in specific areas—*Dioptric, Meteors,* and *Geometry.* (For *Geometry,* see pp. 295-353.) To these three "essays of the method," he added as a preface the *Discourse on Method,* written in a direct, personal style, setting forth in autobiographical form how he came to his principles and inviting his readers to tell him what they thought of them. This first published work, comprising the three essays and the *Discourse*, was published in 1637, when Descartes was forty-one years old and well advanced in his career as a philosopher and scientist.

His principal philosophical works, setting forth his complete system of thought, appeared later. His *Meditations on First Philosophy*, together with "Objections" made by eminent thinkers of his time and his replies to the objections, were published in 1641. (See pp. 68-293.) And the *Principles of Philosophy*, summing up his system and dedicated to a refugee princess who admired his work—Princess Elizabeth of the Palatinate—appeared in 1644. His work on ethics and psychology, *Treatise on the Passions of the Soul*, published in 1649, developed from correspondence with another royal lady admirer, Queen Christina of Sweden, to whom he dedicated the work. It was in compliance with the queen's request to teach her philosophy that Descartes went to live in Sweden, "in the land of bears among rocks and ice," he said, and this led directly to his death. For the queen required him to teach her at five o'clock in the morning, and one bitter winter day, returning from a lesson, he caught a chill and developed a fever from which he died, just about four months after he had arrived in Sweden.

II

Descartes tells us in his preliminary remarks that he has divided the *Discourse* into six parts to make it easier to read, and then enumerates the topics dealt with in each part. This selection comprises Parts I-IV, which present the history of Descartes' philosophical quest and the basic principles and truths he discovered. Parts V and VI deal with the application of these principles to various fields of inquiry and go further into the reasons which led Descartes to write and publish his work. The reader of this guide is invited to read these two parts also, at his leisure; he will find them interesting and instructive about Descartes' way of thinking.

Descartes makes it plain at the start that this work is a *discourse*, a conversation with his fellow men, rather than a treatise, addressed by a specialist to those unfamiliar with his field.

Thus my design is not here to teach the Method which everyone should follow in order to promote the good conduct of his Reason, but only to show in what manner I have endeavoured to conduct my own. (p. 42b)

This is corroborated in a letter to his friend Father Mersenne, where he says he purposely called it a *Discourse on Method* rather than a *Treatise on Method*, "in order to signify that my design is not to teach the method but only to converse about it."[1]

Descartes began his quest for certainty when he discovered that the scholastic training which he had received since childhood was futile so far as attaining "clear and certain knowledge" was concerned. He appreciated the cultivation of the mind which ensued from the "conversation" with the great writers of the past, but he found that their works provided a very shaky foundation for knowledge. Hence at the first opportunity he forsook book learning for the school of experience,

resolving to seek no other science than that which could be found in myself, or at least in the great book of the world . . . (p. 44a)

On the one hand, he felt that the "various predicaments" in which he found himself—urgent life situations—would be much more conducive to sound judgment than meditations in a library far removed from the actual world and the consequences of wrong judgment. On the other hand, he thought that right conduct and the attainment of good things require right judgment.

And I always had an excessive desire to learn to distinguish the true from the false, in order to see clearly in my actions and to walk with confidence in this life. (p. 44b; see also p. 50b)

Hence Descartes spent several years traveling about, meeting all kinds of men and gathering various experiences. The extraordinary diversity of customs he encountered taught him "to believe nothing too certainly of which I had only been convinced by example and custom" (p. 44b; see also p. 46b). His study of "the great book of the world" proved helpful in free-

[1] *Descartes, Philosophical Writings,* trans. Norman Kemp Smith (New York: The Modern Library, 1958), p. 91, fn. 1.

ing his mind from certain errors, but still it did not lead him to the certain basis of knowledge. For this he turned within to the study of himself, and thereby he found the direct road to the discovery of new method.

As he tells us the story in Part II, circumstances so arranged it that he was suddenly transported from society to solitude. Rejoining the army in which he was serving, he found himself immobilized in winter quarters in Germany (at Neuberg on the Danube).

. . . I remained the whole day shut up alone in a stove-heated room, where I had complete leisure to occupy myself with my own thoughts. (p. 44c)

Out of these solitary meditations arose the conviction that he must begin with a completely clean slate in his attempt to attain certain knowledge. An utterly new foundation, consisting of principles reached through his own reasoning, was necessary. He could rely only on such principles, certainly not on those obtained at second-hand from books, teachers, or other authorities.

. . . I thought that the sciences found in books—in those at least whose reasonings are only probable and which have no demonstrations, composed as they are of the gradually accumulated opinions of many different individuals—do not approach so near to the truth as the simple reasoning which a man of common sense can quite naturally carry out respecting the things which come immediately before him. (p. 45a)

And I firmly believed that by this means I should succeed in directing my life much better than if I had only built on old foundations, and relied on principles of which I allowed myself to be in youth persuaded without having inquired into their truth. (p. 45c)

Recognizing that this "simple resolve to strip oneself of all opinions and beliefs formerly received" (p. 46a) would appear to be subversive of all established authority and institutions, Descartes is quick to point out that he abhors such revolutionary purposes. He is not submitting to a program for the reform of the sciences and the schools but is simply telling us the story of how he reformed his own knowledge, with no thought of setting himself up as an example for others.

My design has never extended beyond trying to reform my own opinion and to build on a foundation which is entirely my own. If my work has given me a certain satisfaction, so that I here present to you a draft of it, I do not so do because I wish to advise anybody to imitate it. (p. 45d; see also p. 42b)

As a matter of fact, Descartes did not intend to discard all his former opinions merely because they were old and he had acquired them from others. On the contrary, he proposed to retain any received opinions that could meet the test of first-hand scrutiny.

But as regards all the opinions which up to this time I had embraced, I thought I could not do better than endeavour once for all to sweep them completely away, so that they might later on be replaced, either by others which were better, or by the same, when I had made them conform to the uniformity of a rational scheme. (p. 45b-c)

This rare combination of daring and caution is shown again as Descartes lets us know that he was confident of his own power to discern truth from falsehood, and that not finding anyone else who had hit upon the right path to knowledge, he decided to do it himself. But he also lets us know that he possessed the prudence and patient care that is necessary for success in rebuilding the whole edifice of knowledge for oneself.

But like one who walks alone and in the twilight I resolved to go so slowly, and to use so much circumspection in all things, that if my advance was but very small, at least I guarded myself well from falling. I did not wish to set about the final rejection of any single opinion which might formerly have crept into my beliefs without having been introduced there by means of Reason, until I had first of all employed sufficient time in planning out the task which I had undertaken, and in seeking the true Method of arriving at a knowledge of all the things of which my mind was capable. (p. 46c)

III

Descartes began by searching among such disciplines as logic, geometry, and algebra for a hint as to the proper method in inquiry. Dissatisfied for various reasons with what he found in these studies, he decided to start afresh with a few simple rules and to stick to them consistently on all occasions. He arrived at these four precepts:

1. Accept nothing as true unless it is presented to the mind so clearly and distinctly that it cannot be doubted.
2. Divide each problem into as many parts as possible, in order to reach the most adequate solution.
3. Proceed in gradual order from the simplest and most easily understood objects to knowledge of the most complex.
4. Make complete and comprehensive surveys and checks to ensure that nothing has been omitted.

(See p. 47a-b.)

Descartes was convinced that with these few and simple rules he had arrived at a method for acquiring knowledge in all things which was comparable to that by which geometricians arrive at demonstrable and certain truths.

. . . provided only that we abstain from receiving anything as true which is not so, and always retain the order which is necessary in order to deduce the one conclusion from the other, there can be nothing so remote that we cannot reach to it, nor so recondite that we cannot discover it. (p. 47b)

Elsewhere Descartes has left us an account of the dream experience and the religious vow which followed his memorable discovery, and he names the precise day, "the 10th of November 1619, when filled with enthusiasm, I discovered the foundations of a wonderful science."[2] He had a series of three dreams, starting forebodingly and ending on a mild and pleasant note, which he took to be a sign that he had been inspired by the Spirit of Truth in his meditations. The next day he prayed to God for guidance and support in his quest, and also to the Virgin Mary, to whom he made a special vow to make a pilgrimage to the shrine of Our Lady of Loreto in Italy. He fulfilled this vow four years later. Thus we find the origin of a revolution in philosophical thought marked by an act of simple and sincere religious piety.[3]

Within two or three months, the use of the newly discov-

[2] Harald Höffding, A History of Modern Philosophy (New York: Dover Publications, Inc., 1955), Vol. I, p. 213.

[3] For a description of Descartes' dreams, see Norman Kemp Smith, New Studies in the Philosophy of Descartes (New York: St. Martin's Press, Inc., 1953), pp. 15-17, 33-39; and Jacques Maritain, The Dream of Descartes (New York: Philosophical Library, 1945), pp. 13-15.

ered method bore startling results, far beyond Descartes' initial expectations. He found that by adhering conscientiously to his four rules, he had solved some of the main previously unsolved questions in geometrical analysis and algebra and was on his way to solving the others. Starting from the simplest truths, he proceeded to the more complex, "making each truth that I discovered a rule for helping me to find others" (p. 47d). Simplicity and order were the keynotes of his method. Take one thing at a time, in due order, and understand it as much as it can be understood by the human mind—this is the way to arrive at certain knowledge, he found.

However, the main advantage which Descartes obtained from the first use of his method lay not in the actual results but in the confidence that he gained in the power of his reason to solve difficulties in all the sciences.

But what pleased me most in this Method was that I was certain by its means of exercising my reason in all things, if not perfectly, at least as well as was in my power. And besides this, I felt in making use of it that my mind gradually accustomed itself to conceive of its objects more accurately and distinctly; and not having restricted this Method to any particular matter, I promised myself to apply it as usefully to the difficulties of other sciences as I had done to those of Algebra. (p. 48a)

Descartes modestly recognized that at the time he was not equipped with the knowledge of first principles which was required for the accomplishment of such a great undertaking. He realized that he would have to mature—he was only twenty-three—and prepare himself for the task he had proposed to himself by discarding all his false opinions, gathering abundant experience, and exercising himself in the new method.

I V

The time had now come for Descartes to leave his stove-heated room and return to the society of his fellow men. But one thing more was necessary for the man who had decided to hold all his former intellectual judgments in doubt. He valued the practical conduct of life and recognized its dependence on our judgments. Hence, he knew that he would have to have some temporary mental edifice in which he could dwell while he was engaged in the building of a new one. Therefore, he says, "I formed for myself a code of morals for the time being" (p. 48c).

He arrived at the following four moral maxims to set off against his four rules of method:

1. To obey the laws and customs of his country, to adhere to the religion he had been raised in, and to direct his conduct by the most moderate opinion in all other matters.
2. To be resolute in action, once he had made a decision, even where the grounds were uncertain, recognizing that it is better to follow a definite course, even if based on mere probability, than none at all.
3. To try to conquer and change himself and his desires, not the fixed order of things, and to accustom himself "to believe that there is nothing entirely within our power but our own thoughts" (p. 49c).
4. To choose from the various occupations of men the one best suited to him, which turned out to be his present one of cultivating his understanding and attaining knowledge of the truth, following his new method.

(See pp. 48c-50b.)

Thus bolstered with "a code of morals for the time being," and holding on to his religious beliefs, Descartes was prepared to junk all the rest of his opinions and sally forth into society again.

He spent the next nine years in gathering all kinds of experience, in observing and reflecting carefully on everything that he encountered, and in practicing his method on various types of problems. He assiduously doubted any opinions or judgments that seemed dubious, not for the sake of doubting or to remain in doubt but in order to attain certainty. And he discovered that doubt always led to certainty, even if it were only the certainty that a particular judgment was utterly uncertain. He found that the pathway of knowledge led from the very shaky to the quite secure. Thus, though to the outward eye he might have seemed a man of leisure, enjoying a pleasant though virtuous life, all the time, he says,

. . . I did not cease to prosecute my design, and to profit perhaps even more in my study of Truth than if I had done nothing but read books or associate with literary people. (pp. 50d-51a)

But the task still remained of discovering the first principles upon which all knowledge must be based. So many eminent thinkers had endeavored to accomplish this without success that he felt inadequate to do it himself. He was pushed into attempting it, however, by the public rumor that he had already done so. Hence, he tells us in his characteristically disarming, humble way, he decided to try his utmost to earn the reputation which had undeservedly been bestowed on him.

Thus at the end of his nine years' plunge into society and experience, he returned to solitary meditation, choosing a place (Holland) where he could "live as solitary and retired as in deserts the most remote" (p. 51b). The stage was now set for his great discovery of the absolute rock upon which all knowledge could be built, for the great moment in Descartes' mental life and in the history of Western philosophy. That moment is described in Part V.

V

In these new meditations, Descartes proceeded to doubt everything that was the least bit dubious until he came upon something entirely certain. This extreme procedure involved doubting the reports of the senses, the validity of reasoning, and even the reality of the waking as compared with the dream state. Our senses may deceive us, our reasoning may be false, and we cannot be sure that our waking thoughts are truer than those in our dreams. Thus, doubting everything, Descartes came upon one thing that could not be doubted—that the doubter himself existed.

"*I think, therefore I am*" (p. 51d). Here was the first principle of philosophy, starting from which Descartes could build the foundations of knowledge. It was utterly incontrovertible,

. . . so certain and so assured that all the most extravagant suppositions brought forward by the sceptics were incapable of shaking it . . . (p. 51d)

Descartes went on to perceive that the indubitability of the existence of the "I" lay in its thought.

. . . I knew that I was a substance the whole essence or nature of which is to think. (p. 51d)

And he really meant "the *whole* essence or nature," for the "I" essentially needs nothing else to exist—neither place, nor body, nor any external thing.

> . . . this "me," that is to say, the soul by which I am what I am, is entirely distinct from body, and is even more easy to know than is the latter; and even if body were not, the soul would not cease to be what it is. (pp. 51d-52a)

That man is a thinking substance, is essentially mind or soul, is the first assertion that Descartes drew from his first principle.

He went on to seek the basis of certainty in our propositions about things, taking as his model the immediate certainty of the primary statement, "I think, therefore I am." Examining the latter, he saw that its certainty lay in the fact "that I see very clearly that to think it is necessary to be" (p. 52a). Hence, he decided to

> . . . assume, as a general rule, that the things which we conceive very clearly and distinctly are all true . . . (p. 52a)

That the truth of our thoughts lay in their clarity and distinctness was the second assertion that Descartes drew from his first principle.

However, he perceived that the certainty which he had arrived at arose from the immediate experience of an imperfect, finite being. Something more perfect was required as the objective ground of knowledge. Doubting is a proof of the doubter's existence, but of a very imperfect existence. Descartes "saw clearly that it was a greater perfection to know than to doubt" (p. 52a). But where did the idea of such perfection come from?

It could not have come from himself, Descartes reasoned. The thought of a greater perfection must have come from a more perfect being, which had placed it in Descartes' mind—namely God. Hence, he concluded, this more perfect being necessarily exists, and he was dependent on it for his existence and all that he had. All the imperfections of which he was cognizant pointed to "some other more perfect Being" which had all the perfections that he lacked and which was the basis of all less perfect levels of reality.

The necessary existence of God is "a metaphysical certainty" which certifies all the rest of our knowledge—which adds objective validity to our merely "moral assurance" about the reality of things. The reason that clear and distinct ideas are true—that is, reflect actually existing things—is that they come from God, a perfect being, who cannot have obscure and vague ideas about things, but necessarily conceives them as they are.

. . . that all the things that we very clearly and very distinctly conceive of are true, is certain only because God is or exists, and that He is a Perfect Being, and that all that is in us issues from Him. From this it follows that our ideas or notions, which to the extent of their being clear or distinct are ideas of real things issuing from God, cannot but to that extent be true. . . . But if we did not know that all that is in us of reality and truth proceeds from a perfect and infinite Being, however clear and distinct were our ideas, we should not have any reason to assure ourselves that they had the perfection of being true. (p. 53d)

It is reliance on this perfect and truthful being that stills our anxiety about the truthfulness of our waking ideas. The ideas that we have of things, whether they come to us in our sleeping or waking state, and whether they are adequate or not, have some basis in truth—otherwise God would not have placed them in us. In the final analysis, our reason, as distinct from our imagination and our senses, must be the judge of the truth of our ideas; and our reason tells us that truth is more likely to be found "in our waking experience rather than in that of our dreams" (p. 54b).

As regards Descartes' basic principle, "I think, therefore I am," it is interesting to note that a much earlier thinker, St. Augustine, had voiced a similar insight.

For if I am deceived, I am. For he who is not, cannot be deceived; and if I am deceived, by this same token I am. (*The City of God*, Vol. 18, p. 337a)

When this passage was pointed out to him, Descartes replied that he did not claim any uniqueness and originality in this regard, that anyone might have this simple insight; and that, besides, it played a far different role in his thought than in Augustine's. He says in a letter, written in November 1640,

I am obliged to you for telling me about the passage in Saint Augustine to which my *"I think, therefore I am"* has some relation. I went to read it today in the library of this city [Leyden], and I find that actually he uses it to prove the certainty of our being, and then to show that there is in us some image of the Trinity, in that we are, we know that we are, and we love this being and this knowledge that are in us. I, however, use it to show that this "I" that thinks is an *immaterial substance* which has nothing corporeal about it. These are two different things. And to infer that we exist from the fact that we doubt is something so simple and natural that it might have come from anyone's pen; nevertheless, I am glad to be in accord with Saint Augustine on this principle, if only to silence those small minds who have tried to quibble about it.[4]

And in another letter, written probably in May 1644, he says,

I am greatly obliged to you for pointing out to me the passages in Saint Augustine which may serve to authorize my opinions; some of my other friends have also done so, and it gives me great satisfaction to know that my thoughts are in agreement with those of such a holy and excellent personage. For I am not of the same character as those who wish their opinions to appear to be new; on the contrary, I adapt my opinions to those of others, as much as truth will allow me to do so.[5]

VI

What does Descartes mean by "clear and distinct?"

According to Descartes' first rule of method, a perception that is clearly and distinctly present to the mind is indubitable. His model of this kind of perception is the statement "I think, therefore I am," to which the mind assents immediately. The fact that I think necessarily involves the fact that I am.

Descartes' "clear and distinct" perceptions, then, seem to be the same as the traditional "self-evident" propositions, such as that the sum of two and two is four, or that the whole is equal to the sum of its parts. Once the terms are grasped, the relation or implication is grasped "immediately" or "directly," by an act of mental vision.

The "clear and distinct," then, is what is directly evident. Are the terms "clear" and "distinct," however, similar or different in meaning? They usually have about the same meaning in

---

[4] *Essential Works of Descartes,* trans. Lowell Bair (New York: Bantam Books, 1961), p. 210.
[5] *Ibid.,* pp. 222-223.

our common speech. Is Descartes, then, using the two terms to reinforce one another? Or does "distinct" add something to the meaning which is not contained in "clear"? If so, what?

Could there be clear ideas or perceptions which were not distinct, or distinct ideas or perceptions which were not clear? Does "clear" refer to the unobstructed, direct view of something, and "distinct" to the precise discernment of what is presented?

In other writings, Descartes distinguishes between objects which are merely clear and those which are both clear and distinct. He takes his examples of merely clear objects from sense experience—a pain, a blur in the distance, a stick that appears bent when partly submerged in water. We perceive these things clearly but not distinctly, he says, for we do not precisely distinguish what they are—of what physical process the pain is symptomatic, whether the blur is a mist or a crowd, or that the stick is actually straight. On the other hand, an object that is both clear and distinct appears to the mind precisely as it is. Such objects are best shown in the simple ideas of mathematics and metaphysics, such as unity, existence, cause, straight, point, etc.

Is clarity and distinctness an adequate criterion of truth?

In his four rules of method, Descartes presents the elements of precise and rigorous knowledge. First, he says, start with clear and distinct ideas or perceptions, then, by a combination of analysis and synthesis, proceed from the simplest to the more complex things, arriving at the utmost knowledge possible to man. This procedure, with the final admonition to make a complete survey to insure that nothing has been omitted, seems to be logical, rational, and good common sense.

The objection might be made, however, that Descartes, by his criterion of clarity and distinctness, has arbitrarily limited beforehand what is knowable and true. Can this criterion extend beyond Descartes' model discipline of mathematics? Is physical reality knowable only through clear and distinct ideas? What about biological processes and organic development? And can we arrive at a satisfactory and illuminating knowledge about man, his nature, his mind, and his history through clear and distinct ideas?

William Temple once raised the question of whether Descartes' criterion excluded from certain knowledge such religious experiences as Isaiah's vision of God. "Why," he asked, "is my perception that $2 + 2 = 4$ to be regarded as either more clear and distinct, or more compelling of acceptance, than Isaiah's perception of the Holiness of God?[6] Similarly, Alfred North Whitehead asserted that Descartes' criterion is utterly inadequate as far as aesthetic experience is concerned. He said that those "elements in experience which are neither clear nor distinct" but are rather "dim, massive, and important . . . provide for art that final background of tone apart from which its effects fade."[7]

What would be Descartes' answer to such criticisms? On the basis of his own procedure, would he be able to exclude religious experience from the realm of certain knowledge because it is private or because it involves a supernatural object and origin? Must all certain knowledge, for Descartes, be based on ideas originating in the human mind and grasped by the natural power of reason? Would aesthetic experience fall into the category of the merely "clear," such as a pain in the stomach or a blur in the distance, but not of the "clear and distinct," and hence into the sphere of the uncertain?

This issue of the criterion of certain knowledge—of truth—obviously evokes the question of the nature of reality. For Descartes, what is really real is apprehensible in clear and distinct ideas, and what is comprised in the rest of our experience falls into the realm of mere appearance, of vague and confused becoming. For thinkers like Whitehead, on the other hand, it is the dim elements of our experience which more directly reflect reality, while the clear and distinct ideas are the more attenuated appearances in our consciousness.

[6] William Temple, *Nature, Man and God* (London: Macmillan & Co., Ltd., 1951), p. 86.

[7] Alfred North Whitehead, *Adventures of Ideas* (New York: The Macmillan Co., 1952), p. 358.

Is the statement "I think, therefore I am," indubitable?

If I try to doubt everything, says Descartes, I find that I can doubt the existence of all external things. However, I cannot doubt the basic process of doubting that is going on in me. I cannot doubt that I doubt or think (doubting is a form of thinking). This I know for sure. I can then say with certainty, "I think." But I can also say, "I am," for the "I" who doubts or thinks must exist—"to think it is necessary to be."

If we critically examine Descartes description of how he arrived at this statement, however, we may question whether it is simply an expression of immediate insight. Has he, for example, assumed at the beginning the "I" he claims to have discovered, sneaking it into the "I think"? Has he really put all previous concepts in doubt, or does his immediately certain statement depend on the traditional idea of "substance," that is, on the assumption that a function such as thinking necessarily implies a subject that does the thinking. Is "I think, therefore I am" actually a syllogism, with the major premise, "all things that think exist," left out?

Descartes himself makes the following response to this line of criticism, in his replies to the objections advanced against his *Meditations on First Philosophy:*

But when we become aware that we are thinking beings, this is a primitive act of knowledge derived from no syllogistic reasoning. He who says, "*I think, hence I am, or exist,*" does not deduce existence from thought by a syllogism, but, by a simple act of mental vision, recognises it as if it were a thing that is known *per se.* This is evident from the fact that if it were syllogistically deduced, the major premise, *that everything that thinks is, or exists,* would have to be known previously; but yet that has rather been learned from the experience of the individual—that unless he exists he cannot think. For our mind is so constituted by nature that general propositions are formed out of the knowledge of particulars. (p. 123a-b)

Descartes insists that this is an existential proposition arising out of the concrete experience or self-consciousness of the individual, not an abstract thought arrived at through logical deduction.

But is the "I" of "I think" given in immediate experience? Would it not be more proper to begin with the observation, "thinking is going on," and then to go from that to the statement of a something or "somewhat" in which the thinking is going on? Should we then use the term "mind" or "soul" for this something? Is that the same as the "I" of Descartes' "I think"? Is it the same as the "I" of his "I am"?

Does his famous assertion, then, mean only that a particular process of thought shows that the mind in which it occurs exists? Or does Descartes mean something far more by the self whose existence he asserts in his "I am"? Is he asserting the existence of the concrete, historical, empirical, integral René Descartes?

Why must Descartes prove his existence by the fact that he is thinking? Why could he not say, "I breathe, therefore I exist," or "I yawn, therefore I exist," or "I am hungry, therefore I exist"? Why must the primary, irreducible, undeniable experience be that of thought?

Does Descartes make existence dependent on thought?

Following is an excerpt from Graham Greene's novel *Our Man in Havana*.[8] The scene is the bar of the Seville-Biltmore Hotel in Havana. Dr. Hasselbacher is talking to his friend Mr. Wormold about a possible winning of $140,000 on a lottery ticket he has purchased.

"Pardon me," a voice whispered out of the shadows. "Has this guy really won a hundred and forty thousand bucks?"

"Yes, sir, I have won them," Dr. Hasselbacher said firmly before Wormold could reply, "I have won them as certainly as you exist, my almost unseen friend. You would not exist if I didn't believe you existed —nor would those dollars. I believe, therefore you are."

"What do you mean I wouldn't exist?"

"You exist only in my thoughts, my friend. If I left this room . . ."

"You're nuts."

"Prove you exist, then."

"What do you mean, prove? Of course I exist. I've got a first-class

[8] Graham Greene, *Our Man in Havana* (New York: The Viking Press, Inc., 1958), pp. 39-40.

business in real estate; a wife and a couple of kids in Miami. I flew here this morning by Delta. I'm drinking this Scotch, aren't I?" The voice contained a hint of tears.

"Poor fellow," Dr. Hasselbacher said, "you deserve a more imaginative creator than I have been. Why didn't I do better for you than Miami and real estate? Something of imagination. A name to be remembered."

Is this spoofing in accord with Descartes' procedure? Can we think or unthink the existence of other persons? Do we by doubting negate the existence of things outside us? Does Descartes actually doubt the existence of the external world?

As regards this issue, see what Descartes himself has to say in his replies to the objections to his *Meditations,* pp. 206d-207a.

The following questions are designed to help you test the thoroughness of your reading. Each question is to be answered by giving a page or pages of the reading assignment. Answers will be found on page 301 of this Reading Plan.

1 What subjects did Descartes study at school?

2 What was Descartes' opinion of the philosophy taught in the schools?

3 What insight does Descartes try to convey through the metaphor of buildings planned by a single architect?

4 Which two classes of mind are unfit to engage in a reformation of knowledge?

5 What defects in geometrical analysis and algebra make them unfit to serve as models for the new method?

6 What is the example of the child who correctly adds a sum supposed to prove about the rules of method?

7 What three qualities or functions does Descartes list as constituting mental activity?

SPINOZA

Ethics

Part I

Vol. 31, pp. 355-372

To see one changeless Life in all the Lives,
And in the Separate, One Inseparable.

With Spinoza, we come to a culminating point in our survey of Western philosophy. His *Ethics* presents a rational account of the whole of reality and of man's place in it. This combination of a rational "system" of things with a guide to man's role in it is in accord with the traditional philosophical concerns with metaphysics and morals, from Plato to Descartes. We should, therefore, not find it too bizarre that Spinoza's metaphysics is presented in a work entitled *Ethics*.

We may justly be surprised, however, to find Spinoza's account of reality begin with a discussion of God, like a traditional theological treatise, instead of with a reflection on human experience. And we may also be surprised to find that he uses the terms "God" and "Nature" interchangeably, and that the physical world, for him, is an aspect of God. Furthermore, this is a metaphysical ethics, or theological cosmology, which sees no supreme end, purpose, or good in the universe, indeed no purpose at all, and which denies freedom of the will. And, although we are familiar with Descartes' praise of the geometrical method, most readers may be somewhat bewildered to find a philosophical work presented in geometrical form.

Thus, though Spinoza shares the traditional concerns of Western philosophers, his approach to these concerns is markedly different from that of his predecessors. The ordinary reader who approaches this work for the first time, however, should take heart in the fact that what Spinoza deals with is a universal human concern which has been urgent in all times and cultures—the nature of ultimate reality and man's relation to it. To understand even vaguely what Spinoza is talking about, we must put ourselves in the position of men who envision the whole of reality and the relation of the parts to the whole; who ask and answer the question of the relation of ultimate, infinite, eternal reality to proximate, finite, temporal existence; who point to an experience of at-oneness with the whole of things.

This is, of course, a religious as well as a philosophical theme. The great mystics and the poets have dealt with it, too. Spinoza deals with it here as a philosopher and answers this eternal question in terms of rational discourse. His is one of the classical answers, and its presentation in the *Ethics* makes that work one of the milestones in the history of thought.

Tenth Reading

I

Spinoza, for various reasons, has been an odd figure in the history of Western thought. Some commentators, confronted with the seeming anomaly of his presence in the grand line of Western philosophers, have tried to label him as a misplaced Oriental who would have been more at home in Indian thought. Coming to his work, as we do now, after a survey of selections from Plato to Descartes, we will be more disposed to see the close connection between him and his great predecessors in the Western tradition. We can see, for instance, that he is considering themes similar to those considered in Aristotle's *Metaphysics* and in Lucretius' *On the Nature of Things,* and that his emphasis on mathematical method in philosophy is related, more or less closely, to Plato's and Descartes'. And if we were to turn to philosophical writings not considered in this Reading Plan, we would see a certain similarity between what Spinoza has to say on certain matters and what Epictetus and Hobbes have to say. (See the Reading Plan *Ethics: the Study of Moral Values,* Fifth and Seventh Readings.) However, the differences between Spinoza and previous great thinkers are as important as the similarities, and he combines qualities—mystical and rational, spiritual and material—which we usually think of as opposed and as represented by different figures in the history of thought.

Modern scholarship has revealed Spinoza's background in three literatures—Hebrew, Arabic, and Latin. In this he bears a certain resemblance to medieval Scholastic thinkers, such as Thomas Aquinas. Many of the basic terms and ideas he uses and the themes he deals with come from a common store of knowledge. But there is one important and per-

haps decisive distinction between Spinoza and other thinkers represented in *Great Books of the Western World*. Spinoza was a Jew, with a traditional Jewish education in Biblical
and Talmudic literature and an intimate, first-hand knowledge of Jewish philosophical and mystical writings. Hebrew
was his first learned language, and his name was Baruch long
before it was Benedict. Undoubtedly the basic philosophical
ideas he gained through Hebrew sources were neo-Platonic
and Aristotelian in origin, and were in common use in the various medieval literatures where they dealt with the problem
of the relation of God and the world, of the infinite and the
finite. Yet there is a special emphasis on the unity of God, the
immanence of God in the world, and the unification of reality
in the Jewish tradition—in its mystical writings, in its prayer-
books, and in its liturgy as well as in its philosophical works—
which may have contributed to the direction of Spinoza's
thought, as well as accounted for its seeming strangeness.

The "new philosophy" of Descartes played an important
role in Spinoza's transition from this Jewish and medieval
sphere of thought to the world of modern philosophy. He studied Descartes' thought thoroughly, taught it, and wrote one
of his early works on Descartes' philosophy. In a certain sense,
he might be regarded as the heir of Descartes, who brought
his ideas to fulfillment and presented the whole system of
reality in geometrical order. But there is an essential distinction
between a thinker who made thought the basic reality which
assures us of our existence, and a thinker for whom thought cannot be dissociated from body in any being, including God; between a thinker who requires a transcendent God to assure us of
the certainty of our knowledge, and a thinker for whom God is
only immanent and for whom our thought is a mode of God's
thought; between a thinker who asserts the freedom of the
will and a thinker who denies it. Spinoza made it clear quite
early that he did not accept the philosophy of Descartes as a
whole, and his deviations became more evident in his later
works, such as the *Ethics*.

In one respect, though, Spinoza carried Descartes' thought
to its n'th degree, when he used the geometrical method to

present his own philosophy as well as Descartes', something that Descartes never did himself on a full scale. Spinoza's work on Descartes' thought is called *Descartes' Principles of Philosophy Geometrically Demonstrated,* and consists of definitions, axioms, postulates, and propositions in the order of a geometry book. The *Ethics,* too, is presented in this form, indeed even more so, since it lacks even the prefatory remarks which introduce the work on Descartes. We have to start out cold with lists of definitions and of axioms, followed immediately by the propositions which set forth Spinoza's thought on the ultimate nature of things.

This is a most unusual form for the presentation of philosophical thought, unique among the major philosophical works in the Western tradition. Its strangeness presents a certain barrier to the comprehension of Spinoza's thought even before we get into it. But we should recall that in the previous selections we have encountered various forms of philosophical writings, from Plato's dramatic dialogues and Aquinas' question-and-answer format to Descartes' autobiographical confession. However strange it may seem at first sight, let us accept the fact that this is the way Spinoza wrote the book and go on from there to apprehend the thought that is thus presented—thought which has had a powerful influence on minds far removed from the geometrical mode of reasoning.

For a consideration of the various reasons that may have led Spinoza to the use of this particular form of presentation, we refer the reader to what we have already said in the Reading Plan *Ethics: the Study of Moral Values,* Ninth Reading, pp. 159-162. Spinoza apparently considered the geometrical order the best form in which to present a system of reality in which all things and events are necessarily connected with one another and with the whole. The subtitle of the *Ethics* begins with the words "Demonstrated in Geometrical Order . . .," which, however, we are advised to interpret as "set forth in geometrical order" rather than as "proven with geometrical necessity." Spinoza himself seems not to have taken his geometrical form literally and to have used such terms as "definition," "axiom," and "proposition" rather loosely. Actually, the definitions become meaningful and the axioms evident for the reader only after he has worked his way through the propositions. Hence we would also be well advised not to take the geometrical method too rigorously and not to become bogged down in the details at the start.

It is not necessary fully to understand and accept each one of Spinoza's axioms, definitions, and propositions before going on to the next. They hang together in the whole that Spinoza is constructing as he goes along, and we cannot really understand any one of them fully until we have seen the whole picture. (*Ethics: the Study of Moral Values*, p. 161)

I I

In view of the peculiar difficulties of Spinoza's mode or presentation, let us vary our method of approach in this case and start out with a summary of the basic ideas presented in Part I, and then proceed to a detailed survey of the definitions, axioms, and postulates. Let us first get a glimpse of the whole before proceeding to the parts.

Spinoza says in Part I that reality is an organic whole. Everything that exists is an integral part of one ultimate reality which he calls "substance," "God," or "Nature."

There is and can be only one substance—an absolutely infinite and all-inclusive being which is the necessary ground and cause of everything that exists. The ultimate substance is the cause of its own existence. It is a being "whose essence involves existence," that is, one "whose nature cannot be conceived unless existing," whose existence follows necessarily from its own nature. Such self-causation or necessary existence cannot be ascribed to the finite things of our experience, which depend upon one another and ultimately on the one reality or substance for their existence.

Substance has infinite "attributes" (essential characteristics or aspects) of which two are known to us—thought and extension (matter). All things—stones and flies, as well as men—have a mental and a physical aspect; for the attributes are "infinite," not only in the sense of being innumerable but also in the sense that each of them extends over the whole of reality. (See Part II, Prop. 13, Schol., p. 378a-b.)

Spinoza's technical term for the particular form in which

the attributes are present is "mode." We might, then, equate *modes* with *things* and consider them the finite forms in which the infinite attributes are present. This is not quite true, however, because although finite things—a tree, a dog, a mountain—are in fact considered "modes" by Spinoza, he distinguishes between these and what he calls "infinite modes," which intervene between the infinite attributes of substance and their manifestation in finite forms. The infinite modes, like the attributes, are coextensive with the whole of reality. For example, one of the infinite modes of extension is "motion and rest," or the total movement of energy in the universe; and one of the infinite modes of thought is the absolutely infinite understanding, or the whole of knowledge. In any case, the modes, finite or infinite, are "modifications" or "affections" of the infinite attributes.

The attributes "express the eternal and infinite essence" of reality, of the very nature of God, of the source of things. The modes are the concrete manifestations of the attributes, the way in which the infinite attributes are present in things. Spinoza differentiates the one reality, substance, or God, into (1) the core, origin, or source, which he calls *natura naturans* (or "nature creating"), and (2) its concrete manifestations or outflowing, which he calls *natura naturata* (or "nature created"). This, of course, is not a distinction between God and a world created by Him and apart from Him, for "God" here includes both the source and the manifestation. Ultimate reality is one and is present in the modes, as they are present in it.

The order of reality thus envisaged is completely determined. Whatever is, exists necessarily. All action is necessary action. In the case of God, or substance, or the whole of things, this causation is "free" in the sense that it arises out of the divine essence or nature, but it is necessary in the sense that it cannot be other than it is. Everything else, the whole realm of the *natura naturata,* the manifestations of this essence, is the necessary result of God, the one "self-caused cause" and hence the one "free cause." God is the one true cause of things and events, both of their coming to be and their continuing to be. He causes them to be not in order to accomplish any end, such as the good, but as the necessary expression of the divine fullness and perfection. There are no final causes, no purposes or ends, in nature.

III

Let us now see how Spinoza works out this view of things in the definitions, axioms, and propositions of Book I. He lists eight definitions, describing what he means by self-cause, finite, substance, attribute, mode, God, free and necessary existence (or causation), and eternity. He follows this by a list of seven axioms—the basic principles or assumptions upon which his propositions are to be based and which also underlie the definitions already stated. For instance, Axioms 1 and 2, distinguishing between the existence of a thing in itself or in another, and the conception of it through itself or through another, are related to the definitions of substance and of mode. Similarly, Axiom 7 is related to and amplifies the definition of self-cause. Axioms 3 and 4 assume that there is a necessary relation of causes and effects in things, and that knowledge of the effect depends on knowledge of the cause; in other words, that knowledge of things is knowledge of their causes. Axiom 5, asserting that things that have nothing mutually in common cannot be mutually understood, reveals its significance in Prop. 3, asserting that such things cannot have a causal relation with one another, the point being that there must be something in common in things, and particularly between infinite substance and its modes, to make the existence of things comprehensible. Axiom 6, assuring us that a "true" idea must agree with that of which it is the idea, echoes Descartes' view that "clear and distinct" ideas are true, as becomes plain in Prop. 8, Schol. 2. (See p. 357b.)

One thing to note in these definitions and axioms is that the necessary relations described and assumed are necessary both in existence and in thought. A thing must exist either in itself or in another, and it must be conceived either through itself or through another. Thus substance is defined as that "which is in itself and is conceived through itself"—it needs nothing else in order to exist, and the conception of it needs no other conception in order to be conceived. So also with the definition of mode as "that which is in another thing, through which also it is conceived."

Spinoza begins his statement on the nature of ultimate reality ("Of God") in Part I with the argument that there is, can be, and must be only one substance. He begins with the apparently mild statement that substance is naturally prior to its modes, or "affections." Granted Definitions 3 and 5 and Axioms 1 and 2, this seems obvious and unexceptionable. Essence is "prior" to its manifestations, the whole to its parts, and the universal to the particulars. Spinoza now proceeds to argue, on the basis of this proposition and of various definitions and axioms, that it is impossible for there to be more than one substance.

If there were more than one substance, reality would be incomprehensible. There could be no cosmos, no ordered whole, in actuality or in thought. We recall that, according to Axiom 4, knowledge of things involves the knowledge of their causes and that, according to Axiom 5, things having nothing mutually in common cannot be mutually understood. All that we know of substance, we know through its attributes and its modes. But two or more substances, by definition, would each have different attributes, since they would have different essences or natures, expressed by their attributes. They would have nothing in common, one substance could not be the cause of another, and their coexistence would be inexplicable. (See Props. 1-6.)

Substance, by definition, is that which exists in itself and is thinkable through its own conception alone. Nothing whatsoever outside itself can be its cause. It is self-caused and exists necessarily from its very essence. (See Prop. 7.) But such characteristics can be ascribed only to the infinite whole of things. To say that there cannot be more than one substance is the same as to say that there can be no finite substance. If there were two or more substances they would be parts of reality, limited, and not self-sufficient, self-caused, etc. The unitary whole of reality is boundless, unsurpassable, incomparable, unique, "perfect." "*Every substance is necessarily infi-*

nite." (See Prop. 8.) Far from being negative, as the term "infinite" (not finite) might connote, this is the absolutely positive, full, all-inclusive reality as distinct from the partial, limited, conditioned. "Finiteness is in truth partly negation, and infinitude absolute affirmation . . ." (p. 356d).

The assertion of this positive, full, infinite substance leads to the assertion of infinite attributes and to the ascription of conception through itself and necessary existence to each of the attributes. Since, by definition, an attribute expresses the essence of substance, *"the more reality or being a thing possesses, the more attributes belong to it"* (Prop. 9, p. 357d); or, more specifically, "the more attributes it possesses expressing necessity or eternity and infinity" (Prop. 10, Schol., p. 358a). This argument for an absolutely infinite substance with infinite attributes, each of which expresses its eternal and infinite essense, brings us in a full circle back to the definition of God as just such a being. Whatever has been said thus far about the technical philosophical term "substance" and its attributes applies to the traditional religious term "God." And whatever will be said about God in the following propositions will apply to substance and will show that "only one substance exists, and that it is absolutely infinite." (See p. 358a-b.) Hence Prop. 11 begins with the words *"God, or substance . . ."*

I V

The God whose existence Spinoza tries to prove through various traditional methods in Prop. 11 is the substance which he has described in Props. 1-10. God, so conceived, is strikingly different from God as conceived by medieval Jewish and Christian theologians and philosophers. This becomes obvious when we combine what has been said about substance in Props. 1-10 with what is now said about God or substance in Props. 13-15. These all bear on the nature of the relation between God and the world.

Spinoza has implied that there is and can be only one substance which exists necessarily, which is absolutely infinite, and the essence of which is expressed in each of its attributes. Now he adds in Props. 12-13 that substance cannot be separated from any of its attributes (such as thought or extension) and that as absolutely infinite it is utterly indivisible. Substance is one and simple. In Props. 14-15 he ascribes this unique unity and simplicity of substance to God.

PROP. 14. *Besides God, no substance can be nor can be conceived.* (p. 359d)

PROP. 15. *Whatever is, is in God, and nothing can either be or be conceived without God.* (p. 360a)

From these quiet assertions, it soon becomes plain, follow revolutionary conclusions: that God is material, that He did not create the world, that there are no divine purposes or Providence, and that there is no freedom of the will. In this, as he points out, Spinoza is completely opposed to traditional Jewish and Christian views of the nature of God and His relation to man and the world. He has, for instance, retained the affirmation of the unique unity of God proclaimed in Maimonides' "Thirteen Principles of the Faith," but he has interpreted that unity in such a way as to deny what is said about God and His relations in the rest of this traditional Jewish creed.

Let us first follow Spinoza's argument for the all-important and extraordinary assertion that God is material as well as spiritual. If we accept the definitions of substance and mode and the axiom that everything exists either in itself or in another, we must conclude that nothing exists but substance (together with its essential attributes) and its modes or manifestations (which are the "affections" or "modifications" of the attributes). If we also accept what has been said about the unity, infinity, and simplicity of substance, and about the identification of God with substance, and keep in mind that no attribute can be separated from substance (Prop. 12), we must conclude that God is physical as well as mental. For, granting what is obvious in common experience, that "corporeal or extended substance" exists, and that all that exists is caused, we must either ascribe extended substance to a mysterious act of divine creation or see it as an "affection" or "modification" of the divine attributes. But since, as we have seen, substance cannot be produced by anything else, and God is the only conceivable substance, we must conclude "that

extended substance is one of the infinite attributes of God"
(p. 360c). (In Part II, Prop. 2, this is considered equivalent
to saying that "God is an extended thing.")

Some readers may feel that Spinoza has begged the question and indulged in a bit of verbal sleight-of-hand by using
the term "corporeal or extended substance." But what he
means by it is simply the world of objects extended in space,
including our own bodies (the extension immediately known
to us), and he is asserting that this reality, in its material aspect, is an expression of the nature of ultimate reality and not
something completely distinct from it. He opposes the ordinary implications of statements such as the one in Maimonides'
creed, that God "is not a body, and that he is free from all the
properties of matter, and that he has not any form whatsoever."[1]

The trouble with thinkers who hold such a view of God, says
Spinoza, is that they can only conceive of physical reality as
finite and consisting of discrete parts. By "body" such thinkers
mean "a certain quantity possessing length, breadth, and
depth, limited by some fixed form" (p. 360b), and hence they
are unable to ascribe bodily extension to God, the absolutely
infinite being. If corporeal substance can be divided into separate parts, as they assume, then it "is unworthy of the divine
nature, and cannot pertain to it" (p. 360d), for that would
mean that God can "suffer" (undergo action), which contradicts the definition of God as an absolutely perfect being.

The error here, says Spinoza, is first, the failure to distinguish between ultimate reality with its attributes and their finite manifestations; and second, the failure to see their organic
connectedness. Actually, the physical aspect of things is infinite
and indivisible. What makes all things material is a universal
quality which as such, as material substance, cannot be divided into cut-off finite parts. We must remember

that matter is everywhere the same, and that, except in so far as we
regard it as affected in different ways, parts are not distinguished in it;

[1] Joseph H. Hertz, *The Authorised Daily Prayer Book* (New York:
Bloch Publishing Company, 1961), p. 251.

that is to say, they are distinguished with regard to mode, but not with regard to reality. (p. 361c)
(Read "substance" here for "reality.")

Water, for instance, may be divided into parts, but the material substance which underlies water and all physical things is "infinite, one, and indivisible." The reason that water or any other material form exists is that substance exists and is expressed materially, that there is infinite substance with infinite extension. We must look at things in their organic totality and connection, not in bits and pieces, if we wish to understand their essential nature and causes. Reality is a continuous whole, without gaps or real, essential separations. Any universal quality present in the concrete world, in finite things, must first be present in the ultimate, infinite essence of which it is the manifestation.

All things, I say, are in God, and everything which takes place takes place by the laws alone of the infinite nature of God, and follows . . . from the necessity of His essence. (p. 361d)

Clearly, then, God must be material, that is, infinite and eternal matter (not "a body" or "any form whatsoever"). Otherwise there would be nothing to account for the origin of the physical world and its forms. And God cannot be said to suffer from something which is the active expression of His own essence and which follows from the laws of His own nature. As against what the traditional philosophers and theologians say, matter indeed is worthy of the divine nature.

V

The statement of the materiality of God requires a non-dualistic interpretation of the causal relation between God and the world. Spinoza distinguishes between God as substance, which exists in itself and is conceived through itself, and the modes which follow from its nature and attributes. Yet "substance" and "modes" are by no means two realities—God and not-God—but are one reality, divided into two aspects—the *natura naturans* or essential core of things, corresponding to substance and the attributes, and the *natura naturata* or concrete manifestations, corresponding to the modes. (See p. 366c.) The latter follows necessarily from the former; everything that exists is the necessary result of the divine nature and attributes, not as separated and set off from them, but as included in them. Since "all things are in God," then He must be the "immanent" (internal) rather than the "transitive" (external) cause of things. He is not a divine artificer standing apart from and over things, creating the world out of a primal stuff or out of nothing, nor does the world flow out from some intermediary being between Him and the world. He is one with the things that follow from His nature—they are parts of Him.

Individual things are nothing but affections or modes of God's attributes, expressing those attributes in a certain and determinate manner. (p. 365b)

Hence when Spinoza speaks of God as the cause of all things, he means that He is the universal principle or ground of all existence, the "first cause" of all things—not indirectly as a purely "spiritual" principle above and apart from the world, but directly, through His infinite attributes, including materiality as the active, "efficient" cause of the existence of things, causing them to come into being and to continue in being. (See Prop. 24, Corol.) This means that God is the direct cause of every individual thing (see pp. 357b-d and 366a), and since His nature and attributes are infinite, He is the cause of "*infinite numbers of things in infinite ways*" (p. 362a). It also means that everything which exists exists necessarily and that the actual world in which we exist is the only world that could have existed.

God is a "free cause," in the sense that He "acts from the laws of His own nature only, and is compelled by no one" or nothing outside Himself. He is the only free cause, existing and acting from the necessity of His own nature, while everything else necessarily is caused from without, "determined to existence and action in a fixed and prescribed manner" (Def. 7, p. 355b)—that is, necessarily follows from the divine nature. But God is not "free" in the sense that He could arbitrarily choose to make or not to make a world or to make a different world from this one. "All things which can be conceived by the infinite intellect . . . must necessarily follow" (p. 362a), must come into existence. Furthermore, "there is no cause, *either external to God or within Him,* which can excite Him to act except the perfection of His own nature" (p. 362b, italics added). Far from impairing the absolute perfection and omnipotence traditionally attributed to God, this seeming "limitation" on His action upholds them. To assert that He can create things through an arbitrary fiat, one way or the other, is the same as to say that He could make it come to pass that the angles of a triangle should not equal two right angles. The divine mind would have to be in a state of self-contradiction, or there would have to be two Gods, which is an absurdity. (See Prop. 17, Schol.; and Prop. 33, Schol. 2.)

Insofar as will and intellect can be attributed to God, they must be understood in a sense different from the one which they have when they are applied to man. For God's will and intellect, so far as we can speak of them at all, must pertain to God's eternal essence, and hence must be immutable; and whatever is in God's intellect must necessarily come to be. God's eternal intellect (which Spinoza considers the same as His will or power) is the cause of both the essence and the existence of things. God's omnipotence is described as having "been actual from eternity" (p. 362d; see also p. 368b-c).

The consequence of this view of divine causality is the assertion that "*there is nothing contingent, but all things are determined from the necessity of the divine nature to exist and act in a certain manner*" (Prop. 29, p. 366b). Or, put in another way, "*things could have been produced by God in no other manner and in no other order than that in which they have been produced*" (Prop. 33, p. 367b). This amounts, as soon becomes clear, to a denial of "final causes"—of design and purpose—in nature, and to a denial of freedom of the will— the sense of a choice or decision between alternative possibilities—either in God or in man. "*The will cannot be called a free cause, but can only be called necessary*" (Prop. 32, p. 367a), says Spinoza, and he means this about the will whether conceived "as finite or infinite" in God or in man.

Thus far, Spinoza has argued against the traditional position while accepting the traditional assumptions that intellect and will are attributes of God. Now, however, he asserts his own view—that God's intellect, *as actual or operative,* and His will are not essential attributes of His nature but are infinite modes of the attributes of thought (just as motion and rest are modes of the attributes of extension). They belong to the consequential manifestations of the divine nature (to the *natura naturata*) and are themselves necessarily determined by the original causal power of God's nature (of the *natura naturans*). It follows "that God does not act from freedom of the will," and that God's will stands in no closer relation to Him than the infinite mode of motion and rest which follows from His attribute of extension, or indeed, "than other natural things" (p. 367b). (See Props. 29-32; see also p. 362c.)

This view of God's will is directed not only against the view that God's will is arbitrary and that He can do whatever He wants, but also against the view that the divine will acts for the sake of the universal good, for a supreme end. Indeed, the latter view, in Spinoza's opinion, is even more wrong than the former, for it sets up something outside God as a model or mark for Him to aim at, implying not only that God is imperfect but also subjecting Him to the external power of fate. (See pp. 368d-369a.)

Spinoza has now reached his goal, and at this point he sums up what he has accomplished in the eight definitions, seven axioms, and thirty-six propositions, with accompanying demonstrations, corollaries, and scholia, of Part I.

I have now explained the nature of God and its properties. I have shown that He necessarily exists; that He is one God; that from the necessity alone of His own nature He is and acts; that He is, and in what way He is, the free cause of all things; that all things are in Him, and so depend upon Him that without Him they can neither be nor can be conceived; and, finally, that all things have been predetermined by Him, not indeed from freedom of will or from absolute good pleasure, but from His absolute nature or infinite power. (p. 369b)

These words seem to be the natural rhetorical close of Part I, but actually they are the first paragraph of the Appendix. For Spinoza is not quite through—he returns once more to the attack on final causes and to an exposure of the reasons why men believe in them. It is a polemical, contentious attack, delivered in straightforward and often salty prose. The object of his attack is the belief

. . . that all things in nature, like men, work to some end; and indeed it is thought to be certain that God Himself directs all things to some sure end, for it is said that God has made all things for man, and man that he may worship God. (p. 369c)

The reasons for this belief, says Spinoza, are ignorance and self-centeredness. Men begin by falsely ascribing their own actions to their freely willed decisions to accomplish consciously chosen ends. They then project this illusory belief onto natural things and events, and finally conclude that all things have a design and purpose, supernaturally willed to serve man's desires. From this error follow such instances of "amazed stupidity" as ascribing to God's will the death of a man killed by a falling stone or attributing the supposedly "wonderful" structure of the human body to the deliberate purpose of a divine creator. All man's judgments of good and evil, of order and confusion, and of beauty and ugliness are the result of this anthropocentric view of things as designed for man's benefit. Men read into nature an order that is pleasing to their senses and adapted to their imagination, assuming that God has arranged nature to fit man's sense of proper ends.

This anthropocentric view turns things upside down, considering as causes what are actually effects, making the first to be last and treating the absolutely perfect as imperfect. For to believe that all things and principles in nature serve human ends amounts to making what is closest to God and immediately an effect of the divine power (such as the infinite modes) inferior to what is further away (the merely finite mode, man). Moreover, as we have seen, it assumes an imperfection in God in regarding Him as working to achieve ends that are outside Himself.

Hence, Spinoza finds it easy to handle the question how imperfections can arise necessarily from "the most perfect nature of God," for instance, ugly and disgusting things, and "confusion, evil, crime." He answers that

... the perfection of things is to be judged by their nature and power alone; nor are they more or less perfect because they delight or offend the human senses, or because they are beneficial or prejudicial to human nature. (p. 372c)

As to question why men exist who are not "controlled by the dictates of reason alone"—an obvious defect in natural power —Spinoza answers:

... Because to Him material was not wanting for the creation of everything, from the highest down to the very lowest grade of perfection; or, to speak more properly, because the laws of His nature were so ample that they sufficed for the production of everything which can be conceived by an infinite intellect, as I have demonstrated in Prop. 16. (p. 372c-d)

V I

Is Spinoza's "one reality" one or two?

Spinoza has emphasized, as we have seen, the positive and all-inclusive nature of an infinite and perfect substance or God. Yet he distinguishes between substance and its modes, between God as the first cause of things and the things themselves, between the *natura naturans* and the *natura naturata*. In what sense are God and the world one? In what sense, if any, are they two?

Spinoza's term "God or Nature" and his emphasis on the materiality of God seem to invite us to identify God with the physical universe. Yet the establishment of a causal relation between substance and modes, and the definition of mode as something which exists and is thought in another thing, seem to indicate some kind of duality. And the discernment of infinite as well as finite modes, and of both "immediate" and "mediate" infinite modes, seems to indicate a plurality of levels of reality. In what sense, then, are they one? Or, asked another way, in what sense are they real? Are finite things—stones, trees, and men—as real as God?

Spinoza's favorite analogy between substance and modes is that between the whole and its parts. He speaks in Part II of the concept of "the whole of nature . . . [as] one individual, whose parts" are all the bodies in the universe. (See p. 380a-b.) But is the whole simply equivalent to the sum of all the things that make up the world? Is substance identical with the aggregate of physical phenomena? Or is it a whole in some other sense? What kind of whole is this which is present in all its parts and in which all its parts exist?

One way to approach this is on the analogy of the less general to the more general, of particular to universal, of species to genus; as "animal" is the whole of which men, horses, dogs, etc., are parts. The universal here, of course, would be the one true universal for Spinoza, namely, substance or being, which includes all existence.

Another way to approach this is from the viewpoint of infinitude and limitation. Ultimate and essential reality is unlimited, as we have seen. The finite modes are the delimited, separated segments of this boundless whole. Looking at things in a certain way, we see them in their piecemeal, finite, determinate state. Looking at them in another way, we see the infinite reality of which they are expressions.

If we see things in their finite aspect, are we seeing them falsely, not as they really are? Is their reality only the substance of which they are modifications? Are there grades of reality or perfection from God down to atomic particles?

How can there be more than one infinite attribute?

Spinoza asserts that there is one, and only one, infinite substance, but that it has infinite attributes. Now, an attribute may be "infinite" in the sense that it is all-inclusive and boundless, like substance. Spinoza's attributes are certainly infinite in this sense. But they are also infinite in number, i.e., innumerable. *"The more reality or being a thing possesses, the more attributes belong to it"* (Prop. 9, p. 357d). And God, the absolutely infinite Being, consists of infinite attributes, "each one of which expresses eternal and infinite essence" (Def. 6, p. 355b). That is, God consists of an infinite number of attributes, each of which is itself infinite.

Actually, the problem boils down to how there can be even two infinite attributes, let alone an infinite number. Two or more of anything implies limitation, as Spinoza himself has pointed out. Yet he assures us that thought and distinction are two distinguishable attributes and that there are many, indeed, infinitely more, each *expressing eternal and infinite essence.*

We might seek the solution in some subjectivist interpretation of the attributes, taking them as the way in which the finite human mind conceives of substance. Indeed, the definition of attribute is "that which the intellect perceives of substance, as if constituting its essence" (Def. 4, p. 355b). The "as if" seems to give credence to the subjectivist interpretation, but Spinoza himself later on states flatly that each attribute "expresses the reality or being of substance" (p. 358a), and consistently treats the attributes as actually existing and practically equivalent to substance.

We might also try to solve this problem by treating the attributes as actually modes, for plurality and distinction belong to the realm of the *natura naturata.* It is true that what we know of the attributes we know in the "modifications" and "affections" of substance. But nevertheless Spinoza clearly insists that the attributes belong to the *natura naturans,* to the "creative" primal reality, and introduces "infinite modes," immediate and mediate, between the attributes and the finite modes.

Whatever solution we adopt, we must abandon the spatial picture of infinity, for mind and body are parallel and interchangeable orders in Spinoza's system of reality, running through all things, not separate "lots." Thinking substance and extended substance are the same thing. We may think of it either way. Bergson suggests the analogue of two translations, or better yet, of the physical circle described on the blackboard and the mathematical equation, both of which express the essence of the circle. That essence may be expressed either in extension or in thought, or in any of the other innumerable attributes unknown to the human mind.

Yet all this has to do with the realm of delimited and measured existence and does not solve the problem of an apparent plurality in the one, simple substance. That problem is linked with the question of how the finite, concrete world arises from an infinite, simple substance.

How can the finite, temporal world arise from infinite, eternal substance?

Spinoza's main charge against the old theology and metaphysics was that by conceiving ultimate reality as utterly devoid of materiality, it made the origin and existence of material reality completely incomprehensible. Whatever is in finite existence, he argued, must first be in ultimate reality in a superlative and infinite way. However, he himself appears to be open to a somewhat similar charge, to have failed to account adequately for the derivation of the many from the one, of the changing from the eternal, of the finite from the infinite.

Hegel, for instance, in the preface of his *Phenomenology of Mind*, dismisses Spinoza's "One Substance" as mere "inert, abstract simplicity," a mere undifferentiated uniformity, a "night in which . . . all cows are black," which is completely disjunctive with concrete reality and becoming.[2] Similarly, Bergson in his *Creative Evolution* says of such philosophers as Spinoza, that "after having concentrated in God the whole of the real, it became difficult for them to pass from God to things, from eternity to time."[3] Bergson recognizes that Spinoza's substance is not merely something before and apart from concrete reality but is pre-eminently present in things, but he sees a baffling contradiction in this co-presence of eternality and temporality.

Is this criticism justified? Does Spinoza give an essentially abstract and static picture of reality? Does he fail to take the temporal aspect of things seriously? Is novelty possible in his universe? Is the divine substance present in historical events too? Could time be one of the divine attributes for Spinoza? What would happen to his view of things, if it were?

Do you think that Spinoza is open to the charge of contradiction and absurdity that he has leveled against the "immate-

---

[2] G. W. F. Hegel, *The Phenomenology of Mind* (London: George Allen & Unwin, Ltd., 1910), pp. 78 ff.

[3] Henri Bergson, *Creative Evolution* (New York: Random House, Inc., Modern Library, 1944), p. 383.

rialists"? Does his ascription of materiality to the essence of God or substance decisively remove him from the difficulties of those who see ultimate reality as pure Spirit, Mind, Thought, etc.?

Spinoza himself was by no means unaware of the difficulties raised by the question of the relation between substance and its modes, between God and the world. He was supremely confident in the power of the human mind to set up a consistent and necessary system of reality, and he believed that he himself had accomplished that task. Nevertheless, he recognized his obvious human limitations. For example, when one correspondent asked him to tell "how each part of Nature accords with the whole of it, and in what way it is connected with the other parts," Spinoza answered, "I do not know *how* the parts are really interconnected, and *how* each part accords with the whole; for to know this it would be necessary to know the whole of Nature and all its Parts." All that he offers to do is to present the reason for believing *"that* each part of Nature accords with the whole of it."[4]

[4] *The Correspondence of Spinoza,* trans. and ed. by A. Wolf (London: George Allen & Unwin, Ltd., 1928), p. 209 f. (italics added).

The following questions are designed to help you test the thoroughness of your reading. Each question is to be answered by giving a page or pages of the reading assignment. Answers will be found on pages 301 and 302 of this Reading Plan.

1 Why can't the reason why twenty men exist be found in human nature?

2 Can we have true ideas of nonexistent modifications of substance?

3 Does the reason why a circle or triangle exists lie in its nature or in the order of physical nature generally?

4 Why does the identification of ability to exist with power lead to the conclusion that absolutely infinite Being necessarily exists?

5 Does the divine intellect differ from the human with regard to both its essence and its existence?

6 Do the attributes express God's existence as well as His essence?

7 Is an idea of God in thought finite or infinite?

LOCKE

An Essay Concerning Human Understanding
"Of Knowledge and Probability"; Book IV, Ch. 1-4

Vol. 35, pp. 307-329

Whereas the last two readings dealt with two continental rationalist philosophers, namely, Descartes and Spinoza, the next three readings take up three British empiricists, Locke, Berkeley, and Hume. Of these, Locke is already known to us for his contributions to political thought (see the Reading Plan *A General Introduction to the Great Books and to a Liberal Education*), his views on religion and religious tolerance (see the Reading Plan *Religion and Theology*), his ethical theory (see the Reading Plan *Ethics: The Study of Moral Values*), and his theory of the origin and nature of ideas (see the Reading Plan *Biology, Psychology, and Medicine*). This, then, is the fifth time that Locke appears in the reading plans, and here we are concerned with his theory of knowledge. The mere fact that we have five different readings from Locke would be proof—if any were needed—that Locke is one of the major figures in the history of philosophy.

Locke's importance frequently tends to be minimized, when he is compared with such famous philosophers of antiquity as Plato or Aristotle, or even when he is judged in the light of his followers Berkeley and Hume. Yet he has a philosophical system that is almost as all-embracing as that of Plato or Aristotle; and Berkeley and Hume, being Locke's followers, naturally built on the foundation he laid.

That foundation is empiricism, a thoroughgoing and wholehearted empiricism. This basic tenet of his philosophy frequently gets Locke into difficulties; as we shall see in this reading, it makes difficulties for his theory of knowledge. Locke's basic dilemma, and that of empiricists in general, is stated by a twentieth-century philosopher as follows:

. . . we know the world only by experience, not by reasoning; yet what we know is not the world, but only experience. We must defer to facts, but there are no facts, only ideas.[1]

[1] John Herman Randall, Jr., *The Career of Philosophy* (New York: Columbia University Press, 1962), p. 617.

Eleventh Reading

I

Book IV is the last book of the *Essay* and, accordingly, it is the coping stone in the edifice of empiricism which Locke has built. Book I contains Locke's refutation of the doctrine of innate ideas, Book II treats of the ideas which we acquire from experience, and Book III deals with language. Book IV, finally, is devoted to knowledge—its degrees, extent, and reality.

Locke begins with a definition of knowledge:

Knowledge then seems to me to be nothing but *the perception of the connexion of and agreement, or disagreement and repugnancy of any of our ideas.* In this alone it consists. Where this perception is, there is knowledge, and where it is not, there, though we may fancy, guess, or believe, yet we always come short of knowledge. For when we know that white is not black, what do we else but perceive, that these two ideas do not agree? When we possess ourselves with the utmost security of the demonstration, that the three angles of a triangle are equal to two right ones, what do we more but perceive, that equality to two right ones does necessarily agree to, and is inseparable from, the three angles of a triangle? (p. 307a)

When two ideas agree, one idea can be affirmed of the other; i.e., if the idea of apple and the idea of red agree, I can say that the apple is red; and when I perceive that this affirmation can be made, then I am in a state of knowledge. Similarly, when two ideas disagree, I cannot affirm the one idea of the other; and when I perceive this, I also have knowledge.

This definition of knowledge is in accord with what Locke, in the immediately preceding paragraph, tells us is the object of knowledge:

Since the mind, in all its thoughts and reasonings, hath no other immediate object but its own ideas, which it alone does or can contemplate, it is evident that our knowledge is only conversant about them. (p. 307a)

It is immediately apparent that Locke has made a problem for himself at the very beginning of his treatment of knowledge. The problem is that of the "reality" of knowledge: what assurance do we have that when we know something, our knowledge refers to anything actual outside the mind? Since, according to Locke, the mind has no object except its own ideas, and since knowledge consists in the perception of the agreement or disagreement of ideas, it is very difficult to see how a man knows something "real," i.e., something beyond the ideas in his mind.

Although this problem is raised by the very first words in Book IV, Locke delays addressing himself to it. He waits until the fourth chapter (entitled "Of the Reality of Knowledge"), but then he does face his difficulty squarely. Here is how he himself expresses the objection to his view:

If it be true, that all knowledge lies only in the perception of the agreement or disagreement of our own ideas, the visions of an enthusiast and the reasonings of a sober man will be equally certain. It is no matter how things are: so a man observe but the agreement of his own imaginations, and talk conformably, it is all truth, all certainty. (p. 324a)

And if a man's imaginings, no matter how fanciful, can constitute knowledge, then we may indeed wonder what the utility of knowledge is:

"But of what use is all this fine knowledge of *men's own imaginations*, to a man that inquires after the reality of things? It matters not what men's fancies are, it is the knowledge of things that is only to be prized: it is this alone gives a value to our reasonings, and preference to one man's knowledge over another's, that it is of things as they really are, and not of dreams and fancies." (p. 324a)

As might be expected, Locke has an answer ready, and it is the standard answer that philosophers have always given when this problem comes up: Although what we know immediately are ideas, we also know things by means of ideas. Our knowledge does not stop with our own ideas, but rather reaches out beyond them to reality and to things:

. . . the mind knows not things immediately, but only by the intervention of the ideas it has of them. (p. 324b)

We know ideas *immediately*, but things only *mediately*,

namely through the medium of our ideas. When is knowledge real, then? That is, when is knowledge knowledge of reality? Locke answers, when knowledge does not stop with our own ideas, but when, through them, it is about the things of reality:

Our knowledge, therefore is real only so far as there is a *conformity* between our ideas and the reality of things. (p. 324b)

What does Locke mean by "idea"? This is the subject of the second book of the *Essay*, and here in Book IV Locke assumes that the reader knows how he uses the term. Actually, the most concise definition of the term "idea" is found in the "Introduction" to the *Essay:*

[Idea] being that term which, I think, serves best to stand for whatsoever is the *object* of the understanding when a man thinks, I have used it to express whatever is meant by *phantasm, notion, species,* or *whatever it is which the mind can be employed about in thinking;* and I could not avoid frequently using it. (p. 95c)

Our knowledge is real and not just fanciful when our ideas conform to the things of reality. But how shall we know, Locke asks quite properly, that there is such conformity?

How shall the mind, when it perceives nothing but its own ideas, know that they agree with things themselves? (p. 324b)

Is there any way by which I can tell whether this idea which is now in my mind is real (i.e., corresponds to something in reality) or is imaginary (i.e., has no counterpart in reality)? Locke answers that we can be certain of the reality of an idea, provided it is one of two kinds of ideas.

First, if an idea is simple, then it has reality, for all simple ideas are conformable to things. Simple ideas, such as those of "white," "hot," etc., are not made up by the mind. They are produced in us by things outside us which are white, or hot, etc. These simple ideas conform to things in the way in which an effect conforms to a cause.

Second, if an idea is complex, then it has reality. The only exceptions are complex ideas of substances. To understand this we must go back to earlier parts of the *Essay*. Complex ideas, except when they are of substances, are *"made by the understanding"* (p. 263d); whereas simple ideas are passively received by the mind. Furthermore, these complex ideas are made arbitrarily, *"without patterns, or reference to any real existence"* (p. 264a). Locke explains this in more detail:

> To understand this right, we must consider wherein this making of these complex ideas consists; and that is not in the making any new idea, but putting together those which the mind had before. Wherein the mind does these three things: First, It chooses a certain number; Secondly, It gives them connexion, and makes them into one idea; Thirdly, It ties them together by a name. (p. 264b)

Now because complex ideas are made by the understanding and are made arbitrarily, therefore, they necessarily have reality:

> . . . All our complex ideas, *except those of substances*, being archetypes of the mind's own making, not intended to be the copies of anything, nor referred to the existence of anything, as to their originals, cannot want any conformity necessary to real knowledge. For that which is not designed to represent anything but itself, can never be capable of a wrong representation, nor mislead us from the true apprehension of anything, by its dislikeness to it: and such, excepting those of substances, are all our complex ideas. (p. 324d)

This reasoning does not apply to the complex ideas of substance. For those ideas are intended to refer to something outside the mind (viz., to real substances), and hence there is a genuine question as to whether a complex idea of a substance conforms to it adequately. In fact, Locke tells us elsewhere (in Book II) that no idea of a substance can be adequate. For such an idea must refer either to the essence of a thing or else to the collection of properties and powers that constitute the thing. Now real essences, in Locke's view, are unknowable, so that no idea can possibly be adequate to an essence. As for complex ideas that try to achieve adequacy by enumerating all the properties and powers of a thing, this clearly is a task doomed to failure, because of the many unknown properties that anything has.

> . . . those qualities and powers of substances, whereof we make their complex ideas, are so many and various, that no man's complex idea contains them all. (p. 242a)

But an idea that is not adequate to a thing clearly lacks reality; for it does not conform to a thing, to whatever extent it is inadequate to it.

Let us look back over Locke's total defense against the charge that in his theory knowledge has no reality. Has he succeeded in countering the opponent's argument? His account seems pretty weak. Consider, first of all, his contention that all simple ideas are real because they are directly caused by bodily qualities. The idea of whiteness, Locke says, conforms to whiteness, because it is whiteness that causes the idea of whiteness in us. But what kind of conformity is it that exists between cause and effect? Is it the kind of conformity that assures reality to an idea? Could greenness not cause the idea of whiteness? In fact, is this not what happens when we experience optical illusions?

The case against the reality of ideas seems all the stronger because Locke has a theory of primary and secondary qualities. According to this theory, such qualities as colors are not really "in" things. The ideas of red, blue, etc., are caused by certain combinations of primary qualities (such as extension and motion). Hence it seems that the idea of blue does not conform to anything blue in reality.

Although Locke's argument for the reality of complex ideas is impeccable, it does not prove much. For complex ideas seem to have "reality" only because they do not refer to anything real. In other words, the problem of reality does not arise for ideas which are not claimed to be anything except fictions of the mind. Complex ideas, such as mathematical ideas, therefore seem to have all the reality that can be asked of them— but that is not much.

Finally, it appears that the lack of reality in the complex ideas of substance is a serious flaw in Locke's theory of knowledge. In effect, the most important part of reality—the individual thing—is declared to be unknowable by man.

What, we may well ask, is left of reality for man to know? Does it not seem as though man knows his ideas, but lacks contact with reality?

II

There are two other problems of knowledge which Locke considers in these chapters. (Actually he turns to them before treating of the reality of knowledge.) These problems are that of the *degrees* of knowledge and that of the *extent* of knowledge.

As Locke uses the terms, knowledge is said to vary in degree when it varies in clearness. Accordingly, Locke tells us that basically there are two degrees of knowledge: *intuitive* knowledge and *demonstrative* knowledge. The names are good indications of the characteristics of these kinds of knowledge. In intuitive knowledge, the mind apprehends the agreement or disagreement of two ideas in a flash of intuition. (Knowledge, it will be remembered, is nothing but such apprehension of the agreement or disagreement of ideas.) In demonstrative knowledge, on the other hand, the agreement or disagreement between two ideas must be demonstrated to exist, since it cannot be seen immediately.

As examples of intuitive knowledge, Locke mentions the apprehension that white is not black, that three equals two plus one, and similar statements. Intuitive knowledge is the clearest we have; and when we have it, we also immediately know *that* we know.

This part of knowledge is irresistible, and, like bright sunshine, forces itself immediately to be perceived, as soon as ever the mind turns its view that way; and leaves no room for hesitation, doubt, or examination, but the mind is presently filled with the clear light of it. (p. 309c)

We have demonstrative knowledge when the agreement or disagreement of two ideas is not immediately evident but can be made evident by the intervention of other ideas. Thus, Locke says, we cannot immediately and intuitively perceive whether the two ideas "interior angles of a triangle" and "two right angles" agree or disagree. One or more ideas must be interposed between these two before we can decide whether the angles of a triangle are equal to two right angles or not. This interposition of ideas is called *reasoning*.

Those intervening ideas, which serve to show the agreement of any two others, are called *proofs;* and where the agreement and disagreement is by this means plainly and clearly perceived, it is called *demonstration* . . . (p. 310b)

Demonstrative knowledge is just as certain as intuitive knowledge, but it usually is not quite so clear. This is due to the fact that the several intermediate steps tend to take away some of the clarity of our cognition. Each of the intermediate steps must itself be based on intuitive knowledge or be reducible further to other ideas which are intuitively known. Intuitive knowledge alone needs no further warrant for its validity; demonstrative knowledge must be either reducible to it or else it is not truly knowledge.

In addition to these two forms of knowledge which pertain to general truths, Locke admits that there is one further degree of knowledge. This is what he calls sensitive knowledge; by this he means that we affirm the existence of particular sensible things as a result of our perception of them. For example, when we perceive a tall, green tree, we then know that there exists a tall, green tree.

> . . . I think, we may add to the two former sorts of knowledge this also, of the existence of particular external objects, by that perception and consciousness we have of the actual entrance of ideas from them, and allow these three degrees of knowledge, viz. *intuitive, demonstrative,* and *sensitive:* in each of which there are different degrees and ways of evidence and certainty. (p. 312d)

With respect to sensitive knowledge, Locke considers a very interesting objection: how can we be certain, the objection runs, that there exists more than our idea; how can we know that there is something outside us corresponding to the idea in our mind? Frequently, the objector adds, we have ideas in our mind without there being anything outside the mind corresponding to them. For example, this is the case when we dream.

Locke has very little patience with this objection. His words sound as though he is eager to dismiss it quickly because it so obviously appears absurd to him. He notes that we have very little difficulty in distinguishing between our dreams and our waking perceptions. He adds, in apparent pique, that if everything is a dream, then there is no point to arguing with the objector at all, since in that case "reasoning and arguments are of no use, truth and knowledge nothing" (p. 312c). The objection and Locke's reply are noteworthy because they are related to the basic doctrine of Berkeley's *Principles of Human*

Knowledge, which constitutes the next reading. We shall defer further consideration of this objection until then.

III

The third problem with regard to knowledge concerns its extent. Locke deals with this matter in Chapter 3 of Book IV. The question to be answered is: how much do we, or can we, know? What are the limitations to which our knowledge is subject?

The answer to the question follows from what Locke has already said concerning the nature and degrees of knowledge. We should not be surprised to learn that the extent of our knowledge is quite limited. Locke begins by making six general points.

1. Since knowledge has been defined as the perception of the agreement or disagreement of our ideas, the first limitation on its extent consists in the fact that it can extend no further than our ideas.

2. It follows, from this definition of our knowledge, that its extent is limited to that area where we can perceive agreement or disagreement of our ideas. This means that it is limited to the agreements or disagreements which can be perceived either by intuition or by reason (i.e., by demonstrative knowledge) or by sensation.

3. Intuitive knowledge does not extend to all the relations of ideas. On the contrary, only some agreements or disagreements of ideas are immediately intuited; most of them are not.

4. Demonstrative knowledge (or, as Locke calls it here, rational knowledge) also does not extend to all our ideas. Very frequently we may have two ideas but be unable to connect these two by intermediate ideas of such a sort that we can go from one of the original ideas to the other one by a series of intuitive steps.

5. Sensitive knowledge, since it pertains only to the actual existence of the things which are present to our senses, quite obviously does not extend as far as our ideas.

6. From the five previous points, Locke concludes that the extent of our knowledge is not only smaller than the domain

of reality but also smaller than the extent of our own ideas. No doubt, we can always know much more than we do at a given time; i.e., we can know many more agreements and disagreements of our ideas. But we shall never be able to extend our knowledge to all our ideas; concerning some of our ideas, we will not be able to say that they agree or disagree with one another. As an example of such ideas, Locke mentions those of "matter" and "thinking"; he does not believe that we shall be able ever to ascertain whether God might not make a mere material substance possess thought.

Locke next turns to the limitations arising from the fact that knowledge consists in the perception of agreement or disagreement between two ideas. Such agreement or disagreement may have to do with (1) the identity or diversity of ideas, (2) the coexistence of ideas, (3) other relations between ideas, and (4) real existence.

Knowledge of the identity or diversity of ideas extends as far as the ideas themselves. For there is no idea in the mind which the mind does not perceive, sooner or later, to be what it is and to be different from another idea.

By contrast, the next category of knowledge is very limited. Only very infrequently can we perceive that two ideas either coexist or do not coexist. Yet this category of knowledge is perhaps the most important, since almost all our knowledge of substances depends on the knowledge of coexistence.

This point needs a little explication. Locke does not mean that we never perceive two coexisting ideas; on the contrary, we very frequently do. For example, in examining a piece of gold, we notice that it is yellow, hard, malleable, etc. In fact, whenever we describe a particular substance, we do so by listing the qualities which we find coexisting in it.

The difficulty arises when we inquire what *other* qualities coexist with those which are apparent in gold, or other substances.

When we would know anything further concerning these, or any other sort of substances, what do we inquire, but what *other* qualities or powers these substances have or have not? Which is nothing else but to know what *other* simple ideas do, or do not co-exist with those that make up that complex idea? (p. 315c)

This kind of question is almost always impossible to answer, because we do not really know anything about the essences of substances; all we know are the qualities that we perceive. And these qualities, just because they do not pertain to the essences of things, do not reveal to us anything about other qualities which are necessarily found in things. We must realize, of course, that Locke is inquiring about other qualities which *necessarily* coexist with those that we perceive. For instance, if we understand gold to be something yellow, hard, and malleable, we want to know what other essential qualities it has, or what other qualities are necessarily going to be found in gold. This kind of knowledge can hardly ever be had.

The reason whereof is, that the simple ideas whereof our complex ideas of substances are made up are, for the most part, such as carry with them, in their own nature, no *visible necessary* connexion or inconsistency with any other simple ideas, whose co-existence with them we would inform ourselves about. (p. 315d)

This difficulty looms large with regard to secondary qualities. We are caused to perceive them by the action on us of primary qualities (such as extension, motion, etc.). But we do not know what combinations of primary qualities produce a sensation of yellow, sweet, etc., in us. Hence we cannot hope to discover that one group of secondary qualities—for example, those which are part of our complex idea of gold—must necessarily be connected with another group of secondary qualities.

In vain, therefore, shall we endeavour to discover by our ideas . . . what other ideas are to be found constantly joined with that of *our* complex idea of any substance: since we neither know the real constitution of the minute parts on which their qualities do depend; nor, did we know them, could we discover any necessary connexion between them and any of the secondary qualities: which is necessary to be done before we can certainly know their necessary co-existence. (p. 316b-c)

Locke goes on to show that it is equally difficult, if not impossible, to know the coexistence of other ideas. This topic—that there is no certain but only probable knowledge concerning the necessary connection between two ideas—is one of the major topics in Hume's *Enquiry Concerning Human Under-*

standing. We shall have something to say about this matter in the thirteenth reading.

Locke is a little vague about the next point—the extent of the agreement or disagreement of our ideas with respect to other relations than that of coexistence. The science of mathematics is, of course, based on the perception of agreements or disagreements of ideas in quantitative relations (such as being equal to, greater than, less than, etc.). With the example of mathematics in mind, Locke ventures the opinion that there may be a great deal of knowledge—much more than we suspect—to be derived from the perception of some relations hitherto unexplored.

Finally, Locke asks how far our knowledge extends in the matter of real existence. Here he notes that all three kinds of knowledge—intuitive, demonstrative, and sensitive—contribute to our knowledge of existence. We have an intuitive knowledge of our own existence, demonstrative knowledge of God's existence, and sensitive knowledge of such things as are present to the senses.

Because the examination of the extent of our knowledge has led him to the conclusion that knowledge is very limited, Locke proposes to examine human ignorance—what causes *it* and how extensive *it* is. In general, he says, our lack of knowledge is due to three causes: first, our lack of ideas; second, our inability to discover connections between the ideas which we do have; and third, our failure to trace and examine our ideas.

He begins by investigating the lack of ideas. Why do we not have more ideas? One reason lies in our sensory apparatus. Locke thinks it is likely that there may be other ideas which could be discovered by beings with different and better senses; all such ideas will, of course, forever remain hidden to us. Next, consider ideas which theoretically we are capable of having; i.e., ideas that can be perceived by our senses. We are far from having all those ideas; a great many sensible qualities will not be discovered by us because they are too far from us. For example, we do not know the color, shape, etc., of things on other planets because they are too far away to be seen by us. Other qualities are not known to us because they are in things which are too minute. (It should be noticed that these last two imperfections of human knowledge are remediable by the improvement of instruments such as telescopes and microscopes.) Our knowledge, therefore, does not extend to all material beings; and, in addition, we are in complete ignorance of spiritual substances.

Secondly, when we do have ideas, we very often cannot discover whether there is any connection between them. Examples of this are ideas of primary qualities and ideas of secondary qualities. We have both kinds of ideas, but we remain in ignorance of how primary qualities cause secondary qualities. Equally unknowable and perhaps even more mysterious is the connection between the ideas of mind and body. Again, we are completely unable to explain how the mind can cause the body to do certain things—such as walk, speak, etc.

Thirdly, we frequently are in a state of ignorance because we fail to see an existing connection between ideas. This is the case, for example, in mathematics. We may have the idea of triangle and we may have the idea of two right angles, but we may be ignorant of the fact that these two ideas are connected by the relation of equality, simply because we have not studied mathematics; i.e., we have not examined the relevant ideas. Ignorance of this kind most frequently results from the abuse of words, in Locke's opinion. Because of this, a good portion of Book III of the *Essay* is devoted to correcting the abuse of words and language.

I V

What is the distinction between actual and habitual knowledge?

We have actual knowledge when the agreement or disagreement of ideas is actually before the mind. For example, if I perceive that this cloth is red, I am then in possession of actual knowledge.

Habitual knowledge may result from actual knowledge. If I once knew that some proposition is true, then when I am asked whether it is true, I may remember that it is true. If I do, then I have habitual knowledge of that proposition's truth. This habitual knowledge, Locke says, may itself be of two kinds. When I remember that the proposition in question is true, I may either remember the demonstration by which it was proved, or I may only remember that I once grasped the demonstration and then knew that the proposition was true.

Obviously, the former kind of habitual knowledge is more perfect; in fact, it closely approximates actual knowledge. If somebody asks me about some elementary proposition in geometry—for example, whether the angles of a triangle are equal to two right angles—I may, if I am a geometrician, immediately remember the three or four basic steps that lead to the conclusion that the proposition is true. It is this kind of habitual knowledge which a teacher needs in order to instruct his students. If the students ask the teacher a question, he must be able to produce the requisite proofs out of his store of habitual mathematical knowledge.

The other kind of habitual knowledge seems much less perfect. In fact, should it be called knowledge at all? Basically, it seems to be a memory of knowledge once possessed, joined perhaps with the conviction that the actual knowledge could be restored. He who has this kind of knowledge seems to say: "I knew this once and I remember that I demonstrated this proposition before; consequently, I am sure I could do it again." Perhaps it would be more appropriate to call this state of mind by some other name than "knowledge." Should it not be called simply "conviction"? To be sure, it is conviction based on a reasonable ground, viz. the memory of former ability to prove something. But it seems better not to call this by the honorific name "knowledge."

Is this kind of "knowledge" or "state of conviction" very frequently encountered? Could human beings get along without it? Is it more common than habitual knowledge properly so called? In Aristotle's theory, science is an intellectual virtue and therefore (since the virtues are habits) an intellectual habit. Is this the same sort of habitual knowledge as Locke's?

Does mathematics have a special place as the most precise and certain of the sciences?

In many theories of knowledge, mathematics is given a place of eminence because, given its basic principles, its conclusions are arrived at with absolute certainty. Very often, mathematics is held up as the model for all other sciences.

Locke agrees that mathematical propositions possess certainty, but he denies that mathematics is the only science so privileged. May it not be the case, he asks, that we simply have not applied ourselves sufficiently or correctly in other sciences? In other words, he does not think that mathematical ideas—extension, number, figure, etc.—are in a crucial way different from the ideas used in other sciences, such as ethics.

For whatever ideas we have wherein the mind can perceive the immediate agreement or disagreement that is between them, there the mind is capable of intuitive knowledge; and where it can perceive the agreement or disagreement of any two ideas, by an intuitive perception of the agreement or disagreement they have with any intermediate ideas, there the mind is capable of demonstration: which is not limited to ideas of extension, figure, number, and their modes. (p. 311b)

And a little later he adds:

This at least I believe, that the *ideas of quantity* are not those alone that are capable of demonstration and knowledge; and that other, and perhaps more useful, parts of contemplation, would afford us certainty, if vices, passions, and domineering interest did not oppose or menace such endeavours. (p. 317d)

More specifically, Locke thinks that the science of morality is just as capable of demonstration as mathematics is. As examples of propositions which are as certain as any mathematical propositions he gives two: "Where there is no property there is no injustice" and "No government allows absolute liberty" (p. 318a-b).

Locke recognizes, of course, that in fact the science of morals seems to be much less fully worked out than the science of mathematics. There are far fewer propositions that evoke universal assent in ethics than there are in mathematics. Locke, however, believes that this is not due to some intrinsic imperfection in the science of morals, but rather to two causes, both of which can be overcome. The first cause is an advantage which mathematics has over morals. The mathematician can use diagrams and figures in his demonstrations; this makes it less likely that mathematical ideas will be used with different meanings in a proof. By contrast, the moralist must depend entirely on words, and words are notoriously difficult to understand and to pin down. The second cause is a disadvantage which morals suffers: its ideas are generally much more complex than those of mathematics. Consequently, demonstrations in morals may be expected to be more difficult to achieve than are demonstrations in mathematics.

What are the remedies which Locke proposes in order to bring morals up to the standards of mathematics? Do you think his proposals would work? Do you agree with Locke that we can know moral truths with as much certainty as those of mathematics?

Is there any knowledge that is general or universal in its extent?

Direct sense experience provides us only with ideas that are of particular application; i.e., that here there is something yellow, soft, and so on. If our knowledge is to extend further, we must turn to abstract ideas.

For what is known of such general ideas, will be true of every particular thing in whom that essence, i.e. that abstract idea, is to be found: and what is once known of such ideas, will be perpetually and for ever true. (p. 323c)

The problem of general knowledge, therefore, becomes the problem of knowing general or abstract ideas. This problem is discussed by Locke in the following chapters. On the basis of what Locke has said of knowledge so far, do you think he can show that there is valid, general knowledge? Does such knowledge fit the general definition of knowledge?

The following questions are designed to help you test the thoroughness of your reading. Each question is to be answered by giving a page or pages of the reading assignment. Answers will be found on page 302 of this Reading Plan.

1 What are the four kinds of agreement or disagreement between ideas?

2 Is demonstrative knowledge as clear as intuitive knowledge?

3 How does Locke describe the manner in which the sensation of whiteness is produced in us?

4 Can a material thing have two colors at the same time?

5 Does mathematical knowledge have reality?

6 In order that knowledge have reality, must it be about really existing things?

7 What are the principles of morality from which, Locke asserts, the science of morality could be developed demonstratively?

8 Can man have any knowledge of spiritual substances like angels?

BERKELEY

The Principles of Human Knowledge

Vol. 35, pp. 403-444

Like the Roman emperor Hadrian, the Russian czar Peter, and the American president Washington, the Irish philosopher and bishop George Berkeley is honored by having a city named after him. Such a distinction is only rarely conferred even upon rulers and statesmen, and it is probably unique in the annals of philosophy. Bishop Berkeley was greatly interested in America, especially in improving the system of higher education in the colonies. He spent three years at Newport, Rhode Island, but the city named for him is in California—not then or ever a British colony.

Although Berkeley was educated in Dublin, at Trinity College, and later became a fellow of Trinity, he spent considerable time in London. His wit, charm, and articulateness—qualities evident in his writings— won him acceptance in the polite society of London, where he moved in the same circles as Swift, Pope, Addison, and Steele.

A Treatise Concerning the Principles of Human

Knowledge, Berkeley's greatest and best-known work, appears to be largely destructive. It severely criticizes both John Locke and Sir Isaac Newton. A lesser man than Berkeley could hardly have expected any success in attacking these two giants, but Berkeley's arguments, even if we do not agree with him, are so well taken and so to the point that they arouse nothing but respect in us. We should also realize that Berkeley's intent, in spite of the appearance, was to be constructive in philosophy and religion. Indeed, one of the main purposes of the book was to combat both skepticism and atheism.

Twelfth Reading

I

Berkeley's theory of knowledge is sometimes chosen—by laymen—as the prototype of philosophy gone wild. Many persons, already suspicious that philosophy is at best useless and at worst harmful, find their opinion reinforced by the popular misconception of Berkeley's doctrine. He is thought to maintain that the things we see around us "don't really exist." He also is said to believe that if I stop looking at a tree before my eyes, then that tree ceases to exist, until I look at it again, at which point it instantaneously and miraculously is recreated.

Common sense rebels against a theory of this sort and refuses to take it seriously. Nor should common sense be ignored. Far from it. But those who scornfully reject the theory often attributed to Berkeley should realize that they are not fighting against Berkeley: that is not his theory, nor does Berkeley scorn common sense. On the contrary, he regards his theory as coming to the rescue of common sense, which he thought had been badly mauled by the views of Isaac Newton and John Locke. Indeed, Berkeley writes in his notebooks, prior to the publication of the *Principles*: "I side in all things with the Mob."[1]

By "siding with the mob" Berkeley no doubt meant that he wished his theory of knowledge to agree with the common-sense opinions of mankind. Common sense maintains that when we see a tree and know a tree, our knowledge is real (not fictitious or imaginary) and valid. In general, common

[1] *Philosophical Commentaries*, Notebook A, Note 405, in *The Works of George Berkeley*, ed. by A. A. Luce and T. E. Jessop (London: Thomas Nelson & Sons, Ltd., 1948), Vol. I, p. 51.

sense tells us that our senses do not usually deceive us. The existence of sensory illusions does not argue against this; the very fact that we recognize them as illusions indicates that, on the whole, the senses report truly to us. When we know a tree (by perceiving it), what we know really is a tree.

Berkeley desired to develop a theory of knowledge in accordance with these common-sense tenets. He felt that Locke, following the lead of Newton, had violated common sense with his theory of primary and secondary qualities. In Locke's view, only the so-called primary qualities—extension, figure, motion, rest, impenetrability, number—really appertain to existing things. The secondary qualities—all other sensible qualities—exist only in us. They are caused in us by the primary qualities, but they themselves are not "real." The quality *blue* is caused in us not by something that is really blue but rather by a certain assemblage of the primary qualities which act in such a fashion on our visual sense that we perceive blue.

The ideas we have of these [secondary qualities] they acknowledge not to be the resemblances of anything existing without the mind, or unperceived, but they will have our ideas of the primary qualities to be patterns or images of things which exist without the mind, in an unthinking substance which they call Matter.

. . . .

They who assert that figure, motion, and the rest of the primary or original qualities do exist without the mind in unthinking substances, do at the same time acknowledge that colours, sounds, heat, cold, and suchlike secondary qualities, do not—which they tell us are sensations existing in the mind alone, that depend on and are occasioned by the different size, texture, and motion of the minute particles of matter. (pp. 414d-415a)

To Berkeley, it seemed that this view of sense experience jeopardized the reality of knowledge. For it amounts to saying that when we perceive sensible qualities such as "blue," "hot," "soft," etc., there really exists nothing that is blue, hot, or soft. All these secondary qualities are mere fictions of sense; they do not represent reality. Reality, in the Newtonian and Lockean picture, consists of "solid, massy, hard, impenetrable, moveable particles." (This quotation is from Newton's *Op-*

tics, Vol. 34, p. 541b.) Our perceptions, however, tell us nothing of these solid, massy particles; they tell us of things that are blue, hot, etc. Consequently, our knowledge is not real, by Locke's own test of the reality of knowledge. Our ideas (blue, hot, etc.) do not agree with things, as Locke told us they should. (See Locke, *Essay Concerning Human Understanding*, Book IV, Ch. 4, p. 324b.)

Berkeley's effort, in the *Principles*—as well as in his other writings—is directed to recasting the picture of the world and the account of knowledge in such a fashion that knowledge will assuredly be real.

II

The problem of the reality of knowledge in Locke's epistemology may be stated as that of knowing whether there is conformity between our ideas and the things of which they are ideas. Berkeley solves this problem in one fell swoop: he denies the distinction between ideas and the things of which they are ideas. What we know, he says, are our ideas, and there is nothing outside the mind to which these ideas refer—or if there is, it is totally unknowable anyhow and in no way affects our knowledge. When I see a tree, I have an idea of a tree; and when I have an idea of a tree, I know a tree (because I know the idea). There is no need to go any further; in fact, it is foolish to try to have knowledge beyond the realm of our ideas.

When I say, "This tree exists," I mean only, "I perceive this tree." There is no *thing* called "tree" in addition to my idea "tree." The tree does not exist apart from its being perceived, either by me or by someone else.

. . . as to what is said of the absolute existence of unthinking things without any relation to their being perceived, that seems perfectly unintelligible. Their *esse* is *percipi*, nor is it possible they should have any existence out of the minds or thinking things which perceive them. (p. 413d)

Here is the famous phrase *"esse est percipi"*—to be is to be perceived. Sensible, perceivable things have no existence except insofar as they are actually perceived.

Berkeley notes, with some irony, that the opinion he advances is not the common one of mankind.

It is indeed an opinion strangely prevailing amongst men, that houses, mountains, rivers, and in a word all sensible objects, have an existence, natural or real, distinct from their being perceived by the understanding. (p. 413d)

But this involves a manifest contradiction:

For, what are the forementioned objects but the things we perceive by sense? and what do we perceive besides our own ideas or sensations? and is it not plainly repugnant that any one of these, or any combination of them, should exist unperceived? (pp. 413d-414a)

How can a mountain exist and yet be unperceived, Berkeley asks, when obviously the mountain I am talking about is my perception of the mountain? It is not possible for my perception of the mountain to be unperceived by me.

Before we delve more deeply into this doctrine, let us ask: Does it solve the problem in response to which Berkeley proposed it? Does this doctrine, in other words, solve the problem of the reality of knowledge? The answer must be affirmative: if there is no distinction between a thing and the idea of the thing, or better, if there is not anything that is a thing simply, but there are merely ideas of things, then I need not worry about the conformity of an idea to anything else. Since in fact thing and idea become synonymous, an idea in conforming to its thing merely conforms to itself.

Berkeley is very pleased with his solution, for it seems to him that it undercuts the arguments of skepticism.

. . . so long as men thought that real things subsisted without the mind, and that their knowledge was only so far forth *real* as it was conformable to *real things*, it follows they could not be certain they had any real knowledge at all. For how can it be known that the things which are perceived are conformable to those which are not perceived, or exist without the mind? (p. 429d)

The distinction between ideas and things, between appearance and reality, involves us in skepticism. For since, on the assumption of this doctrine, we know only the appearances of things, reality will remain hidden from us:

. . . for aught we know, all we see, hear, and feel may be only phantom and vain chimera, and not at all agree with the real things existing in *rerum natura.* All this scepticism follows from our supposing a difference between *things* and *ideas,* and that the former have a subsistence without the mind or unperceived. (p. 430a)

The solution to all this skeptical doubt consists in eliminating the distinction between ideas and things:

But, all this doubtfulness, which so bewilders and confounds the mind and makes philosophy ridiculous in the eyes of the world, vanishes if we annex a meaning to our words, and not amuse ourselves with the terms "absolute," "external," "exist," and suchlike, signifying we know not what. I can as well doubt of my own being as of the being of those things which I actually perceive by sense; it being a manifest contradiction that any sensible object should be immediately perceived by sight or touch, and at the same time have no existence in nature, since the very *existence* of an unthinking being consists in *being perceived.* (p. 430b)

Thus the problem of the reality of knowledge has been solved; or perhaps we should say that the problem has been eliminated. The specter of skepticism has been banished as the result of just one principle—that there are no material substances. This is a price that Berkeley is more than willing to pay. Berkeley sees the world as consisting of *spirits* (which are active and perceive) and of *ideas* (which are passive and are perceived). Ideas exist in spirits, namely, insofar as they are perceived by them; since the being of an idea lies in its being perceived, an idea clearly cannot exist (be perceived) in an unperceiving substance. There is no need for any unperceiving, material substance to support ideas, in the way in which substance is said to support accidents in scholastic philosophy.

Still, granted that there is no need for such material substances, might it not be the case that these substances exist and that our ideas are copies of them? Berkeley dismisses this theory on the ground that ideas can only be like ideas. If these alleged material substances are not ideas and yet ideas are similar to them, we would have something visible, such as the idea of a color, being like something that is not an idea, and therefore not visible. Berkeley contends that such a state of affairs is on the face of it absurd.

If we give up the existence of unthinking, material substances, then of course we must also give up the distinction between secondary and primary substances. In the Newtonian-Lockean scheme of things, primary qualities were those possessed by massy, hard particles; but if these particles do not exist, their so-called qualities do not either. This does not mean, however, that such qualities as hardness, extendedness, and so on, are now less real than they were in Locke's scheme. On the contrary, these qualities are just as real as the qualities formerly called "secondary." All qualities are real—they exist when they are perceived, and that is their only reality and existence.

The doctrine that matter does not exist is, of course, bold and unusual. Small wonder, then, that it meets with many objections. Berkeley considers a whole series of them in Sections 34-84. Some of them are trivial, but others are quite powerful. We will consider just a few of the important objections, omitting those that are obviously without merit and those that merely repeat earlier arguments.

In many of the objections, the basic claim is that Berkeley has done away with the reality of things by denying the existence of matter. Berkeley answers that we should not be talking about things, but about ideas, and that ideas have all the reality anyone could want; they are real because they exist, and they exist when they are perceived.

To be sure, when we substitute the expression "idea" for "thing," we come up against such oddities as having to say that we eat ideas or drink ideas. Berkeley agrees that this sounds unusual and awkward. But we can and should retain the ordinary way of speaking as long as we know what we mean:

> If therefore you agree with me that we eat and drink and are clad with the immediate objects of sense, which cannot exist unperceived or without the mind, I shall readily grant it is more proper or conformable to custom that they should be called things rather than ideas. (p. 420a)

In general, Berkeley says that we should "'think with the learned, and speak with the vulgar'" (p. 422d). He points out that men speak of the rising and setting of the sun, even if they are convinced of the truth of the Copernican hypothesis.

"A little reflexion on what is here said will make it manifest that the common use of language would receive no manner of alteration or disturbance from the admission of our tenets" (p. 422d).

Berkeley also considers the objection that in his doctrine there is a constant creation and annihilation of things. It seems, the objection runs, that there is a tree when I look at it (for I then have an idea of it); but when I shut my eyes, the tree is annihilated together with the idea of it. Yet if I open my eyes again, there is the tree once more, created anew. This objection, of course, is based on a distinction which Berkeley denies: that between "real existence" and "being perceived." The objection assumes that it is possible to mean something by the expression "the tree exists" other than that it is being perceived. If we realize that the latter is the only meaning there is, we will not be tempted to talk about annihilation and creation of things. We will realize that when we no longer perceive a tree, then we no longer perceive a tree —nothing else need or can be said.

Furthermore, when I no longer perceive a tree, there may still be some other mind that perceives it, and so it would still exist:

Wherever bodies are said to have no existence without the mind, I would not be understood to mean this or that particular mind, but all minds whatsoever. It does not therefore follow from the foregoing principles that bodies are annihilated and created every moment, or exist not at all during the intervals between our perception of them. (p. 422a-b)

III

What are Berkeley's theories of space, time, and infinity?

We have already mentioned that Berkeley is opposed to Newton's theories of nature and matter, especially as these are transmitted in Locke's *Essay Concerning Human Understanding*. But Berkeley disagrees further with Newton, namely, with the latter's theories of space and time.

Newton, at the beginning of the *Mathematical Principles*, distinguishes between absolute and relative space, time, place, and motion: "Absolute, true, and mathematical time, of it-self, and from its own nature, flows equably without relation to anything external. . . . Absolute space, in its own nature, without relation to anything external, remains always similar and immovable" (Vol. 34, p. 8b). The other two concepts are subsidiary to these two, place being a part of space (either absolute or relative) and motion being the translation of a body from one place to another.

We can easily see what Berkeley's objections to these abso-lute entities are. First, they seem to be abstract ideas, and as we shall see in the following question, Berkeley maintains that abstract ideas do not exist. Belief in them is the cause of much philosophical mischief. Second, Berkeley objects to ab-solute space and time because Newton's definition of them quite clearly implies that these are separate entities, existing outside the mind "without relation to anything external." Just as Berkeley denies the existence of trees, mountains, etc., ex-cept insofar as they are perceived ideas, so he denies the ex-istence of an absolute space or absolute time, except insofar as they are perceived, in connection with the motion of bodies. That absolute space "cannot exist without the mind is clear upon the same principles that demonstrate the like of all other objects of sense" (p. 435d).

Denial of the existence of absolute space has another ad-vantage which appeals to Berkeley, the clergyman. Newton's absolute space seemed to many people to have almost god-like qualities, for it was conceived to be eternal, unchanging, infinite, and so on. "The chief advantage" arising from the de-nial of absolute space, Berkeley writes,

. . . is that we are freed from that dangerous dilemma, to which several who have employed their thoughts on that subject imagine themselves reduced, to wit, of thinking either that Real Space is God, or else that there is something beside God which is eternal, uncreated, infinite, indivisible, immutable. Both which may justly be thought pernicious and absurd notions. (p. 436a)

Berkeley's attack on infinity is also mainly directed against Newton, who dealt with "infinitesimals" in his *Principles*. Berkeley maintains that there is no infinite in extension—there is no infinitely long line and there is no line with infinitely many parts. His proof of this contention is quite simple. A line, like everything else, exists only as an idea in the mind. But I can have no idea of a foot-long line divided into 10,000 parts, for the individual parts are too small to be imagined. Quite obviously, then, I cannot have an idea of a line divided into infinitely many parts.

If it is said that a diagram, such as we ordinarily use in geometry, is often so small that the lines in it cannot even be divided into 20 or 50 parts, Berkeley replies that the lines in the diagram are merely *signs* for other lines that are large enough to be divided into the requisite parts. But no line can be the sign of a line long enough to have an infinite number of parts. Thus Berkeley categorically denies the infinite divisibility of geometrical extension. (See Sections 123-134, pp. 437c-440a.)

What are the consequences of such a denial? Does Berkeley think he is able to demonstrate all the ordinary propositions of geometry? Or does his denial involve constructing a new geometry?

Does geometry, as mathematicians ordinarily conceive it, maintain that a line has an infinite number of parts? Does it make sense to say a line has an infinite number of infinitely small parts?

Aristotle, in the *Physics*, distinguishes between an actual and a potential infinite. Berkeley denies that there is an actually infinite line, or a line with an actually infinite number of parts. Can he take refuge in the conception of a potential infinite, or does his theory of ideas prevent him from saying that a line has potentially an infinite number of parts?

What are Berkeley's arguments against abstract ideas?

His main argument is that he does not believe that men have the faculty of abstracting in such a way that the products are "abstract ideas." Other men may claim that they can form an idea of "man" or "humanity," in which all particular qualities, such as the color, height, etc. of a man are omitted, but Berkeley denies that he can perform such a feat of abstraction.

Whether others have this wonderful faculty of abstracting their ideas, they best can tell: for myself, I find indeed I have a faculty of imagining, or representing to myself, the ideas of those particular things I have perceived, and of variously compounding and dividing them. I can imagine a man with two heads, or the upper parts of a man joined to the body of a horse. I can consider the hand, the eye, the nose, each by itself abstracted or separated from the rest of the body. But then whatever hand or eye I imagine, it must have some particular shape and colour. Likewise the idea of man that I frame to myself must be either of a white, or a black, or a tawny, a straight, or a crooked, a tall, or a low, or a middle-sized man. I cannot by any effort of thought conceive the abstract idea above described. (pp. 406d-407a)

Berkeley argues similarly that in mathematical proofs we do not employ the abstract idea of a triangle, for example, if by such an abstract idea we mean a triangle that is neither scalene, nor right-angled, nor obtuse. Every idea of a triangle must be one of these three, he says, since I cannot imagine the triangle in any other way. Berkeley does not deny that we have general ideas, but he denies that these general ideas are abstract. All ideas are particular, but some particular ideas may become general in the sense of signifying other ideas beside themselves. That is what happens in the case of mathematical ideas. Every idea of a triangle will be a particular one, but it may stand for other triangles beside itself and in that way become general. Nor need a proof suffer in generality because it applies in the first place to a particular triangle. If the proof in no way depends on the fact that the triangle is, say, scalene, then the proof will equally apply to other, non-scalene, triangles and hence be a general proof.

Universal notions are not formed by abstractions,

. . . *universality*, so far as I can comprehend, not consisting in the absolute, positive nature or conception of anything, but in the relation it bears to the particulars signified or represented by it; by virtue whereof it is that things, names, or notions, being in their own nature *particular*, are rendered *universal*. (p. 409a)

If men do not have this faculty of abstraction, why then do they insist on thinking that they do? What is the cause of the belief in abstract ideas?

What do you make of Berkeley's insistence that it is impossible to have an abstract idea because it cannot be imagined?

Do those who believe in abstract ideas deny that any imaginable triangle must be either scalene, right-angled, or obtuse? Must all ideas be imaginable?

Do we know anything besides ideas?

Although Berkeley often writes as though our knowledge were limited to our ideas and nothing else, it is obvious that knowledge must extend a little farther, even in his theory. For example, he makes a distinction, early in this book, between passive, perceived ideas and active, perceiving spirits. How does he know this? There cannot be an idea of a spirit, for, if there were, spirit would be something passive like all other ideas. Hence we must know spirits in some other fashion.

Having despatched what we intended to say concerning the knowledge of IDEAS, the method we proposed leads us in the next place to treat of SPIRITS—with regard to which, perhaps, human knowledge is not so deficient as is vulgarly imagined. (p. 440a)

Berkeley concedes that we do not have ideas of spirit, or mind, or substance, but he thinks that we do know something about these.

In a large sense, indeed, we may be said to have an idea or rather a notion of *spirit;* that is, we understand the meaning of the word, otherwise we could not affirm or deny anything of it. (pp. 440d–441a)

But a notion is not an idea, and hence our way of knowing other spirits, minds, or substances is different from the way in which we know ideas. We know other active spirits by their operations; i.e., when we see things happening that are obviously due to an active agent, yet are not due to us, then we know that other agents like ourselves exist.

It is also in this way that we know the existence of God. We know Him through His works, through His effects as we experience them in the perceived world of nature. It is only through God's operations that we know other men:

There is not any one mark that denotes a man, or effect produced by him, which does not more strongly evince the being of that Spirit who is the Author of Nature. For, it is evident that in affecting other persons the will of man has no other object than barely the motion of the limbs of his body; but that such a motion should be attended by, or excite any idea in the mind of another, depends wholly on the will of the Creator. He alone it is who, "upholding all things by the word of His power," maintains that intercourse between spirits whereby they are able to perceive the existence of each other. (p. 442b)

Is this theory of "notions" as distinguished from "ideas" convincing? Does it weaken Berkeley's general theory? Is the way in which we know active spirits any less mysterious than the faculty of abstraction?

If it were not for God, and the way in which he upholds communication between men, would Berkeley's theory lead to a solipsism? That is, would each man know only himself and his ideas?

The following questions are designed to help you test the thoroughness of your reading. Each question is to be answered by giving a page or pages of the reading assignment. Answers will be found on page 302 of this Reading Plan.

1 What other purposes, besides communication, are served by language?

2 What causes ideas in us?

3 How do we perceive that things are at a distance from us?

4 How does Berkeley explain what appear to be relations of cause and effect among things?

5 How does the doctrine of the existence of matter support atheism and anti-Christian sentiments?

6 Are there abstract ideas of number?

7 Is the fact that man cannot see God an argument against his existence?

HUME

An Enquiry Concerning Human Understanding

Sections I-VIII

Vol. 35, pp. 451-487

Locke, Berkeley, and Hume are often grouped together under the single name of "British Empiricists." Indeed, they do belong together. Berkeley was aware that he was extending and modifying many of Locke's views; the title of Hume's essay is almost identical with Locke's, indicating his great affinity with the earlier philosopher. Together, these three Britishers gained a decisive victory over European rationalism, such as that of Descartes, Spinoza, and Leibniz. Yet only a few years elapsed before German idealism as propounded by Kant and Hegel superseded empiricism.

Fashions in philosophy come and go as they do in other fields. Although empiricism seemed definitely to have lost its appeal to philosophers during the nineteenth century, it has made a decisive comeback and is probably the dominant school of philosophy in the twentieth century. And almost all contemporary empiricists look upon David Hume and his *Enquiry* (as well as his *Treatise of Human Nature*) as the source of most of their doctrines.

These works are the output of a young man. This is especially the case with the *Treatise of Human Nature*. Hume published it in 1739-1740 when he was 28 years old. He expected great things from it, but much to his disappointment the book attracted almost no notice. He recast the first part of the *Treatise* and in 1748 published it as *An Enquiry Concerning Human Understanding*. Hume tells us in the "Advertisement" to the *Enquiry:*

Most of the principles, and reasonings, contained in this volume, were published in a work in three volumes, called A Treatise of Human Nature: A *work which the Author had projected before he left College, and which he wrote and published not long after. But not finding it successful, he was sensible of his error in going to the press too early, and he cast the whole anew in the following pieces, where some negligences in his former reasoning and more in the expression, are, he hopes, corrected.* (p. 450a)

The third volume of the *Treatise* was recast by Hume in 1751 and published as *An Enquiry Concerning the Principles of Morals.*

Thirteenth Reading

I

Hume's empiricism has two aspects; it is both *observational* and *subjective*. Of these, the former is far more important than the latter. For Hume, as for Locke, the origin of all ideas lies in our sense impressions; observation lies at the root of all knowledge. Berkeley, it will be remembered, went beyond this. In his view, *what we know* are our ideas (Locke had already stated this), and these ideas are not the means of knowing something else. We have no right, therefore, to assume that these ideas refer to anything material outside ourselves. Each person knows his own ideas only.

Hume occasionally talks in Berkeley's subjective fashion, but for the most part he seems to take the existence of material things for granted. Much more important to him is the conviction that confusion, error, and ignorance can be eliminated if we are consistent in our adherence to empiricism.

All knowledge comes originally from the senses. However, in addition to sense perceptions, we also have "ideas," namely, when we remember something, or when we imagine something. Still, it is easy to distinguish between direct sense perceptions and remembered or imagined ideas. The former are much more lively and forceful than the latter. There is quite a difference, Hume tells us, between being in love and imagining being in love.

Here therefore we may divide all the perceptions of the mind into two classes or species, which are distinguished by their different degrees of force and vivacity. The less forcible and lively are commonly denominated *Thoughts* or *Ideas*. The other species want a name in our language, and in most others; I suppose, because it was not requisite for any, but philosophical purposes, to rank them under a general term or appellation. Let us, therefore, use a little freedom, and call them *Impressions* . . . (p. 455d)

Impressions can give rise to new ideas because the mind has the "faculty of compounding, transposing, augmenting, or diminishing the materials afforded us by the senses and experience" (p. 456a). This is how we obtain such ideas as those of a golden mountain or a mermaid.

From this basic position concerning the origin of ideas, Hume derives a proposition which seems to him to make possible the resolution of any and all disputes in philosophy. Ideas, especially the more abstract ones, are apt to be pretty confused, Hume tells us. Still, if we have become familiar with an idea, we are likely to think that it signifies something definite when it really does not. The remedy is obvious:

When we entertain, therefore, any suspicion that a philosophical term is employed without any meaning or idea (as is but too frequent), we need but enquire, *from what impression is that supposed idea derived?* And if it be impossible to assign any, this will serve to confirm our suspicion. By bringing ideas into so clear a light we may reasonably hope to remove all dispute, which may arise, concerning their nature and reality. (p. 457b)

II

One of the virtues of Hume as a philosopher and as a writer is his directness. When he finds a result that seems to him indubitable, he does not hesitate to announce it or stick to it, even if it appears to lead to consequences that are unusual or difficult to believe.

This directness characterizes Hume's famous discussion of cause and effect. He begins by dividing everything that men know into two categories: (1) the relations of ideas, and (2) matters of fact.

Mathematical knowledge is an example of the first category: it consists of propositions that concern the relations between ideas. All such propositions "are discoverable by the mere operation of thought, without dependence on what is anywhere existent in the universe" (p. 458b). Hume adds that it makes no difference whether any of the mathematical entities, such as triangles, circles, or numbers, actually exist in the world of reality. The propositions concerning these mathematical things are true, independently of what is the case in fact. Furthermore, these mathematical propositions (and all propositions concerning the relations of ideas) are not only true but necessarily true. That is to say, the contradictories of such propositions are not only false but impossible. Given Euclid's definitions, postulates, and axioms, the opposite of any of his propositions is inconceivable.

Things are decidedly different when we are dealing with propositions concerning matters of fact. Here propositions can be true without being necessarily true. "The contrary of every matter of fact is still possible; because it can never imply a contradiction, and is conceived by the mind with the same facility and distinctness, as if ever so conformable to reality" (p. 458b-c). Even though it is true, for example, that "this chair is yellow," it is still possible to conceive that this might be false and that the proposition "this chair is red" is true.

Hume uses a different, slightly more complicated example. He considers the two propositions "The sun will not rise tomorrow" and "The sun will rise tomorrow." Neither can be *demonstrated* to be true or false, he says; and both propositions can be equally clearly conceived by the mind. However, in addition to being propositions about a matter of fact (the sun's rising), they are propositions about a *future* matter of fact. Consequently, an additional question arises, namely, how do we conclude anything about future matters of fact on the basis of past experience? This is an important and interesting problem and one to which Hume turns later on. At this point, however, it serves merely to becloud the issue. For the moment, we need only see that propositions concerning matters of fact have no logical necessity. They are all contingent. Their opposites are just as possible as they are themselves.

Some matters of fact are directly known by the senses. But how do we obtain any knowledge concerning matters of fact that are not susceptible to direct sense experience? This is a problem not only as regards knowledge of *future* events. We can also ask the same question concerning present or past events. Hume asks: How do we know that men once inhabited a deserted island? He answers: From the artifacts, such as watches and houses, which they left behind. To give another example, drawn from the conditions of the twentieth century: if the engine in our automobile sputters and dies, we say "the car is out of gasoline." On the basis of examples like these, Hume states that all reasoning concerning matters of fact (as contrasted with mere perception) is based on the relation of cause and effect.

In both of our examples, we perceive an effect. In the first example, the effect is the presence of artifacts; in the second example, it is the malfunctioning of the engine. From these effects, we conclude that a particular cause exists. In the first example, the cause is the prior presence of human beings; in the second example, it is the lack of sufficient gasoline. Hume maintains that whenever we make a statement concerning a matter of fact that is not at that moment present to our senses, the basis for that statement must be the relation of cause and effect. "By means of that relation alone we can go beyond the evidence of our memory and senses" (p. 458d).

Hume immediately goes on to ask whence comes our knowledge of cause and effect. He quickly concludes that all such knowledge comes only from experience. A priori (i.e., prior to actually observing what happens), we cannot know that event A causes event B. It may sometimes seem that we do have such knowledge without prior experience, but brief examination reveals that the phenomena involved in such cases are always so familiar that we think we always knew that A caused B, although in fact our first knowledge was based on observation. Without first observing the phenomenon, Hume writes, we could never know that the smoothness of two slabs of marble would cause them to stick together so tightly that a great force is required to separate them. Similarly in other cases: our knowledge that such and such an event causes such and such a phenomenon is always based on prior observation. Sarcastically, Hume writes, "A man must be very sagacious who could discover by reasoning that crystal is the effect of heat, and ice of cold, without being previously acquainted with the operation of these qualities" (p. 460d).

Hume is well aware that he has not yet solved all difficulties with regard to knowledge of matters of fact. On the contrary, the real difficulties are just beginning.

But we have not yet attained any tolerable satisfaction with regard to the question first proposed. Each solution still gives rise to a new question as difficult as the foregoing, and leads us on to farther enquiries. When it is asked, *What is the nature of all our reasonings concerning matter of fact?* the proper answer seems to be, that they are founded on the relation of cause and effect. When again it is asked, *What is the foundation of all our reasonings and conclusions concerning that relation?* it may be replied in one word, Experience. But if we still carry on our sifting humour, and ask, *What is the foundation of all conclusions from experience?* this implies a new question, which may be of more difficult solution and explication. (pp. 460d-461a)

In Part II of Section IV, Hume gives a negative answer to this question; i.e., he shows us that something which may be supposed to be the basis of our conclusions from experience cannot in fact be so. Hume explains that the conclusions which we draw from experience are not drawn by any process of reasoning. There is no logical process which enables us to draw those conclusions from experience which in fact we do draw. Hume by no means denies that all of us learn from experience: if thing A, with sensible properties x and y, possesses the power M, then we readily assume that thing B, if it possesses the same sensible properties x and y, will also possess the power M. But such a conclusion, though it may be true, is in no way logically justified. There are no logical principles which enable us to draw conclusions concerning future or present matters of fact on the basis of past matters of fact.

If a body of like colour and consistence with that bread, which we have formerly eat, be presented to us, we make no scruple of repeating the experiment, and foresee, with certainty, like nourishment and support. Now this is a process of the mind or thought, of which I would willingly know the foundation. (p. 461b)

Hume repeats again and again that he is not unaware of the fact that such inferences are constantly made; he admits that he himself, in his daily life, depends on such inferences. But he denies that the inference from the observed past to the unobserved future is made by a chain of reasoning. "If you insist that the inference is made by a chain of reasoning. I desire you to produce that reasoning" (p. 461d). Hume says he knows of no medium which connects the one set of propositions (concerning the past) with the proposition about the future. Perhaps there is such a connecting medium, Hume admits; but if there is, he wants to be shown what it is. Unless and until he is shown, he insists that a proposition does not in any way "reach out" to make connections with other propositions.

The matter may also be put this way. From past experience we might be able to make inferences to the future, if we knew with certainty that the course of nature is always the same and that the future is always in accordance with the past. But Hume denies vigorously that we know that this proposition is true. We, of course, *believe* that the seasons repeat themselves as they have for thousands of years and that it will be hot in July and cold in January, but we have no *reason* for this belief. There is nothing intrinsically impossible about the opposite state of affairs. Our judgment that nature is pretty uniform is, in other words, a probable judgment of experience. Obviously, therefore, the uniformity of nature—being itself based on a judgment of experience—cannot be used to justify arguments of experience:

We have said that all arguments concerning existence are founded on the relation of cause and effect; that our knowledge of that relation is derived entirely from experience; and that all our experimental conclusions proceed upon the supposition that the future will be conformable to the past. To endeavour, therefore, the proof of this last supposition by probable arguments, or arguments regarding existence, must be evidently going in a circle, and taking that for granted, which is the very point in question. (p. 462b)

If the judgment that "nature is uniform" is to be used in support of generalizations derived from particular judgments of experience, then "nature is uniform" itself must not be a generalization of this kind. For if it were, we should then have to *assume* that nature is uniform, in order to prove this uniformity. And such an argument would, of course, be circular.

This concludes the negative part of Hume's argument. Judgments which go from present experiences to anticipated future experiences are not based on any logical principles. Since, however, we do make such judgments, what is the basis for them? Hume's positive argument consists in assigning a ground or basis for these inductive judgments. The basis is not logical, however, but psychological. Judgments of this sort are made, he says, because of *custom* or *habit.*

> Custom, then, is the great guide of human life. It is that principle alone which renders our experience useful to us, and makes us expect, for the future, a similar train of events with those which have appeared in the past. (p. 465c)

The answer is ingenious, because it takes us by surprise. The previous discourse has not prepared us for this answer. In effect the answer merely repeats the question. The question is: "Why do we always infer that similar-appearing things will have similar powers?" And the answer which Hume now proposes is: "Because we always do."

However, Hume accomplishes two things by his answer. In the first place, he clearly indicates that uniformity cannot be *proved* inductively, that it is not self-evident, and that it cannot be established by logic. He now tells us that the answer is to be found in the nature of man's mind, in his psychological make-up, which is such that we customarily assume that the future will be like the past. In the second place, Hume spends quite a few paragraphs in analyzing this customary belief and tries to tell us what it is.

Hume finds it difficult to explain just what belief is. We all know what it is, he says, even if we cannot precisely define it. Finally, he arrives at this description: "The sentiment of belief is nothing but a conception more intense and steady than what attends the mere fictions of the imagination, and . . . this *manner* of conception arises from a customary conjunction of the object with something present to the memory or senses . . ." (p. 467c).

We believe in the existence of things outside the mind because the conception of such things is accompanied by a sense impression or by the memory of one. Similarly, when we believe that something which always has happened in the past will also happen in the future, we have a sense impression, together with the conception of cause and effect:

> When I throw a piece of dry wood into a fire, my mind is immediately carried to conceive, that it augments, not extinguishes the flame. This transition of thought from the cause to the effect proceeds not from reason. It derives its origin altogether from custom and experience. And as it first begins from an object, present to the senses, it renders the idea or conception of flame more strong and lively than any loose, floating reverie of the imagination. (p. 469a)

After giving another example, Hume concludes:

> But what is there in this whole matter to cause such a strong conception, except only a present object and a customary transition to the idea of another object, which we have been accustomed to conjoin with the former? This is the whole operation of the mind, in all our conclusions concerning matter of fact and existence . . . (p. 469a-b)

There is, Hume observes, a kind of pre-established harmony between the operation of nature and the operation of our mind. Though we do not know the secret and hidden ways in which nature operates, the ways in which the human mind thinks and believes are such that we can act perfectly well and successfully, even if we cannot explain, by any chain of reasoning, why we should believe what we do.

III

Hume returns to the discussion of cause and effect in Section VII of the *Enquiry Concerning Human Understanding*. In Sections IV and V, the discussion of cause is secondary to Hume's analysis of the operations of the human mind; our knowledge of matters of fact is seen to be dependent on our knowledge of cause and effect. In Section VII, the idea of cause, or of necessary connection, constitutes the major topic.

Hume begins by noting that the idea of necessary connection is obscure, and he proposes to remedy this by using what he considers to be his infallible method of clarification. Since all ideas originally come from sense impressions, we need only go back to those impressions in order to remove any obscurity that may have attached itself to the idea as a result of our having used it so much that it seems to have taken on added content. Such investigation, by going back to the source of our ideas, constitutes "a new microscope or species of optics, by which, in the moral sciences, the most minute, and most simple ideas may be so enlarged as to fall readily under our apprehension . . ." (p. 471d).

What, then, are the original sense impressions that give us the idea of necessary connection? Hume considers three possible kinds of events that might be thought to provide such impressions. First, there are the interactions of material objects; for example, one billiard ball imparting motion to a second one. Second, there are the actions of our body, resulting from volition; for example, we will to raise our arm and then proceed to do so. Third, there are actions of the mind which perhaps cause other actions of the mind; for example, we seem able to recall a certain idea in order that we may consider it.

Hume examines these three sorts of events one by one in order to determine whether any of them provide us with a sense impression of necessary connection. The result of his investigation is completely negative. To begin with the actions of material bodies: none of them gives us the idea of a power in one body to cause necessarily some action in another. To be sure, from long familiarity, we expect that a moving billiard ball will, upon hitting another billiard ball, transmit part of its motion to the second ball. But, says Hume, when we see this sort of phenomenon for the first time, we are completely ignorant of what is going to happen. There is nothing in the moving billiard ball which conveys to us the sense impression that it must bring about this rather than that result.

It is impossible, therefore, that the idea of power can be derived from the contemplation of bodies, in single instances of their operation; because no bodies ever discover any power, which can be the original of this idea. (p. 472b)

Things are no better when we turn to the influence of the will over bodily motions. In fact, they are worse. Hume asks: "Is there any principle in all nature more mysterious than the union of soul with body; by which a supposed spiritual substance acquires such an influence over a material one, that the most refined thought is able to actuate the grossest matter?" (p. 472d). Furthermore, the will is not always able to accomplish its commands; there are many bodily actions which refuse to be subject to the will. Although we can control the movement of our arms and legs, we are powerless with regard to other bodily functions, such as breathing or the motion of the heart. Finally, to show that there is no sense impression of a cause or of necessary connection to be found there, Hume notes that the will does not act directly even where it controls bodily motion; the direct action of the will appears to be on muscles, nerves, etc., and, generally, on such minute and hidden parts of the body that there certainly cannot be any sense impression of them.

We may, therefore, conclude . . . that our idea of power is not copied from any sentiment or consciousness of power within ourselves, when we give rise to animal motion, or apply our limbs to their proper use and office. That their motion follows the command of the will is a matter of common experience, like other natural events: But the power or energy by which this is effected, like that in other natural events, is unknown and inconceivable. (p. 473b-c)

Finally, Hume investigates the manner in which the human mind exercises power over itself to see whether the idea of necessary connection could have arisen here. But he denies that we feel any power of the will to bring up a desired idea. "We only feel the event, namely, the existence of an idea, consequent to a command of the will: But the manner, in which this operation is performed, the power by which it is produced, is entirely beyond our comprehension" (pp. 473d-474a). Besides, it is hard to see how this kind of operation could give rise to the idea of necessary connection, since in fact the power of the mind over its own operations is limited. The mind, far from being able necessarily to cause itself to think about this or that, is often unable to do so. This inability stems from such causes as the violence of passions or bodily sickness.

The only impression which experience gives us, therefore, in all these events, is that of a temporal *conjunction* of something with something else, not of necessary *connection* between them. From where, then, do we obtain the idea of necessary connection? Hume cannot deny that we do have such an idea; yet, if we cannot find any sense impression on which this idea is based, we seem to be led to the conclusion that this idea is void of all meaning.

When we observe an event, such as one billiard ball striking another, for the first time, we can merely say that we see two conjoined events—the motion of the first billiard ball, followed by the motion of the second billiard ball after being struck. If, now, we observe many instances of this sort of thing, we are eventually led to pronounce that these two events are not merely conjoined but actually connected. Yet there is nothing about the twentieth such instance that differs from the first. What is different, however, is our mind:

. . . after a repetition of similar instances, the mind is carried by habit, upon the appearance of one event, to expect its usual attendant, and to believe that it will exist. . . . The first time a man saw the communication of motion by impulse, as by the shock of two billiard balls, he could not pronounce that the one event was *connected:* but only that it was *conjoined* with the other. After he has observed several instances of this nature, he then pronounces them to be *connected*. What alteration has happened to give rise to this new idea of *connexion?* Nothing but that he now *feels* these events to be *connected* in his imagination . . . (p. 476c-d)

And so Hume concludes:

When we say, therefore, that one object is connected with another, we mean only that they have acquired a connexion in our thought, and give rise to this inference, by which they become proofs of each other's existence . . . (p. 476d)

Thus cause, or necessary connection, according to this analysis, cannot be observed in reality. That A is the cause of B means only that A is always followed by B or that if we have the idea of A in our mind then the idea of B follows it. On the objective side, therefore, "cause" is reduced to conjunction; from the subjective point of view, cause is a tendency of the mind, a feeling, or a habit. After observing many instances of A followed by B,

We then *feel* a new sentiment or impression, to wit, a customary connexion in the thought or imagination between one object and its usual attendant; and this sentiment is the original of that idea which we seek for. (p. 477c)

When we have found the source or original of any idea, then we are in a position to understand its true meaning and to strip away any ambiguities. Hume's analysis shows that the source of the idea of cause is a tendency of the mind, not the observation of actual causes. This does not mean that Hume denies the existence of causes or necessary connections; he merely denies that we can observe them and maintains that we observe only conjunctions. The study of the idea of cause belongs, according to Hume, to psychology rather than metaphysics.

I V

What is Hume's theory of chance?

In general, there are three possible views which may be held concerning chance. First, it may be considered to be a kind of cause, though a cause of a special kind. This was Aristotle's view, who called chance "an incidental cause" (Vol. 8, p. 273d). In his theory, if A, which was intended to produce B, also happens to produce C—without the intention of the agent—then A is the incidental, or chance, cause of C.

A second view is that a chance cause is no cause at all. To say that X happened by chance is to say that it happened without any cause at all—a chance event is an event that occurred without being caused to occur. Usually, if this is the way in which chance is understood, it is added that there is no such thing as chance, because every event must have a cause.

A third view is directly related to the second. If there are no uncaused events—so that there is no chance in the second meaning of the term—there may still be events whose causes are unknown to us. Such events may be called chance events, relative to us. In this view, chance refers not to anything real but only to a condition in us, viz., ignorance.

Hume takes the third position:

> Though there be no such thing as *Chance* in the world; our ignorance of the real cause of any event has the same influence on the understanding, and begets a like species of belief or opinion. (p. 469d)

Chance, therefore, is wholly subjective. It is relative to an observer. If he does not know the cause of an event, then, to him, the event is happening by chance.

Probability is a similar subjective condition. It, too, is relative to an observer and to his evidence. If a man has observed a great many throws of a die and has found that a certain marking comes up 65% of the time, he will then believe that it is 65% probable that this same marking will come up again in the next throw. Probability, therefore, refers not to an objective state of affairs but to a subjective condition, namely, belief.

> . . . when we transfer the past to the future, in order to determine the effect, which will result from any cause, we transfer all the different events, in the same proportion as they have appeared in the past, and conceive one to have existed a hundred times, for instance, another ten times, and another once. As a great number of views do here concur in one event, they fortify and confirm it to the imagination, beget that sentiment which we call *belief*, and give its object the preference above the contrary event, which is not supported by an equal number of experiments, and recurs not so frequently to the thought in transferring the past to the future. (p. 470c-d)

Are there other possible views of what chance is? Similarly, are there other theories of probability that occur to you? Would all theories of probability necessarily be subjective; i.e., depend on the evidence available to a given person?

Does Hume think there is any human freedom of choice?

The "free will problem" is one of the oldest and most vexing in the history of philosophy. Hume, however, makes short work of the entire matter. Here, as elsewhere in philosophy, the important thing is to clear up what we are talking about. If we understand all the terms of the dispute, we shall see that there is no problem left, Hume tells us.

Hume begins by investigating the meaning of "necessity." We can clarify its meaning by going back to the original sense impressions from which we derive the idea of necessity. Now what are these sense impressions? Actually, Hume says, we have no impressions of necessity. The only thing which we observe in nature is the constant conjunction of certain events. This constant conjunction, combined with the idea of the uniformity of nature, causes us to infer that these events are necessarily connected—i.e., that one is the cause of the other:

Our idea, therefore, of necessity and causation arises entirely from the uniformity observable in the operations of nature, where similar objects are constantly conjoined together, and the mind is determined by custom to infer the one from the appearance of the other. These two circumstances form the whole of that necessity, which we ascribe to matter. Beyond the constant *conjunction* of similar objects, and the consequent *inference* from one to the other, we have no notion of any necessity or connexion. (p. 479a)

Now, says Hume, if this is how we get the idea that certain events in nature are necessarily related (i.e., that one event is the cause of another event), then this is no different from what we observe in events involving human action and volition. For we observe exactly the same uniformity in human actions as in other events: "The same motives always produce the same actions: The same events follow from the same causes" (p. 479b).

The reason that men benefit from experience lies in this uniformity of human actions. We know what to expect from our fellow men in a given situation, because we are sure they will react in a predictable fashion. And if someone does the unexpected, we believe that this must be due to the action of some hidden and contrary cause:

The most irregular and unexpected resolutions of men may frequently be accounted for by those who know every particular circumstance of their character and situation. A person of an obliging disposition gives a peevish answer: But he has the toothache, or has not dined. A stupid fellow discovers an uncommon alacrity in his carriage: But he has met with a sudden piece of good fortune. (p. 481a)

Hume goes on at some length to indicate not only that this is the correct account of human actions but also that all men agree that there is this necessity in men's doings.

After this, Hume turns to the consideration of liberty. "It will not require many words," he says, "to prove, that all mankind have ever agreed in the doctrine of liberty as well as in that of necessity" (p. 483c). Liberty cannot mean, he tells us, that human actions have no connection with "motives, inclinations, and circumstances." He continues:

By liberty, then, we can only mean *a power of acting or not acting, according to the determinations of the will;* that is, if we choose to remain at rest, we may; if we choose to move, we also may. Now this hypothetical liberty is universally allowed to belong to every one who is not a prisoner and in chains. Here, then, is no subject of dispute. (p. 484a)

According to this theory, liberty is to be opposed not to necessity but rather to constraint. He who is not constrained is free —that is Hume's view. What about him who is not necessitated to act in a certain way—is he free? No, says Hume, for such an unnecessitated person does not exist. Not to be *necessitated* to act in a certain way means not to be *caused* to act in a certain way. Thus "cause" involves "necessitation" or "necessary connection." That A causes B means, according to Hume, that there is a necessary connection between A and B.

Thus Hume is in the position of denying that we can observe the existence of necessary connections, while at the same time asserting that all events arise from necessary connections. Inability to observe necessary connections in things is joined with a conviction that everything which takes place happens necessarily. Apparently Hume thinks that this conviction is shared by everyone: "It is universally allowed that nothing exists without a cause of its existence" (p. 484a) and he goes on to challenge anyone to define "cause" in such a way that the definition does not involve necessary connection. (See p. 484b.)

Is Hume justified in opposing liberty only to constraint, not to necessity? Is it possible to define "cause" in such a way that it does not become equivalent to necessity?

Does Hume have an answer to the objection that his doctrine removes moral responsibility from man, because he is simply one link in a chain of causes and cannot help what he does? What do you think of Hume's answer?

What about the objection that this doctrine impugns God's goodness and wisdom, since it makes God, as the first cause, responsible for all subsequent actions, including evil human actions?

Are the moral sciences as exact as the mathematical sciences?

Most philosophers admire the precision and rigor of the mathematical sciences and deplore, by contrast, the inexactitude of the moral disciplines. It is refreshing to see Hume take a different approach. He finds something to praise in both morals and mathematics.

Mathematics has the advantage of dealing with very precise objects. Circles, ellipses, and so on are (or can be) precisely defined; in the chains of mathematical reasoning, there is no place for difficulties arising from the obscurity of the terms employed. Whenever a mathematical term is employed, we need only substitute the definition for the term (as mathematicians do), in order to remove any doubts or difficulties. On the other hand, the terms employed in the moral sciences, such as virtue, vice, right, wrong, are much more difficult to handle because they are much less clear.

On the other hand, the moral sciences have an advantage in the brevity of the reasoning employed. Mathematical propositions, even the simplest ones, commonly employ very long chains of reasoning; and difficult propositions may take pages and pages for their proof. As a result, mathematical reasoning, no matter how clear in itself, is often very difficult to follow. But reasoning in the moral sciences usually needs only one or two steps before the conclusion. Consequently, moral reasoning is employed without difficulty by the majority of mankind.

In order to advance the moral sciences and make them the equal of mathematics in precision, it is only necessary, therefore, to employ precise terms. Morals already has the advantage of brief reasoning; if it could also employ precise terms, it would be a pursuit far more satisfying and precise than mathematics. This is the goal of Hume's continual emphasis on clarifying the meaning of terms, by going back to the original sense impressions which give rise to the ideas signified by the terms.

Does Hume seem to analyze the mathematical and moral sciences correctly? Are the moral disciplines really easier, because their chains of reasoning are briefer? In fact, is Hume correct in saying that moral reasoning is uninvolved and short? If he is right, what can account for this brevity and clarity? Could not a case be made for the opposite, that the reasoning in the moral sciences is really quite complicated and lengthy, even apart from any obscurity of the terms used?

The following questions are designed to help you test the thoroughness of your reading. Each question is to be answered by giving a page or pages of the reading assignment. Answers will be found on page 302 of this Reading Plan.

1 What are the three ways in which the mind associates ideas?

2 What is the advantage of skepticism as a method of philosophy?

3 How does Hume describe the feeling of "belief"?

4 What is the difference between ideas and impressions?

5 What are Hume's arguments against the doctrine of occasionalism?

6 How does Hume reconcile the occurrence of unexpected human actions with his doctrine that such actions are just as subject to causal determinism as the happenings of inanimate objects?

7 Does Hume think any philosophical doctrine should be abandoned because its consequences seem dangerous to morals?

8 How does Hume answer the charge that the doctrine of necessity makes God the ultimate author of human sin and vice?

9 What kinds of objects are treated in the mathematical sciences?

10 What is Hume's method for clarifying philosophical ideas?

KANT

Critique of Pure Reason

Preface to the First Edition; Preface to the
Second Edition; Introduction; I, First Part

Vol. 42, pp. 1-33

Kant marked one of the great turning points in the history of philosophy, and after him the world would never be the same again. It was as if the old Titan, Cronus, growing weary of the chaos into which things had fallen, had roused himself to shape the world over again and put all its warring elements into a new accord. Kant's philosophy united opposing methods and standpoints into a great synthesis, which aimed to overcome both dogmatism and the skepticism into which dogmatism so easily relapses.

Empiricists had looked upon sense perception as the main source of knowledge, whereas rationalists had taken reasoning—reasoning independent of the vagaries of perception—as the chief source. Kant presented proofs that the roles of both sense perception and reasoning are circumscribed and limited, but then vindicated the authority of each in an astounding reconstruction of the world. Similarly, mechanists had held that nature and man constitute a vast machine. Physics and chemistry were the basic sciences, capable of explaining all phenomena. The teleologists, on the other hand, had insisted that it is purpose which gives mechanical action its impulse and direction and that it is to purpose that we must look for final explanations. These seemed to be irreconcilable viewpoints, but Kant constructed a synthesis in which the opposites, he hoped, could live peacefully together.

In ethics, however, Kant was an extremist. There is only one thing under the sun that is unqualifiedly good, he claimed, and that is the good will. The only actions that are morally good are those which we perform out of pure respect for the moral law. If we are just or merciful to our neighbor because we love or pity him or because the world will then be a happier place, our actions have no *moral* value whatever.

Kant's ethical position has an austere grandeur and is often described as "sublime." It is duty for duty's sake—no matter how grim the results. But the perfect *fulfillment* of the moral life, he argued, implies the existence of God, freedom of the will, and immortality, and happiness too, at least in a future life. *Practical* reason thus allows us to affirm—or adopt—them. Kant's philosophy of religion, like his ethics and scientific philosophy, has had an enormous influence on the world of thought.

Fourteenth Reading

I

The facts of Kant's life are available in many places, and we shall mention only a few essentials. He was born in Königsberg in 1724, and in this cold Baltic city he remained his whole life, except for brief trips to surrounding towns. On his father's side his ancestry was Scotch, which made him half-kin to David Hume, who was to revolutionize Kant's thinking. The Pietism with which he was surrounded in Königsberg might have contributed something to his austere self-discipline and dour outlook on life. His sense of the dignity of the individual, however, was typical and was expressed, from youth on, with earnest passion.

While studying theology at the University of Königsberg, he was obliged, because of his poverty, to tutor sons of prominent families in the vicinity. Some of them, under his influence, became leaders in the struggle for the abolition of serfdom in Prussia. In 1755 he became a lecturer at the university and published at the same time his famous treatise "General Physiognomy and Theory of the Heavens." Assailing Newton's view that mechanical laws could never explain how the solar system came about, Kant propounded his ingenious "nebular hypothesis," according to which the solar system had evolved from a rotating spiral nebula.

Up to about 1763, Kant remained an independent follower of Wolff's Leibnizian philosophy. At this time, as Kant reports, Hume roused him from his "dogmatic slumbers," and we soon have the first beginnings of his "critical philosophy." What had galvanized Kant into thought was Hume's argument—discussed in the last reading—that we cannot know the necessary connection between cause and effect. Experience gives no guarantee of a necessary connection, Hume had argued, and there is no other court of appeal except experience. Kant acknowledged that Hume was right and that Leibnizian rationalism provided no alternative. This meant that the foundations of science had been undermined, and metaphysics, which also depends on causality, had become pure fantasy. Something had to be done.

The *Critique of Pure Reason,* which restored to science the causal necessity destroyed by Hume's arguments, did not appear until 1781. Its involved and often tortured style—so different from Hume's easy lucidity—shows all the labor of thought which the new conception had cost. Kant was now fifty-seven. Up to his forty-sixth year, he had been a mere lecturer (*Privat-docent*), but now he was a professor at the University of Königsberg. The book he had written was soon to bring him great renown—greater than that enjoyed by any other German philosopher.

Kant's solution to Hume's impasse was to disclose the ground of necessity in the subject—in the knower. It is the individual perceiving the world who imposes the bond of necessity on the causal order. As a consequence we know, even before experience, that everything will have a cause, and that the effect will always follow the cause. The solution had already been glimpsed by Hume, when he insisted that, though nature exhibits no necessity, we ourselves develop habits of invariably expecting effect to follow upon cause.

Kant went far beyond Hume. Our subjective faculties give positive assurance of the validity of causal laws, and they also guarantee the rigor of arithmetic and geometry.

The second of Kant's celebrated critiques, the *Critique of Practical Reason,* appeared in 1788. It had been preceded in 1785 by *Fundamental Principles of the Metaphysic of Morals.* Both books sought to lay down the foundations of ethics, but the former was particularly concerned with a justification of religion. Just as Kant had vindicated the laws of science in his first critique—the *Critique of Pure Reason*—he now upheld a moral law in ethics. This too was a "necessary" law, since no one could be rational who disobeyed it. It was not necessary, however, in the sense that *natural* laws are, for one *could* disobey it. One insight that pervades Kant's ethical works is that no one has a right to make an exception of himself—that the duties to which he holds others must be his duties too.

The third critique—the *Critique of Judgment* (1790)—sought to demonstrate that both mechanical laws and teleology have a rightful place in the biological world and that both are necessary to a full explanation. The larger part of the book, however, is devoted to "the aesthetic judgment." It is hard to think that the dry, schematic, methodical recluse to Königsberg had any large aesthetic susceptibilities, yet he wrote a book on aesthetics which is universally admired and which stands second only to Aristotle's *Poetics* in persuasiveness and insight.

Neither Kant's fame as a philosopher nor his piety could save him from censure by the reactionary Frederick William II. In his *On Religion Within the Limits of Reason Alone* (1794), he had described Christianity in its historical aspect, as an ethical idea only. A royal mandate soon expressed the monarch's displeasure and threatened further action. In his answer, Kant refused to recant, but he resolved that silence on the offending topic was his duty as a subject.

Kant died in his eightieth year, after a long period of illness and declining powers. In spite of his continuing efforts to unify the body of human knowledge and aspiration, he left great gaps between science and religion, the realm of mechanical necessity and the realm of freedom, the natural man and the spiritual. It was left to his successors to fill in these gaps as well as they could.

I I

Like most philosophers, Kant distinguished between the *form* and the *material* of knowledge. The material consists of sensations—visual sensations, tactual sensations, auditory sensations, and so on. The form is everything else that you apprehend when you have sensations.

Sitting at your desk you see before you a book with a green cover. In perceiving it you have *knowledge* of its existence and characteristics. What part of this knowledge is material and what part form? The green color is a sensation and so are the markings on the surface and the smoothness and heft as you pick it up. If you let it drop on the desk there is an auditory sensation, and if you turn the pages you see patterns of white (or light gray) flecked with patterns of black (or dark gray) markings.

But where is the form? Consider the judgments you make about the book. In the first place, you call it "a book." Is there a sensation of book, as there is a sensation of green or of smoothness? That what you see is a book is evidently not something given in sensation. The greenness or smoothness belong to the book; they are qualities of the book. The book, on the other hand, is not a quality we ascribe to a thing. It is a thing itself—a thing or a substance; it has qualities but is not a quality. Whence comes this idea that what we see is a book, i.e., a thing or substance? According to Kant, substance is a category of the Understanding; i.e., a faculty of human knowing. When we open our eyes we see *things* automatically, not because *being a thing* is a sensation, for it is not; but because this is the *form* which our understanding gives to what we see. It is a *form* imposed upon the welter of sensations by our faculties.

If we release the book it will fall to the surface of the desk, and then suddenly stop, with a muted bang. You would naturally say that it fell because you released it, and it was subject to gravitational force. The book, once released, is attracted to the center of the earth and moves with an accelerated speed determined by the time of the fall, when it is suddenly stopped by the rigid desk, which represents forces with an upward thrust. Asked about the noise, you would say that anyone can see that it was caused by the book hitting, or striking, the table.

But how much of all this is given in sensation? Is there any sensation of hitting or striking, as there are sensations of green and smoothness? Is there a sensation, or any combination of sensations, equivalent to force or cause? That is, could you put together colors, sounds, or kinesthetic sensations (sensations arising from the contraction of muscles) and form something you could call gravitational force? If not, then we have to look elsewhere for the source of these elements of our knowledge. These formal elements of our knowledge, according to Kant, are contributed by the Categories of the Understanding. On p. 42c you will find all these categories listed in a table, as follows:

TABLE OF THE CATEGORIES

1	2
Of Quantity	*Of Quality*
Unity	Reality
Plurality	Negation
Totality	Limitation

3
Of Relation
Of Inherence and Subsistence (*substantia et accidens*)
Of Causality and Dependence (cause and effect)
Of Community (reciprocity between the agent and patient)

4
Of Modality
Possibility—Impossibility
Existence—Non-existence
Necessity—Contingence

You will note that substance is the first category of relation and that causality is the second. If what we perceive are things and causes or effects, it is because we see *through* the Understanding, which imparts these forms. The third category of relation may be more difficult. It means roughly that the cause cannot be a cause unless the effect permits. A monarch cannot rule unless his subjects (to some degree) submit, and the desk cannot support the book unless the book yields, so to speak, to superior force. In the case of a Greek temple we seem to see the weight of the entablature and roof weighing down upon columns and the vertical thrust of the columns supporting the weight; gravitation and the force of rigidity seem equally and beautifully balanced.

It is obvious, too, that if we think of something as existing or extinct, or as possible or impossible, we are not thinking of sensations or of qualities or combinations of sensations. We are concerned with basic ideas of the intellect; i.e., with categories of the Understanding. The same is true of the other categories listed under *Quantity* and *Quality.* Consider "Unity," for example. This really means "all." When we say "All crows are black," the black is a sensation but "all" could never be derived from sensation.

Similarly, "Negation" could never be given in sensation. You say "Some roses are *not* red," but you do not see not-red roses; you see white or yellow roses. Only by the use of your category of negation can you convert "white roses" into "not-red roses." In the same way, the substance-attribute (noun-adjective) relation presupposed in your assertion is not given in sensation. It is a constant form contributed by your Understanding, and it remains the same, however much the content of your assertions varies.

Does this sound like splitting hairs? It will help to remember that dogs have sensations, but, so far as we know, the ideas of substance, causality, community, possibility, and necessity never enter their heads. It is certainly possible to have sensations without having the intellectual forms which go with them in human experience.

So far we have talked about the Understanding, but there is another faculty of the mind which is prior and more basic, and that is Intuition. It is by Intuition that sensations are given the forms of space and time—of spread-outness and duration. Whatever is apprehended as a substance (a book or a temple, etc.) or as a unity (*all* the members of a class) or as cause or effect must first be perceived as extended in space and time. It must first be given spatial and temporal form. In this sense Intuition is prior to and more basic than the Understanding. Intuition is also the subject of the present reading, for the "Transcendental Aesthetic" deals exclusively with the part played by Intuition in our knowledge.

We have said something about the Understanding first, because its role is easier to comprehend than is that of Intuition. Our thought is obviously cast in the mold of categories which we have just discussed, and it is clear that sensations, by themselves, lack these determinations; and that, accordingly, they must be contributed by the *mind.* It is much harder to believe that the mind must endow sensations with their extension in space and time. We are accustomed to think of sensations as spread out and as having a certain duration in their own right. A musical note lasts for a fraction of a second; the green surface of the book measures four by six inches. Why should the mind have to contribute to sensations what they plainly possess in themselves? Perhaps, then, our brief account of the Understanding will help us to comprehend the work of Intuition.

There is a second reason for acquainting ourselves with the role of the Understanding. Before we settle down to explaining difficult points in the "transcendental Aesthetic," we should try to form a bird's-eye view of the whole knowledge process, as Kant conceived it. It begins with the "thing-in-itself," the unknown (and unknowable) object which was originally supposed to act upon our faculty of sensibility (sense organs) to produce the raw, unordered sensations. It ends with scientific reasoning and investigation. The latter is the work of the Understanding, which, however, cannot be completed in most cases, as we shall see, without confirmation in sense perception—i.e., "intuitions." The general scheme is as follows:

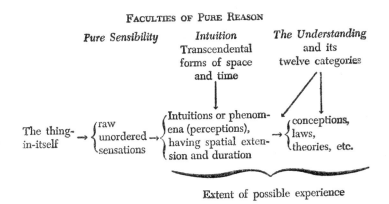

FACULTIES OF PURE REASON

Pure Sensibility — Intuition, Transcendental forms of space and time — The Understanding and its twelve categories

The thing-in-itself → raw unordered sensations → Intuitions or phenomena (perceptions), having spatial extension and duration → conceptions, laws, theories, etc.

Extent of possible experience

Kant started out with the viewpoint of a physicist and thought of the physical object as *causing* sensations by its action on sense organs. In terms of the system he evolved, however, this became impossible, since causality was one of the categories of the Understanding, and thus applies only to phenomena; i.e., only to sensations ordered in time and space. It would be meaningless to say that the object, or thing-in-itself, *causes* our sensations, because it is not perceived and lies beyond possible experience.

Nor are raw sensations perceived. They are automatically determined by the transcendental forms of space and time and are experienced as temporal and spread out. If you pour hot wax into a vase, it takes the shape of the vase. In the same way, our faculty of Intuition determines the structure and order of the sensory material.

The twelve categories similarly mold our thinking and reasoning. We cannot reason without making use of categories such as cause and effect, substance, possibility, and existence. But reasoning would also be impossible if it did not refer back to the spatio-temporal phenomena.

By a glance at the diagram above you can now see how the material and form of knowledge function in Kant's scheme— the question raised at the opening of this section. The matter or material necessary for knowledge consists of raw sensations; the necessary forms are supplied by the faculties of the mind.

III

The Introduction to the "Transcendental Aesthetic" presents important issues and distinctions. We are already familiar with the distinction between *a posteriori* and *a priori* knowledge. Examples of *a priori* truths are $2 + 2 = 4$, 13 is a prime number, and things equal to the same thing are equal to each other. We can know such truths in advance of experience, and we can be sure that they will hold true in any possible situation, no matter how weird it might be in other respects. *A posteriori* propositions, on the other hand, can be known only through and after experience. We cannot establish that "Sugar is sweet" and "Quinine is bitter," except by tasting sugar and quinine.

Propositions, Kant says, can be purely *a priori*, or only partly so. In the latter case, they are *a priori* as propositions but not as regards their terms. "Every change has a cause" is an *a priori* proposition, but the term "change" is derived from experience and could be understood only by someone who has witnessed first-hand the flux and alterations in the sensuous world. The term "cause," on the other hand, is not empirical; it designates one of the transcendental categories, which we have briefly discussed. We do not need to go to experience to understand "cause" or "necessary connections." We know it in advance, for it is one of the ways—our faculties being what they are—in which we necessarily see things. We see things as causes and effects. We "see" the batter (or bat) hit the ball over the fence, but we do not really see (i.e., sense) the hitting. We see the ball come into contact with the bat and then fly away. It is the category of cause which furnishes the necessary connection between the earlier and later motion of the ball.

Now Kant's provocative claim is that the propositions of mathematics are *a priori* only in this sense. They are *a priori* as propositions, but their terms are derived from experience, and they can be known to be true only within possible experience. Numbers and triangles are first known through sense perception—through Intuition.

A priori knowledge is of immense importance for mankind. A science or philosophy is needed, Kant contends, which will be able to demonstrate that such knowledge is possible and to exhibit its nature and limits. This is the task that he sets himself in the *Critique of Pure Reason*. The questions he must answer are:

> How is pure mathematics possible?
> How is pure natural science possible?

Both of these broad fields are *a priori*, in Kant's opinion, but only the former is deemed *a priori* today. Kant would have liked to uphold the *a priori* in metaphysics, but this was impossible in terms of *pure* reason.

To understand Kant's vindication of the *a priori*, it is necessary to distinguish between analytic and synthetic judgments. An analytic judgment is such that its predicate is contained in its subject, whereas a synthetic judgment is one of which this is not true. "All whales are mammals" is analytic, since its predicate, "being a mammal" is part of the definition of "whale." The predicate is thus contained in the subject, and it is necessarily true. It is like saying "the green house is green," or "*A* and *B* contain *B*," or "2 is a number," or "every bachelor is unmarried." Corresponding synthetic judgments would be "the house is green," "*A* contains *B*," "2 is the number of my children," and "every bachelor wishes he were married." Since the predicates here are not contained in the subjects, we must make empirical investigations to determine whether they are true.

You will note at once that the analytic judgment is also *a priori.* Since its predicate is contained in its subject, as *B* is contained in *AB*, we know before experience that it must be true, even in the remote future, or on Mars. *If* a thing is *A* and *B*, then it is *A*. There is no question that analytic judgments are *a priori.* But how important are such judgments? Following Francis Bacon, Kant asserts that analytic judgments add nothing new to our knowledge but only clarify our conceptions. The predicate merely asserts what is already contained in the subject. Some analytic rules, such as *A = A*, are important and indispensable in the sciences, Kant admits, but they are only connecting links, not principles. Where then are we to find the real principles of science? Can they be synthetic?

But how could synthetic propositions qualify as principles of science, which must be true always and on all occasions? We can determine their truth only by reference to sense experience, which changes from day to day. Kant points out that all *a posteriori* judgments are synthetic. "Milk is nourishing," "Wood can be cut with an ax," and "Parasites can cause illness and death," can be known only through experience, by observation, and by means of rules which experience has taught us. All *a posteriori* judgments are unquestionably synthetic.

The crucial question for Kant is whether all synthetic judgments are *a posteriori.* In other words, can synthetic judgments ever be *a priori?* At first glance this appears impossible. How could you know that "wood is combustible" except by lighting a fire to it, or by some other empirical test? And how, even so, could you know that it must always be combustible? Well, perhaps this synthetic proposition is not *a priori.* Others may be.

Consider Kant's famous example $7 + 5 = 12$. It is a synthetic proposition, for the 12 is not contained in the conception of 7 or 5. You could understand the two numbers and the operation $+$ without knowing that 12 is entailed. Of course, if you put down seven dots followed by five dots, viz: .... / ....., and then add them up, you will at once see the identity asserted. But in this case $7 + 5 = 12$ is learned only by an appeal to intuition or sense perception. But how do we know that this equality must hold at all times, and not only for dots but also for cabbages and kings and anything else? If the proposition is *a priori,* we must know in advance of experience that it will always hold.

Another example, taken from geometry, is "A straight line is the shortest distance between two points." Examples given from physics are the so-called law of the conservation of mass and the law that action and reaction are equal. The conservation of mass has given way, since Kant's time, to the conservation of energy, but it is true that laws *of this kind* are fundamental in natural science and are presupposed throughout. It is also true that they are not analytic. This leaves two alternatives. Either they are synthetic *a priori,* as Kant argued, or they are synthetic *a posteriori,* as almost all authorities hold today. In the latter case, however, the foundations of science will be not necessary but contingent, and we cannot be *certain* that they are true.

Kant wants to uphold, as against Hume, the *a priori* necessity of pure science. To this great task the whole of the *Critique of Pure Reason* is devoted.

Kant would like to do the same for metaphysics, but he reluctantly admits that the questions whether God exists or the soul is immortal, and whether space and time are infinite, etc., lie beyond the scope of pure reason and could never be resolved within the framework of Intuition and the Understanding. In the section of the *Critique* which deals with "Transcendental Logic" he shows that the attempt to answer such questions leads to inevitable contradictions. The limits of pure reason, in Kant's view, are here clearly apparent. It is only when we turn to the "practical reason," which is expounded in the *Critique of Practical Reason*, that a way is found to vindicate metaphysical and theological beliefs.

Although Kant considers the critique of pure reason a science, or at least a steppingstone to it, he warns that it must not be supposed to lay down a doctrine. It is essentially a critique. It does not pretend to enlarge our knowledge of the world. It seeks only to explain how *a priori* knowledge of the world is possible, to show where its limits lie, and to demonstrate that the master role is played by the *a priori* mental capacities of man—the two forms of Intuition and the Understanding. It is man's *a priori* capacity to mold his sensory experience into orderly spatial and temporal patterns which make geometry and arithmetic possible that will be our concern in the next section.

I V

Transcendental aesthetic, according to Kant, is "the science of all the principles of sensibility *a priori*" (p. 23d); it lays down the *a priori* principles which govern sense perception. It is thus concerned with the faculty of Intuition. Intuition is divided into an external sense (or form), which furnishes our perceptions with spatial order, consistency, and necessary geometrical relations; and an internal sense (or form), which supplies the order and necessary connections peculiar to temporal experience.

Space and time are expounded in two ways. The metaphysical exposition explains the role of the *a priori* in sense experience, whereas the transcendental exposition shows the possibility, and necessary sources, of the *a priori* structure which our experience assumes.

Whereas the raw sensations—the matter of knowledge—are given *a posteriori*, the forms of Intuition are *a priori*. What does this distinction mean? Sensations cannot be known until we have experienced them. No man can know what blue looks like until he has seen it, nor what hardness is until he has felt it. You can easily see that this is not the case with some of the relations between sensations. You know, even before experience, or *a priori*, that if *a*, *b*, and *c* are tones of a violin, and *a* occurs before *b*, and *b* before *c*, then *a* must occur before *c*. The relation "before" is thus "transitive." There is no question that the relation "before," in the temporal sense, will be transitive for all events in time. "If *a* is before *b*, *b* is not before *a*," is another *a priori* necessity, holding for all possible temporal experiences. It states that "before" is asymmetrical; this we know in advance.

The example is not trivial. If "before," in the temporal sense, were not "asymmetrical," it would be possible for time to turn back on occasion and repeat itself, enabling us to correct bad mistakes we have made. But, as you know, "time waits for no man," and never turns back—never *could*. But how do you know this? Do you learn it from experience? This would be impossible. Experience would tell you only that time has never reversed itself in your memory or in that of other men. It would not tell you that this is *impossible*.

But suppose we *define* time as irreversible? The irreversibility of time would then be analytic, and we would know *a priori* that it could never turn back. But this will not do either. You cannot prevent time from turning back—if it wants to—simply by a definition. Is not Kant's solution, then, the only possible one? If time turned back, we could never experience it; the irreversibility is an *a priori* character imposed on experience by our faculty of Intuition, and is thus assured for all possible experience, but not beyond. "Time is irreversible" is a synthetic *a priori* proposition.

We have just considered two examples of *a priori* temporal intuition, based upon our transcendental capacity of representing time—a capacity shared by all human beings. Let us now consider an example or two of *a priori* spatial intuition: How do we know that parallel lines in the same plane will "meet at infinity," i.e., will never meet? This is called the *postulate* of parallels, because it is not self-evident and cannot be proved, though it is necessary for the proof of certain theorems. Is not the truth of this postulate apparent merely by looking at two parallel lines on the blackboard? If so, could our certainty be explained in any other way than by our *a priori* faculty of representing space?

Consider also Proposition 1 in Euclid's *Elements* (see Vol. 11, p. 2), which reads: *"On a given finite straight line to construct an equilateral triangle."* Starting out with the line *AB,* one draws the circle *CDB,* with center *A* and *AB* as a radius, and then another circle *ACE* with center *B* and the same *AB* as radius:

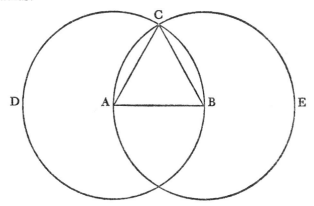

The proof of Proposition 1, as you will see, depends on the definition of a circle (Def. 15); on Postulate 3, which permits you to draw a circle "with any centre and distance"; and on the Common Notion "Things which are equal to the same thing are also equal to one another."

The definition of a circle simply expresses precisely what we mean by a circle, that is, a figure with a center such that all straight lines drawn from this center to the circumference will be equal. But could we be sure that we can always draw such a figure from any point, and of any size, if we had not looked at circles out in space? Once we have drawn a circle with the help of a compass or a piece of string, we suddenly see that it must always be possible to do so. This is the *a priori* spatial intuition Kant is talking about.

Now consider how the Common Notion "Things which are equal to the same thing are also equal to one another" can be known to be true in all cases. How would you go about proving this? Would you see whether it is true for circles and squares, and for measures of cement, corn, and apples, etc., or do you not intuit the truth of this propositon in advance? It is obvious that this is an *a priori* proposition and that it would be foolish to try to prove it inductively; i.e., by seeing whether it works in all sorts of cases.

But is the *a priori* analytic or synthetic? If the proposition is analytic, then, according to Kant's definition, its predicate must be contained in its subject. If you decide that it is not so contained, then will you not have to concede that it is synthetic *a priori,* based upon our *a priori* intuition of space? Not necessarily, for perhaps it is based on our *a priori* intuition of time.

Time is the dimension which makes counting possible, and it therefore makes arithmetic possible too. And in arithmetic, as in geometry, things equal to the same thing are equal to one another.

If you now take another look at the diagram for Proposition 1, you will see more clearly why Kant holds that geometric proof is not analytic but synthetic. Once definitions have clarified the terms involved, we can "see" *a priori,* Kant maintained, that the propositions of geometry must hold in all cases, independently of empirical qualities. And this ability is to be explained only on the theory that our inborn visual capacity determines the intuited structure of perceived things. It does not determine the color, weight, temperature, and other such empirical qualities of things, but it *does* determine their *a priori* necessary structural forms. This is the reason why, when the situation is clear in our minds, we cannot imagine a case in which geometrical propositions would not be true. We cannot imagine, for instance, that opposite angles of intersecting lines in a plane should ever be anything but equal. But we can easily imagine lead which is not heavy and oranges which are not orange.

Everyone will grant that geometrical propositions are *a*

priori. The question is whether they are synthetic *a priori*, as Kant thought, or analytic *a priori*, which is the prevailing view among mathematicians today.

Kant returns again and again to the task of proving that geometric propositions cannot be analytic. He takes as an example " 'Two straight lines cannot enclose a space, and with these alone no figure is possible.' " Try to deduce this, he says, "from the conception of a straight line and the number two" (p. 31b-c).

It will be noted that Kant's example depends directly on the Postulate of Parallels, which cannot be proved deductively, nor is it regarded as self-evident. It is clear, therefore, that his argument at this point has considerable force. Do we not have to rely on our spatial intuition when it comes to the Postulate of Parallels? The modern mathematician would say No. The postulates and axioms (which Euclid called Common Notions) can both be taken as assumptions, and geometry will then consist of the deductions from them. By altering the Postulate of Parallels, non-Euclidean geometries have been evolved. One of these geometries is utilized by Einstein's General Theory of Relativity. According to this modern conception, geometry does not expound the nature of space but only defines possibilities. It is physics which determines which geometry will apply to the world.

But Kant argues that space

. . . is a necessary representation *a priori*, which serves for the foundation of all external intuitions. We never can imagine or make a representation to ourselves of the non-existence of space, though we may easily enough think that no objects are found in it. (p. 24c)

Does this seem to you to be true? You cannot, of course, abstract from space and think of the objects only. But is it not also impossible to imagine space without any objects in it? Would you not at least feel your own body in the empty space, and indeed right in the center of it? Would not sensations from the soles of your feet and from muscles and joints, tell you that you were trespassing on the space supposed to be empty? But perhaps we could think away our own body too! In any case,

Kant concludes that space "is a representation *a priori*, which necessarily supplies the basis for external phenomena" (p. 24c). That our own faculty of Intuition should supply the geometrical structures of the visual world has perhaps appeared very odd to you, from the first. Yet we know that if our eyes were constructed differently we would see things very differently. The perceiver does make this contribution. Note that, as you look out at the world, everything seems to be related concentrically to you, as if you were the hub of the world and everything revolved about you. Every object is *your* object. Kant calls this phenomenon "the transcendental unity of apperception." What we perceive is certainly not all from the outside but partly due to us.

Kant goes on to say that the *a priori* structure which we, as perceivers, confer upon the perceptual world is not "discursive" but intuitive. That is, we find out that things have geometrical relations not by reasoning but by seeing these relations between concrete things. That our faculty of Intuition is one of *pure* intuition is shown by the fact that it is not altered by empirical qualities. It does not matter whether a triangle is white or black, traced with chalk, or built of steel: the sum of its angles must equal two right angles.

That the faculty is purely intuitive is shown again by the fact that we can imagine only one space. "We can only represent to ourselves one space," he says, and

when we talk of divers spaces, we mean only parts of one and the same space. . . . Hence it follows that an *a priori* intuition (which is not empirical) lies at the root of all our conceptions of space. (p. 24c-d)

If this is true, even the space of imaginary cities and countries that we read about must be *thought of* as part of the one physical space, determined by our faculty of representation. Alice in Wonderland must be conceived as going down the mouse hole or "through the looking glass" in England or some other country. And, speaking of a looking glass, what would Kant say about mirror images? Must we think of these as part of the one and only space? How is this possible?

Our faculty of spatial Intuition not only insures the validity of geometry; it also is necessary to our having objects and stating any synthetical relation between them. In a typical sentence, Kant states:

> If, therefore, space (and time also) were not a mere form of your intuition, which contains conditions *a priori*, under which alone things can become external objects for you, and without which subjective conditions the objects are in themselves nothing, you could not construct any synthetical proposition whatsoever regarding external objects. (p. 31d)

Sensations, if we could experience them by themselves, would not be objects. A patch of blue or a feel of hardness would be mere wisps of feeling—not enduring, not objective. According to Kant, sensations are only the materials on which our faculty of representation (Intuition) imprints the character of objectivity. Were there no such faculty, therefore, we should not be able to know that "dogs bark" or that "elephants are larger than horses" or to frame any synthetic proposition; we should have no *objects* to talk about. Is there any other way than this to account for objects and objectivity in our experience? The empiricist has an alternative explanation, but it is not easy. He has to show that, as a result of experiences of the child, the "blooming, buzzing confusion" of the newborn infant is transformed into more or less firm objects.

V

In what sense is time more fundamental than space?

Time and space, as the *a priori* forms of Intuition, have much in common. We cannot think of objects without space, Kant argues, though we can imagine space without objects. Space is therefore *a priori*. Similarly,

> With regard to phenomena in general, we cannot think away time from them, and represent them to ourselves as out of and unconnected with time, but we can quite well represent to ourselves time void of phenomena. Time is therefore given *a priori*. (p. 26c)

Time and space must both be *a priori* fixtures of the mind, for it is impossible for the mind to function without using them. Time also, like space, furnishes the only basis for mathematical and other ("apodeictic") principles, space being the *a priori* basis of geometry, and time that of arithmetic.

Time is like space also in being exclusively *one*. There can be only one time, as there is only one space. Any segment of time which we conceive, even if it is the lifetime of a fictitious hero, must be conceived as a part of this one time, and thus as earlier or later than the present moment. This also goes to show that time, like space, is an *a priori* form of our intuitive faculty.

There are also a number of crucial differences between space and time. Space has three dimensions, time only one. Moreover, the one dimension of time is irreversible. We cannot move backward in time, but only forward. In the three dimensions of space, on the contrary, we can move in any direction we please. We can do so, however, only by virtue of the time order in which we necessarily move. This is a clue to the priority of time. "Time," Kant explains,

> . . . is the formal condition *a priori* of all phenomena whatsoever. Space, as the pure form of external intuition, is limited as a condition *a priori* to external phenomena alone. (p. 27c)

Time is more fundamental than space in the sense that it is the *a priori* condition of all phenomena, of all objects of the senses, whereas space determines only those which are external.

If the forms of space and time are applicable only to sensations, what can be the cause of sensations?

Space and time, as we have seen, are merely forms of human Intuition *a priori*—human ways of organizing the sensory field. Only sensations can have spatial extension or duration. Is this true? Try to think of something that is extended but not colored, or of something that has duration—which lasts a short or long time—but is neither colored nor sonorous nor painful, which is not a kinesthetic, gustatory, olfactory sensation, or any combination of sensations. If you succeed in finding something of the sort, try to describe it. See if you can do so without naming sensations of one kind or another, or combinations of sensations.

But if space and time are limited to the various categories of sensation, what can be the cause of sensations? The physicist says that sensations are produced by the stimulation of our sense organs by physical objects. But physical objects lie beyond the sensory field; they are not themselves sensations.

The flame of a candle is really a process of combustion, which utilizes oxygen and produces carbon dioxide. The process reflects light which strikes our retina, where there is a photochemical response, and a nervous impulse is transmitted to the cortex of the cerebrum. Thereupon we see the flame. Only the final outcome is a sensation; the causal series preceding it is all physical. This is how sensations are produced, according to the customary theory. But how could Kant accept it?

The process of combustion that the physicist describes could have no extension nor duration on his account, or at least we could never know it. Nor could our sense organs and nervous system be known to be spread out or temporal; they are not sensations.

This is a real difficulty in Kant's philosophy. In working out his system, he had assumed that sensations were caused by physical objects, but as the system developed it became clear that this was impossible. In the first place, cause became a transcendental category, applying only to what was given in Intuition. And secondly, space and time, the forms of Intuition, had relevance only to sensations.

The conclusion he reached was that the "thing-in-itself," the real substance that lies beyond any possible experience, is unknowable. He might have avoided this skeptical conclusion by eliminating the thing-in-itself and making sensations the starting point of his system. But this would result in Berkelean idealism, or Humean phenomenalism, neither of which Kant approved. The thing-in-itself therefore remained, though it was completely useless. Its nature could not be known, nor could it be supposed to produce our sensations. It was thus said that you cannot get in Kant's system except by supposing an external cause of our sensations, but once in, you cannot retain this cause. (See the chart on p. [259].)

Does Kant's argument prove the existence of a permanent reality beyond human experience?

Let us consider only the argument included in the present reading (see footnote, pp. 12-13). Here Kant declares:

"But this permanent [reality] cannot be an intuition in me. For all the determining grounds of my existence which can be found in me are representations and, as such, do themselves require a permanent, distinct from them, which may determine my existence in relation to their changes, that is, my existence in time, wherein they change." (p. 12c)

In this difficult passage and in the explanations added, Kant seems to be arguing as follows: My consciousness of my own existence in time presupposes that I am somehow aware of something permanent, for I am conscious of remaining the same subject throughout all changes. "But this permanent cannot be an intuition in me." On the contrary, it must be explained how I come to have this stream of changing intuitions (i.e., sensations) within me. My awareness of this permanent is therefore possible only through a thing outside me, and this could only be given in my perception of things in space. My representation of things in space thus cannot be a *mere* representation.

One of the most plausible interpretations of this argument is that what Kant means by "this permanent" is the external physical object and the sense organs and brain. The occurrence of sensations requires an explanation, and the explanation is that external physical objects act upon sense organs and brain. This interpretation is reasonable and agrees with Kant's writings on mechanics, but is it consistent with what Kant says in the "Transcendental Aesthetic"?

It is well to remember that Kant was a brooding, very complex thinker. Contrary solutions of perplexing problems strove for an advantage within him. One thing he wanted to believe was that just as, in mechanics, physical bodies interact, so in psycho-physics physical bodies can produce sensations. Yet he also wished to overcome Hume's skepticism and to demonstrate how mathematics, with its *a priori* necessities, could be true. This endeavor led to a transcendental philosophy which seemed to exclude the role of physical objects in causing sensations.

We should not be prejudiced against Kant's argument for realism (i.e., for the existence of a permanent material world) just because it may be inconsistent with his doctrine of space and time or his doctrine of causation. Some of the best thoughts of a philosopher may be found inconsistent with his basic doctrine.

The following questions are designed to help you test the thoroughness of your reading. Each question is to be answered by giving a page or pages of the reading assignment. Answers will be found on page 302 of this Reading Plan.

1 Why, according to Kant, has "the queen of all the sciences" fallen into dishonor?

2 What are the two formal requirements of any critique of pure reason?

3 Why does Kant say that anything like a hypothesis must be excluded from his critique?

4 What is meant by saying of a book *"that it would be much shorter, if it were not so short"*?

5 What does Kant mean when he says that logic is "only a *propaedeutic*"?

6 Is physics partly *a priori*, according to Kant?

7 Is metaphysic, in Kant's opinion, entirely independent of the teaching of experience?

8 Can I cognize my soul, according to Kant, as a thing-in-itself?

9 From what does *the hope of a future life* arise?

10 In what sense must metaphysics be regarded as *"given"* and as "really existing"?

11 What must be the case if "All objects are beside each other in space" is to be true?

12 How does Kant answer the argument: Time must be real since changes are real, and occur in it?

WILLIAM JAMES

The Principles of Psychology

Ch. 28

Vol. 53, pp. 851-890

How can we know that some things in our experience are necessarily connected? We see the sun rise every day, or we do whenever we get up in time, but do we know that it will always rise? Everyone knows that sulphuric acid boils at 338 degrees centigrade at sea level, but can we be sure that this will always be so? And how can we be so absolutely certain that $2 + 2 = 4$ and that opposite angles formed by two intersecting straight lines are equal—that this will hold true throughout the universe?

Hume, as we have seen, distinguished between "matters of fact" and "relations of ideas." Matters of fact are facts learned from perception, such as "Crows are black" and "Granite is hard." Here there is no necessity. The crows *might be* white and the granite soft; they just happen to be the way they are. Relations of ideas are patterns of ideas we have combined in our minds. Necessary connections become possible here because the ideas are ours, and we can define them as we please. Combining ideas in axioms and defining required terms, we can develop the sciences of arithmetic and geometry, which consist of necessary propositions. Two examples of such necessary propositions are given in the preceding paragraph, but the other two are contingent matters of fact.

Later in the eighteenth century, as we have seen, Kant gave a very different explanation of our knowledge of necessary propositions. The most important necessary propositions are synthetic. The necessity is imposed on them by the transcendental structure of the mind. We can be absolutely certain of arithmetic and geometry because space and time have an *a priori* structure. We can be absolutely certain of causal laws, within possible experience, because this is the way the human mind necessarily works. In the same way, everything we see while wearing blue glasses becomes blue.

James, at the turn of the twentieth century, had been influenced by Hume and even more by John Locke. His mind rebelled against Kant, but he learned from him nonetheless, almost in spite of himself. His admiration for Darwin was immense; that for the evolutionary philosopher Herbert Spencer something less. Could evolution explain the necessary connections we find in experience, as the latter maintained? Or had they been stamped in by repeated experiences of the individual, as J. S. Mill in England, and Sigwart and others in Germany, had contended? In the present reading we see James denouncing both these views. His own distinctive theory owed much to Locke and Hume, but we see Darwin's influence in it, and even Kant's.

Fifteenth Reading

I

A few facts of the life of William James will help to explain why he left so dazzling a remembrance and such a trail of new ideas. He was born in 1842 in New York, the eldest son of Henry James. This studious, very independent-minded gentleman seemed to be a searcher for an honest religion. Scornful of conventional churches, he was much impressed by the writings of the Swedish mystic Swedenborg. William held his father in loving respect throughout his life and gave a sympathetic account of mysticism—usually tinged with common sense—in his *Varieties of Religious Experience* (1902). He also remained very close to his famous novelist brother, Henry James the younger. The correspondence of the three Jameses, much of which is available in *The Letters of William James*, edited by his son Henry James, is full of fresh impressions, wit, and novel cogitations.

Owing to his father's restless habits, William was schooled, now in New York, now in France and Switzerland. When nineteen years old he entered Harvard as a student of science and then went on to medicine. He broke off his studies to accompany the famous biologist Agassiz on an exploring expedition to the Amazon. In 1867, however, we find him in Germany studying under Helmholtz and other leading physiologists of Europe. Two years later he took his M.D. at Harvard, but was never attracted to the practice of medicine. For the next few years he was not attracted to anything and remained, idle, ill, and depressed, in his father's house.

In 1872 he began to teach physiology at Harvard and later became Professor of Psychology. His morbid symptoms disappeared in 1878, on his marriage with Alice Gibbens, and now his intellectual energies appeared inexhaustible. His two-volume *Principles of Psychology*, which took ten years to compose, came out in 1890. A work of unique charm, depth, and originality, it made a strong impression which has not dimmed to this day.

For a long time James's real passion had been philosophy, and in the 1890's he gave way to it. *The Will to Believe and Other Essays in Popular Philosophy* appeared in 1897. In 1906 he gave his lectures on *Pragmatism* at Harvard and in the following year repeated them at Columbia University. They were published in 1907. *A Pluralistic Universe* came out in 1909, a year before James's death, and *Essays in Radical Empiricism* appeared posthumously in 1912.

James's abundant mind embraced diverse and contrary tendencies. Although he was an arch empiricist, he made a sympathetic study of psychic research and did not rule out miracles. On the other hand, he attempted to explain instantaneous conversion and other religious phenomena naturalistically. He had only contempt—graced with humor—for absolute idealism, which made the individual a dispensable fragment of a vast inhuman whole, but he lent an understanding ear to any vagary of individual religious belief. Philosophy and religion are for the good of men, according to his pragmatic creed, not *vice versa*. A man has a right to believe anything (not disproved) which enriches his life. No wonder he was attacked by empiricists. He went on to argue that the true is simply the useful, and the useful always true. Here his pragmatism had clearly triumphed over his empiricism.

We shall see in the present reading, which deals with necessary propositions, that James again parts company with the empiricists. He always remained faithful, however, to the observed world as he saw it, and especially to facts which, however unusual, had a bearing on the life and aspirations of the individual.

II

James's psychological method is not usually genetic; but it is that in his last chapter, "Necessary Truths and the Effects of Experience." Here he undertakes to see how far the necessary truth which some propositions undoubtedly have can be explained in terms of earlier experience. The difference between a necessary truth and a contingent truth is that the latter *might* be false, whereas the former *must* be true, i.e., could not be false. In order to be sure that the distinction is clear, check the propositions below which you think are necessary.

1. All bats are mammals.
2. All men employ language of some kind.
3. The diagonal of a square is incommensurate with the sides.
4. The sum of the angles of any Euclidean triangle is equal to two right angles.
5. Gravitational attraction of bodies varies directly with the mass and indirectly with the square of the distance.
6. Seven is the number of days in a week.
7. Seven is the number of Jesus' disciples.
8. If men are monkeys, then, since monkeys are arboreal, men live in trees.
9. Men cannot survive without food.
10. $1 \times 1 = 1$

There are six necessary propositions on the list, but they are of different kinds. Numbers 1 and 6 are necessary, but only because the words "bat" and "week" have been defined in a certain way. If "bat" had been defined in terms of some other character the animal has, and a different calendar had been adopted, neither of these propositions would have been necessary. But is not the necessity of propositions 3, 4, and 10 very different? We could change our definitions of terms as much as we pleased, but these would still remain necessary truths.

But note that if we omit "Euclidean" from the fourth statement, it ceases to be necessary; it is in fact false in non-Euclidean geometries. Kant would have said it was true, but he knew nothing of non-Euclidean geometry, which had not yet been evolved. This unforeseen development, as you can imagine, was a crushing blow to Kant's claim that geometrical necessity derives from spatial intuition and is disclosed in perception. Intuition is not a sure guide. Kant was also led to assert that if space is finite it must be bounded. Now with De Sitter we can conceive (though not *imagine*) a three-dimensional space that turns back upon itself, like a snake that bites its tail.

Proposition 8 is still another kind of necessary proposition. It is a hypothetical or "if . . . then" proposition. Its premise "men are monkeys" and the conclusion too are false, but the hypothetical itself is necessarily true. Necessary propositions of this kind are immensely important. You will have noticed how often in geometrical proofs you assume the opposite of what is to be proved and then show that this implies a self-contradictory proposition. Since this cannot be true, the assumption is false, and the proposition to be proved *is* proved. This could be abbreviated as follows:

> The proposition p is to be proved.
> Let us suppose that not-p is true.
> But not-p can be shown to imply q and not-q.
> Thus, not-p is false, and p must be true.

If the proposition not-p can be shown to imply something self-contradictory, then we know it is false, and that p is true. The whole argument is *necessarily* true.

The original elements of experience for James, as for John Locke and other empiricists, consists of sense data—colors, sounds and silence, tastes, kinesthesia, pain and pressure. Here we do not expect to find necessity. That the sky looks blue and ice feels cold are simply facts. It is in the combination of these elements that the question of necessity arises, and it is here that empiricists and apriorists come to blows. Empiricists take the view that experience is sufficient to account for necessity; apriorists claim that we know necessity *before* experience.

The empiricists hold that we feel $2 + 2 = 4$ must be true because we have, on innumerable occasions, added things with this result, and there has never been a negative instance. Moreover, $2 + 2 = 4$ is an integral part of the multiplication table, which has always proved right in experience and never wrong. We may feel for a moment doubtful whether $11 \times 12 = 132$, but there is always a final test; we can add 11 sets of 12 things and banish doubt.

When a proposition has been verified in our experience again and again, we naturally expect it to be verified in the future. Thus we expect "Thunder follows lightning" to be true in all cases. Yet, on reflection, we can imagine an observer so close to the electrical discharge in the clouds that he would hear the thunder as soon as he sees the lightning. It is different with a proposition like $2 + 2 = 4$. We cannot imagine circumstances in which this would be false. Here expectation is overwhelmingly strong. We say a proposition of this sort could not be false and is necessarily true. Empiricists thus try to account for the necessity attributed to propositions, such as those of arithmetic, in terms of experience.

But since Darwin put evolution on the map, James says, empiricists have widened experience to include the experience of our ancestors as well as our own. He quotes a long passage from the British evolutionary philosopher Herbert Spencer, who was the rage at the time.

The strengths of the connections between things—such as "sulphuric acid" and "corrosion"—it is held, depend on the frequency with which they have been conjoined in experience. From this it follows, Spencer says, " 'that an *infinity of experiences* will produce a psychical relation that is indissoluble' " (p. 853a). The connection in the brain between "sulphuric acid" and "corrosion" has a strength determined by the number of times it has been stamped in by experience. If stamped in by an infinity of experiences, the connection would be "indissoluble"; we could not imagine sulphuric acid dropped on cloth without corrosion of the material. The sulphuric acid-corrosion connection, of course, is not of this strength, but perhaps the $2 + 2 = 4$ connection is. If so, its necessity can be explained.

It is obvious, Spencer says, that though no individual could have the infinity of experiences required to stamp in a necessary bond, this is quite possible for the human race. Your ancestors for thousands of generations have confirmed the proposition $2 + 2 = 4$, and the bond of equality has grown stronger in succeeding epochs, until now it is unthinkable that the equation should not hold. What we must suppose is that " 'there is a transmission of induced tendencies in the nervous system' " (p. 853b), that the brain traces or strengthened neural pathways of our ancestors have been transmitted to us.

All of our *a priori* abilities, which Kant included under the transcendental forms of space and time, are thus to be explained empirically by the law of frequency, "'as soon as it is supplemented by the law that *habitual* psychical successions entail some hereditary tendency to such successions, which, under persistent conditions, will become cumulative in generation after generation'" (p. 853b). The necessary propositions of arithmetic and geometry are not superimposed on experience by static transcendental forms, as Kant thought, but are the result of the frequency of individual experience transmitted to succeeding generations throughout a long strand of evolution. As a consequence, mistakes that our remote ancestors made have been gradually eliminated, and we tend to perceive things and connections as they are.

One difficulty of Spencer's theory is at once apparent. It assumes that acquired characters can be inherited. Spencer says nothing about natural selection or the survival of the fittest, but assumes that we have inherited cerebral patterns acquired by our ancestors. We know that Darwin's main principle of evolutionary change was natural selection, but that he sometimes employed the inheritance of acquired characters as a supplementary principle. When Spencer wrote his *Principles of Psychology* (1885), and even when James wrote his criticism of Spencer (1890), it was still possible to believe that acquired characters can be transmitted to offspring. James, however, did *not* believe it, and argued with Darwin that instincts, at least, arose from accidental variations which gave some competitive advantage to the species possessing them and enabled those species to survive and multiply. (See pp. 890-897.) He was not willing to accept this explanation for aesthetic activity, apparently, because he could not see that aesthetic activity had any survival value.

But would natural selection account for logical and mathematical activity? In accord with Darwin, James says that the features of our organic mental structure must "be understood as congenital variations, 'accidental' in the first instance, but then transmitted as fixed features of the race" (p. 851b).

In order to get the "feel" of this unusual hypothesis, let us ask ourselves the following questions: Would not the possession of embryonic logical and mathematical abilities have given some early men an advantage over others less gifted in this respect? If such abilities had survival value would they not have tended to accumulate in the race? And if this is so, would not natural selection be the basic explanation of logical and mathematical abilities? James sometimes waters down his thesis to: "The causes of our mental structure are doubtless natural, and connected, like all our other peculiarities, with those of our nervous structure" (p. 897b). He is not too sure what happened in evolution. We too should begin to ponder the possibilities.

III

James makes a useful distinction, sometimes neglected by Spencer, between two ways in which the brain can be affected by the outside world. External objects can act on the brain in a way to produce reflections of themselves in consciousness, as when we perceive trees or houses. Or they can act upon the brain as hormones, drugs, and infectious substances do, without producing any representation or "cognition of *themselves*" (p. 857a). The latter changes, though not reflected in consciousness, may have the most important indirect effects on experience. Molecular accidents before birth may very well account for the susceptibility to music, though, James significantly adds, "it has no zoological utility; it corresponds to no object in the natural environment ..." (p. 858a).

The influences of the environment which do not produce ideas of themselves are said to enter the mind "by the back door," whereas those which enter via the five senses are said to use "the front door." James proposes to restrict the term experience to *"processes which influence the mind by the front-door-way of simple habits and association"* (p. 858b).

If we are to understand where necessity comes from, we must see how experience, in this sense, arises. Ordinary evolutionists, James says, assume that "the *mere presence* of the various objects and relations to be known must end by bringing about the latter's cognition, and ... in this way all mental structure was from first to last evolved" (p. 859a-b). No instructed evolutionist would say anything like this; yet James is bringing out an interesting point. Our sense organs and cognitive faculties cannot be accounted for *merely* by the effect on us of external stimulation—not in a million years of evolution. Our primitive ancestors could not recognize a dog, or see the dog catch and eat a hare, unless they had sense organs and categories something like *animal, space, action,* and *consummation.* We are apt to forget that seeing something *as* an animal depends on something more than the animal, that it takes two to make such a seeing, and that the one has to be equipped with cognitive faculties.

Once endowed with sense organs and a nervous system, of course, we can have sensations. Yet sensations themselves are not ready-made but have had a history. "Why may they not have come into being by the back-door method," he asks, "by such physical processes as lie more in the sphere of morphological accident, of inward summation of effects, than in that of the 'sensible presence' of objects?" (p. 860a). We know that before the advent of animals with sense organs and perceptions there were other more primitive forms which merely reacted to heat and cold, light and dark, or to chemical stimulation. It is possible that even when sensations appear on the evolutionary scene they are more like cues to action than reflections of outer things.

The effect of things on the organism, then, is not to inevitably produce likenesses of themselves. Even the human mind is not a mirror of the outer world; its perceptions are more determined by the brain than by the qualities of external things. Everyone will have to admit (with Locke) that the secondary qualities we experience are not in physical things, and this fact alone destroys the simple correspondence of inner experience and outer processes that Spencer is prone to assume.

It is true, James says, that time and space are impressed on us from without, that these relations between things *"stamp copies of themselves within"* (p. 861a). As a consequence of seeing fire followed by embers or ashes, or by blackened skin and pain, etc., a habit is formed in us of expecting such effects whenever we see fire. In the same way, we habitually expect the teacup to fall when we drop it, and to smash when it hits the floor; and we count on the snow melting when the sun comes out. There are thousands of such habits, thousands of cases in which the perception of a thing calls up the idea of the thing—now absent—with which it has been associated.

Habits formed by association give rise to judgments. We say "If it rains, the picnic will be canceled" (hypothetical judgment) and "Either it will rain or the crop will be ruined" (disjunctive judgment) and "Will it rain?" (interrogative judgment). Such judgments can be explained by frequencies in experience and association. But James doubts that *abstract categories* can be accounted for in this fashion. Where did the hypothetical and disjunctive forms themselves come from? In logic we have the syllogism: If A is B, and B is C, then A is C. Can the abstract forms of logic and mathematics have arisen by association alone? Can even the theories and laws of natural science have this origin? These questions are an echo of Kant's queries. The answer will not be the same.

"Scientific thought," James says,

goes by selection and emphasis exclusively. We break the solid plenitude of fact into separate essences, conceive generally what only exists particularly, and by our classifications leave nothing in its natural neighborhood, but separate the contiguous, and join what the poles divorce. The reality *exists* as a *plenum* . . . what *comes before us,* is a chaos of fragmentary impressions interrupting each other; what we *think* is an abstract system of hypothetical data and laws. (862a)

If we reduce James's brilliant diction to prosaic terms we have something like this: Whereas the world of sensations is a teeming river of concrete qualities, lush with colors, shapes, sounds, etc., science is radically selective and abstract, for it is not interested in individuals but only in classes, and its laws and theories bear little resemblance to the experience on which they are based. Since James wrote, science has grown so much more abstract and remote from experience that it is perfectly obvious that he was right. Look around at the visible world, and then read an account of the structure of the atom or the virus, or consider Einstein's equation:

$$\text{acceleration} = \frac{(\text{gravitational mass})}{(\text{inertial mass})} \times (\text{intensity of the gravitational field}).$$

We must even be careful when we say that science is *based on* experience. The experiences which are employed to prove scientific theories, according to James, are selected and standardized experiences of the scientist in his laboratory; they are far from being raw sensations. They agree only at crucial points with the elaborate combinations and "ideal relations" which make up scientific thought. Scientific law and theory are in no sense reproductions of the order of perceptual experience. How then can they be true *to* it—true *of* it? James replies that they are "*congruent*" with the time and space relations which, it will be remembered, are not of our making but are impressed upon experience from without. (See p. 866a.) The qualities which perception discloses to us are nothing like the structures of matter which the physicist talks about. With respect to space and time relations, on the other hand, the world of perception and the world of science closely correspond. They are congruent, James says.

Scientific laws are congruent with experience in another respect, namely: they enable us to predict the occurrence even of the secondary qualities, which exist only in our subjective experience. James no doubt has this in mind when he says that though science is as fantastically removed from real experience as poetry is, there is an important difference: "What makes the assumption 'scientific' and not merely poetic, what makes a Helmholtz and his kin *discoverers*, is that the things of Nature turn out to act as if they *were* of the kind assumed" (p. 884a). We still have no direct evidence of ions and atoms, but nature at least behaves *as if* there were such things. That is, if we assume that these strange unseen entities exist, we can predict how visible objects will behave. Nowadays atomic theory enables us to make far more predictions than were possible in 1890. Would you say that this is why the existence of atoms is regarded as more certain today?

I V

However much imagination and mathematical construction goes into the theories of natural science, they have a basis in experience and are confirmed by experience. The pure *a pri-*

ori sciences of classification, logic, and mathematics, on the other hand, cannot be conceived as the *"effect of the order in which outer impressions are experienced."* They correspond to *"portions of our mental structure"* and *"form a body of propositions with whose genesis experience has nothing to do"* (p. 867a). The phrase "portions of our mental structure" may remind of Kant's theory, but James does not mean this. He held that our mental structure has come about by a natural development. (See p. 897b.)

James begins with the question: How do we know that black will always differ from white? By repeated experience of the difference, the Spencerians might say. But would this give us certainty in advance, or *a priori*, that if something is black in the future, it *cannot* be white? What would we say if someone reported that he had seen something that was both black and white? We might answer: "You are probably thinking of a newspaper, but you could not possibly see something that was both black and white all over." James's point, then, is that the absolute difference between black and white is a matter of definition. They exclude each other as do square and circle, long and short, hot and cold. It would follow that a congenitally blind person could know that black is never white. Do you think this is true?

We do not have to consult experience to know that black differs from white, square from circle, hot from cold. We *must* do so to know that snow is white, that table tops are sometimes square and sometimes circular, and that fire produces heat. These facts of space and time we know from experience; they are "empirical propositions." Thus perception and comparison give rise to two kinds of propositions and two kinds of science:

Perceptions or
    experience $\longrightarrow$ Empirical propositions $\longrightarrow$ Natural science
Comparison $\longrightarrow$ Rational propositions $\longrightarrow$ Pure or *a priori*
                                         science

James talks about resemblance and difference, because these are the foundations of classification and definition. The class of triangles, for example, comprises all those things which share the following properties: figure, three-sided, and closed. They differ in at least one of these respects from everything in the world, or in the world of thought. We do not know that triangles have these properties by observation. It would be absurd for a man to say he had found a triangle that did not have all these properties, since a triangle is, by definition, possessed of these properties. We know this, then, *a priori*, or before experience.

The same is true of the classifications of the natural sciences. Observation could never disprove the statement that *mammalia* constitute the highest class of vertebrates, that they suckle their young, etc., since it rests on a definition. Similarly, we know from the definition of "bat" and "whale" that these animals are mammals, because they are vertebrates and suckle their young, etc. Before this was known, of course, it was easy to make mistakes. It is interesting to note that although Aristotle had pointed out that the whale is a mammal, Melville, two thousand years later, insisted that it was a fish. The facts were against him but his *feelings* in the matter were too strong for him. Although it is certain that a whale is a mammal, in terms of our present system of classification, a different system might have been employed if it had proved more useful or intellectually satisfying. (See p. 870.)

James gives fundamental examples of rational propositions. Most of them are concerned with *transitive* relations. An example is the relation "greater than." If A is greater than B, and B is greater than C, then A is greater than C. The relations "predecessor of" and "implies" are also transitive. The first is very important in number theory and wherever series occur in science or practical life. The second is crucial throughout logic and mathematics, where we say: If proposition p is true, then q must be true, and if q then r, and if r then s. Therefore, if p is true, s is true. Another conclusion is possible too. We might say: Since s is false, p is false. In all such cases, transitivity permits us to drop the intermediary terms. Thus James speaks of the "AXIOM OF SKIPPED INTERMEDIARIES" (p. 870a), which he terms "the fundamental principle of inference."

To understand better what transitivity is, it will be helpful to point out relations which are *not* transitive. Although "ancestor of" is transitive, "father of" is not. Nor is the relation "lover." If *A* loves *B* and *B* loves *C*, *A* might hate *C*. But now let us consider the relations basic for classification, namely, resemblance and difference. You will soon see that they are not transitive, for *A* might be similar to *B* in one respect, and *B* similar to *C* in quite a different respect. It would not follow that *A* was similar to *C* in any respect. *A, B,* and *C* could be colors, *A* resembling *B* in hue, and *B* resembling *C* in intensity (the amount of white light). It would not follow, of course, that *A* resembled *C*. You can easily see that the relation of difference, also, cannot be transitive.

There is a question that has been in the air for some time, namely: Does James stick to one meaning of his term "rational"? Are scientific classifications "rational" in the same, sense as the propositions of logic and mathematics are? The latter are rational because they assert transitive and other ordering relations which yield necessary truths, not to be established by experience. The former are rational in the sense that they are not established by experience, but no one would say that they are necessarily true. They are *accepted* because they are useful or intellectually satisfying. Classifications are not necessarily true, since they can be changed at will. Like the propositions of logic and mathematics, however, they result from comparisons and cannot be disproved by experience. They are "rational" in this sense.

We have pointed out that "implies" (or "if . . . then") is a transitive relation. Another transitive relation fundamental in logic is "class inclusion." The following syllogism is an example:

> All mammals have lungs.
> All whales are mammals.
> Therefore, all whales have lungs.

Or, to abbreviate, since all *W* is included in *M*, and all *M* is included in *L*, all *W* is included in *L*. The mathematician Euler illustrated the syllogism by circles. The diagram for the above syllogism is:

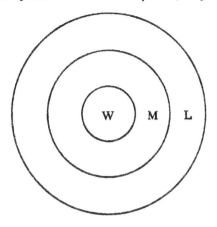

Equally is another important transitive relation. The advantage here again, as James emphasizes, is that intermediate terms can be eliminated. If we determine that $a = b$, $b = c$, $c = d$, we can at once put down $a = d$.

All of this is well known, and elementary. James's real point is that what he calls the axiom of skipped intermediaries could not have been derived from experience—from habit and association. Habit and association, in ordinary experience, lead again and again to false results, whereas the axiom of skipped intermediaries can have only a valid outcome. And the validity has nothing to do with how men actually think. We know the axiom will be true, no matter what habits of thought men have, in point of fact, and no matter what associations they form.

Associations of ideas, as will be remembered, are according to contiguity in space and time, resemblance and contrast, and cause and effect. Now consider an arithmetic proposition such as $2 + 2 = 4$. Could this be proved by associating things contiguous in time and space? No, James seems to say, for numbers are completely abstracted from time and space. Could associations by similarity and contrast have any relevance? No, for it does not make a particle of difference whether the things we add resemble one another or not. Two things of any sort, added to two others, give four things. Nor does it make any difference, of course, whether the items added are causally related.

J. S. Mill, however, insists that frequency of confirming observations is sufficient to explain the certainty of mathematics. He contends that experience teaches us that two pairs of sensations, no matter what shape or size or color—no matter what qualities they happen to have—will add up to four. Innumerable experiences of the sort bring certainty.

James's answer is: "Woe to arithmetic,"

were such the only grounds for its validity! The same real things are countable in numberless ways. . . . How could our notion that one and one are eternally and necessarily two ever maintain itself in a world where every time we add one drop of water to another we get not two but one again? in a world where every time we add a drop to a crumb of quicklime we get a dozen or more?—had it no better warrant than such experiences? At most we could then say that one and one are *usually* two. (p. 875b)

James's argument sounds quite devasting. How could we have become certain that one and one must always equal two in a world in which adding two raindrops gives one—in a world where things, as James says, are not "*unequivocally* numbered" (p. 875b)? What he means by the latter point is that a field, a pasture, an ocean, the expanse of sky, and so on do not come labeled 1. We might assign to each a different number. You say you have 3 meals a day, and that makes 21 a week, but another person, making the same reckoning, might come out with a different answer, namely, 14 meals and 7 morning snacks of coffee and toast.

Let us see if there is anything wrong with James's argument. In the first place, adding raindrops is an unusual case, and most of us have never had occasion to carry out this operation. If we did, we should not be disturbed by the result. We should simply insist on a strict definition of drop in terms of dimensions or surface tension. Moreover, we would point out that *adding* and *physical coalescence* are altogether different processes and should not be confused. If you "add" a lighted match to one stick of dynamite, you get a thousand pieces, but this result is due not to arithmetic but to an explosion. There is an important difference between a physical process which alters objects, and adding, which leaves them unchanged.

James is perfectly aware of this distinction. He is arguing, however, that men in earlier periods of history, when arithmetic began to be evolved, were not aware of it. He is saying that only by having an *a priori* certainty that $1 + 1 = 2$, could they have been sure that this proposition must always hold good in their experience. But does not James neglect certain facts? The things that primitive men added were things that they were passionately interested in, such as game, livestock, ears of corn, which were pretty clearly demarcated from one another. Ten sheep, counted off against 10 fingers, were definitely 10 sheep, and so also the next 10 sheep, counted off against 10 toes; together they made 20 sheep. If lambs mingled with the sheep, the men would have a strong motive for not counting them among the sheep.

Even when adding was necessarily combined with a physical process of mixing the units added, there need have been no confusion. When baskets of grain were to be added to fill a large vat, they were poured together, but the result reached would not be described as "$6 = 1$" but as "6 baskets of grain $=$ 1 vat of grain." Among primitive people, one can imagine, there might be confusion when dream figures and recent ancestors were counted among potentially dangerous persons. But this was perhaps no worse than the common calculation of moderns, in which chickens are counted before they are hatched. In any case, the manner in which arithmetic arises among primitive people calls for anthropological data which James does not mention. Even apart from such facts, there is some reason to think that if men had enough interest in counting things, they had a motive for discriminating the things they counted.

James concludes his treatment of necessary relations with two long quotations from Book IV of Locke's *Essay*, with which he is in full agreement. Once we have derived our ideas from sensory experience, he claims, we can combine them in ways which yield *a priori*, necessary, and eternal relations. Owing to the fact that the relations between ideal angles and triangles are eternally valid, a man can know, from *one* example, that the sum of the angles of any triangle must *always* be equal to two right angles. These eternal relations hold among the ideas which we have combined in definitions. Once we have defined triangle, we see at once that it must have three angles, though this is not included in the definition.

The necessary propositions stating these eternal relations are restricted to logic and mathematics and are not to be found in natural science proper. They do not assert existence, and they apply to the world only hypothetically. We can say only that *if* there exist two things answering to the definition of "triangle," and *if* they have two sides and an included angle in common, *then* they coincide. Similarly, $12 \times 12 = 144$ does not state that 12 things exist, let alone 144 things. The proposition is useful to us because it tells us that *if* there are 12 rows of 12 things, they add up to 144.

It is in this way also that mathematical physics becomes possible. Physics is an empirical science, which reaches existential conclusions about the actual world, whereas mathematics has no concern with existence. Physics and mathematics are combined in mathematical physics—in mechanics, for example, where mathematics is employed to deduce the consequences of empirical hypotheses. If the empirical fact is ascertained that there exist in space bodies of a certain mass, acceleration, and distance from one another, their relative positions at later times can be deduced. The positions, mass, and acceleration of the bodies are known as probable, or highly probable, but the deductions from them, James says, are *a priori* and necessary. By abstracting from all the properties of objects except position, mass, and acceleration, and by employing mathematical deduction, the powerful science of mechanics has evolved. The world of mechanics is poverty-stricken compared to the lush realm of sensations, and its rigor and usefulness depend precisely on that fact.

"Of course it is a world," James adds, "with a very minimum of rational *stuff*. The sentimental facts and relations are butchered at a blow. But the rationality yielded is so superbly complete in *form* that to many minds this atones for the loss" (p. 883a).

Is not James using "rational" here in a new sense? How is the rationality of logic and mathematics related to "rational *stuff*," i.e., "sentimental facts and relations?" This important development will be our concern in the questions to which we now turn.

V

In what sense is metaphysics rational?

We have discussed the sense in which logic and mathematics are "rational." The relations asserted by these sciences are neither derived from nor proved by experience but are necessary *a priori*. We have also seen that the relations on which classifications are based—similarity and difference among the things classified—are "rational" in a different sense and that James is none too clear about this difference. The classification of all bodies according to their position, mass, and acceleration is of great value. It is essential for the science of mechanics. But there are other ways of classifying bodies, as, for example, according to their size, shape, color, etc., which have just as much basis in experience. Thus the classification of bodies employed by mechanics has no *special* warrant from experience, nor is it, of course, necessary or *a priori*. James calls scientific classification "rational" because it is intellectually satisfying, or satisfying to our rational nature, and because it is not based on experience. That is, no classification is preferentially endorsed by experience, over other alternative classifications.

James stretches the term "rational" a little farther in discussing metaphysical axioms. (See pp. 884-886.) Metaphysics was not regarded as a science in James's time, nor is it in our own, yet it is something like a science and has a kind of rationality. An example of a metaphysical axiom is "Nature is intelligible throughout," i.e., comprehensible in every particular or completely explicable by scientific laws and theories. Another is "Everything has a cause and an effect, and cause and effect are necessarily connected." Neither of these so-called axioms can be proved inductively by experience. They are presupposed by the kind of experience which would be needed to prove them. The attempt to prove that the sun *must* always rise in the future, as we have seen in discussing Hume, is circular, i.e., it is an argument that assumes what it wants to prove in its premises.

Nor are such axioms "rational," in the sense of *a priori* and self-evident. We can all see that they *might* be false. Maybe some things would remain inexplicable, however much we knew about nature, and maybe some things have no cause. What is the status of these "axioms," then? In what sense are they rational? James suggests that they should be called "postulates of rationality," meaning that the world would be more "rational"—i.e., more agreeable to our rational nature, or intellectually more satisfying—if they were true. Such postulates are far from barren, James says. They are the lure to scientific endeavor. They give men the zeal and the hope to discover the most remote and hidden connections in nature. It is by hoping they are true that *human* life becomes possible. Cannot we say, then, that they have a very important kind of "rationality"?

Metaphysical postulates are thus rational in much the same sense as scientific classifications are. Yet there is a difference too. The classification of bodies according to their position, mass, and acceleration is based on characteristics which bodies are known to have. But if it should turn out that some bodies do not have all of them, this would not mean that the classification was false but only that it was somewhat less useful, or less satisfying intellectually, than it had previously been. The postulates of metaphysics mentioned above, on the other hand, *might be* simply and straightforwardly false.

Are aesthetic and moral principles "rational" in any sense?

James seems to think that aesthetic principles may be based upon habit to some extent, and perhaps on our common human nature. Many attempts have been made, as a matter of fact, to show that figures of certain proportions are naturally more agreeable to the human eye than others. For example, thousands of measurements were made of vases, doorways, the façades of buildings, etc., to determine whether "the golden section"—a rectangle of certain proportions[1]—is universally preferred to other shapes. The results were not encouraging to the view that aesthetic taste is rooted in human nature.

In his brief comment on aesthetic principles, James makes the individual the chief arbiter. Even metaphysical principles, though defended by logic, are adopted because of individual taste. And here, as in the strictly aesthetic realms of painting, music, poetry, and the like, what is one man's food is often another's poison. Since reason is supposed to be common to the species, but aesthetic preference varies so widely from one individual to another, there is little reason to think that aesthetic taste is "rational" in the sense that arithmetic is. Nor, according to James, can it be mainly due to experience and habit either.

Moral principles, likewise, are not to be explained "*in toto* by habitual experiences having bred inner cohesions" (p. 886b). Here again James opposes Herbert Spencer. Moral judgments and conduct are not mere habits which have been stamped in by the sheer frequency with which our actions have been blamed and approved. Habit plays a part, of course, but what swings the balance in the lonely, fateful decisions of the individual are "subtle harmonies and discords" (p. 887a) felt in the situation he faces. The brain action is certainly as complicated as that involved when we listen to contrapuntal music.

Kant's moral law,[2] James says, overturns habit completely. Instead of looking at things from our own point of view, we adopt a rigorously impersonal standpoint. But could not Spencer reply that this stance is just another higher habit implanted in us by social pressures? Could it be that we permit ourselves no liberty which we do not accord to others, merely because we are punished, in one way or another, if we do the contrary?

James certainly does not desire to see any rigorous, unbend-

[1] The rectangle is such that the width is to the length as the length is to the sum of the other two; i.e., $W : L : : L : W + L$.

[2] See discussion in the last reading.

ing application of the moral law, or the golden rule. He would have agreed with George Bernard Shaw's remark that the trouble with the golden rule is that tastes differ. Here, as always, James is the defender of the individual against the tyranny of general laws and creeds which deprive him of his uniqueness and peculiar worth.

Aesthetic and moral principles are thus "rational" in a weaker sense. They have only this much in common with the principles of logic and mathematics: They are not the simple outcome of repeated outer experiences and habits, but are, on the contrary, elaborate products of the higher centers of the brain.

The following questions are designed to help you test the thoroughness of your reading. Each question is to be answered by giving a page or pages of the reading assignment. Answers will be found on page 302 of this Reading Plan.

1 How does James explain Darwin's use of "accidental," in the expression "accidental variations"?

2 Why does James describe *the order of experience* as "our sovereign helper and friend"?

3 Why does the "experience-philosophy," according to James, have "a halo of anti-supernaturalism about it"?

4 Why does he think he may be suspected of giving aid to obscurantism?

5 What are the seven "elementary mental categories" that James lists?

6 What is meant by: *"the manner in which we now become acquainted with complex objects need not in the least resemble the manner in which the original elements of our consciousness grew up"*?

7 What author is cited as denying that accidental changes in the brain could fit the organism to its environment?

8 In what connection is it said that inner relations engender experiences, rather than *vice versa?*

9 Does the experience of relations of resemblence and difference depend on the space-time order in which they are embedded?

10 What is the *"axiom of constant result"*?

11 What does James mean by saying moral and aesthetic qualities are not of *"the kind's kind"*?

12 Does Helmholtz say that the theoretic division of science seeks "to discover the unknown causes of processes from their visible effects"?

ANSWERS
to self-testing questions

First Reading
1. 373a
2. 376c
3. 377b-c
4. 379c-d
5. 379d-380a
6. 380d-381a
7. 390b

Second Reading
1. 391c, 392a-b, 393c
2. 395b
3. 400a-d
4. 401d
5. 392a
6. 391d
7. 392c

Third Reading
1. 499d-500a
2. 501b
3. 503b
4. 506c-d
5. 508d
6. 509d
7. 510d

Fourth Reading
1. 523d
2. 524c
3. 525c-d
4. 526c-527a
5. 529d
6. 532b
7. 528b

Fifth Reading
1. 2d
2. 6d-7a
3. 8d
4. 11a-b
5. 15a-d

6. 24b-25c
7. 27d-28a

Sixth Reading
1. 94b-c
2. 95c
3. 97b
4. 98a
5. 99b
6. 98b-d
7. 101b-c

Seventh Reading
1. 208b
2. 211c-212a
3. 215d-216b
4. 228c-229a
5. 233a-b
6. 238d-239a
7. 243b-c

Eighth Reading
1. 43c-d
2. 45c
3. 51a
4. 55c
5. 61b
6. 62c-d
7. 66b-c

Ninth Reading
1. 42c-43a
2. 43c-d
3. 44c-45b
4. 45d-46a
5. 46d
6. 47d-48a
7. 41c-d

Tenth Reading
1. 357c-d
2. 357a-b

3. 358c
4. 358d
5. 363b-c
6. 363d-364a
7. 364a-b

Eleventh Reading

1. 307b-308a
2. 310c-d
3. 311c-312a
4. 316d-317a
5. 325a-b
6. 325b-d
7. 318a
8. 321d-322a

Twelfth Reading

1. 410d-411a
2. 417d-418b
3. 420d-421a
4. 425c-426a
5. 431a-d
6. 436c-437c
7. 442b-d

Thirteenth Reading

1. 457a-458b
2. 464a-b
3. 466d-467c
4. 455d
5. 475b-d
6. 480c-481b

7. 484c
8. 487a
9. 458b
10. 457a-b, 471c-d

Fourteenth Reading

1. 1b-d
2. 2d
3. 2d
4. 3d
5. 5c
6. 5d
7. 6c-d
8. 9d
9. 11a
10. 19d
11. 25d
12. 28b-d

Fifteenth Reading

1. 851b
2. 852b
3. 856a
4. 856a
5. 859a
6. 859-860
7. 860b
8. 864a-865a
9. 867-868
10. 869a-b
11. 882b
12. 883b

ADDITIONAL READINGS

This list does not include works in moral philosophy, political philosophy, or the philosophy of nature. For suggested readings in these areas, the reader should refer to the Reading Plans *The Development of Political Theory and Government, Ethics: The Study of Moral Values,* and *Biology, Psychology, and Medicine.*

I. Works included in *Great Books of the Western World*

Vol. 7: PLATO, *Cratylus; Phaedo; Timaeus; Critias; Parmenides; Theaetetus; Sophist*

8: ARISTOTLE, *Categories; Posterior Analytics; Physics; On the Soul*

12: EPICTETUS, *Discourses*

17: PLOTINUS, *The Six Enneads*

23: HOBBES, *Leviathan,* Part I

30: BACON, *Novum Organum*

31: DESCARTES, *Rules for the Direction of the Mind; Meditations on First Philosophy; Objections against the Meditations, and Replies*

42: KANT, *Critique of Practical Reason; Critique of Judgment,* Part II, "Critique of Teleological Judgement"

46: HEGEL, *The Philosophy of History*

II. Other Works

A. Works in Speculative Philosophy and the Theory of Knowledge

ALEXANDER, SAMUEL, *Space, Time, and Diety,* 2 vol. New York: The Macmillan Company, 1920

AYER, A. J., *Language, Truth and Logic.* New York: Oxford University Press, 1936

BERGSON, HENRI, *Creative Evolution.* New York: Random House, Inc. (Modern Library), 1944; *Time and Free Will.* New York: Harper Torchbooks

BERKELEY, GEORGE, *Three Dialogues Between Hylas and Philonous*. Indianapolis: The Bobbs-Merrill Company, Inc. (Liberal Arts Press); *An Essay Toward a New Theory of Vision*. Indianapolis: The Bobbs-Merrill Company, Inc. (Liberal Arts Press)

BOETHIUS, *The Consolation of Philosophy*, trans. by W. V. Cooper. New York: Random House, Inc. (Modern Library), 1943

BOSANQUET, BERNARD, *Logic; or, The Morphology of Knowledge*, 2nd ed. London: Oxford University Press, 1932

BRADLEY, F. H., *Appearance and Reality: A Metaphysical Essay*, rev. ed. New York: Oxford University Press, 1930

BROAD, C. D., *The Mind and Its Place in Nature*. New York: Harcourt, Brace & Company, Inc., 1925.

CASSIRER, ERNST, *The Philosophy of Symbolic Forms*, trans. by Ralph Manheim, 3 vol. New Haven: Yale University Press, 1954-57; *Substance and Function; and Einstein's Theory of Relativity*, trans. by W. C. Swabey and M. C. Swabey. New York: Dover Publications, Inc., 1953

CROCE, BENEDETTO, *Philosophy of the Spirit*, trans. by D. Ainslie, 3 vol. London: Macmillan and Company, Ltd.

DESCARTES, RENÉ, *The Principles of Philosophy*, trans. by E. S. Haldane and G. R. T. Ross; in Vol. I, *Philosophical Works*. London: Cambridge University Press, 1931

DEWEY, JOHN, *Experience and Nature*, new ed. New York: W. W. Norton & Company, Inc., 1929; *Logic, the Theory of Inquiry*. New York: Henry Holt & Company, Inc., 1938; *Reconstruction in Philosophy*. Boston: Beacon Press, 1949

FICHTE, J. G., *The Vocation of Man*, trans. by W. Smith and R. M. Chisholm. Indianapolis: The Bobbs-Merrill Company, Inc. (Liberal Arts Press), 1956

HEGEL, GEORG WILHELM FRIEDRICH, *The Phenomenology of Mind*, trans. by J. B. Baillie, 2nd ed. rev. New York: The Macmillan Company, 1931; *The Science of Logic*, trans. by W. H. Johnston and L. G. Struthers, 2 vol. New York: The Macmillan Company, 1952

HEIDEGGER, MARTIN, *Being and Time*, trans. by J. Macquarrie and E. Robinson. London: Student Christian Movement Press, Ltd., 1962; *An Introduction to Metaphysics,* trans. by Ralph Manheim. New York: Doubleday Anchor Books

HUME, DAVID, *A Treatise of Human Nature,* Vol. I. New York: E. P. Dutton and Company, Inc. (Everyman's Library), 1911

HUSSERL, EDMUND, *Cartesian Meditations: An Introduction to Phenomenology,* trans. by D. Cairns. The Hague: Martinus Nijhoff, 1960; *Ideas: General Introduction to Pure Phenomenology,* trans. by W. R. Boyce Gibson. New York: The Macmillan Company, 1952

JAMES, WILLIAM, *Essays in Radical Empiricism* and *A Pluralistic Universe.* New York: Longmans, Green and Company, Inc., 1943; *Pragmatism.* New York: Meridian Books, Inc., 1955

JASPERS, KARL, *Reason and Existenz,* trans. by W. Earle. New York: Noonday Press, 1957

KANT, IMMANUEL, *Prolegomena to Any Future Metaphysics.* Indianapolis: The Bobbs-Merrill Company, Inc. (Liberal Arts Press)

KIERKEGAARD, SØREN, *Concluding Unscientific Postscript,* trans. by D. F. Swenson and W. Lowrie. Princeton: Princeton University Press, 1941

LEIBNIZ, G. W., *Discourse on Metaphysics; Correspondence with Arnauld, and Monadology,* trans. by G. R. Montgomery. Chicago: Open Court Publishing Company; *New Essays Concerning Human Understanding,* trans. by A. G. Langley, 2nd ed. Chicago: Open Court Publishing Company, 1916

LEWIS, C. I., *Mind and the World Order.* New York: Dover Publications, Inc., 1924

McTAGGART, J. M. E., *The Nature of Existence,* 2 vol. New York: The Macmillan Company, 1921-27

MAIMONIDES, *The Guide for the Perplexed,* trans. by M. Friedländer, 2nd ed. New York: Dover Publications, Inc., 1904

MARCEL, GABRIEL, *The Mystery of Being,* trans. by G. S. Fraser and René Hague, 2 vol. Chicago: Henry Regnery Co., 1951

MARITAIN, JACQUES, *The Degrees of Knowledge*, trans. by G. B. Phelan. New York: Charles Scribner's Sons, 1959.

MILL, JOHN STUART, *A System of Logic, Ratiocinative and Inductive*. New York: Longmans, Green and Company, Inc., 1930

MOORE, G. E., *Philosophical Studies*. New York: Harcourt, Brace & Company, Inc., 1922

NIETZSCHE, FRIEDRICH, *The Will to Power, an Attempted Transvaluation of All Values*, trans. by A. M. Ludovici; in *The Complete Works of Freidrich Nietzsche*, Vol. XIV-XV. New York: The Macmillan Company, 1925

ROYCE, JOSIAH, *The World and the Individual*, 2 vol. New York: Dover Publications, Inc., 1959

RUSSELL, BERTRAND, *The Analysis of Matter*. New York: Dover Publications, Inc., 1954; *Our Knowledge of the External World*. New York: New American Library (Mentor); *Human Knowledge, Its Scope and Limits*. New York: Simon & Schuster, Inc., 1948

RYLE, GILBERT, *The Concept of Mind*. New York: Barnes & Noble, Inc., 1950

SANTAYANA, GEORGE, *Realms of Being*. New York: Charles Scribner's Sons, 1942; *Scepticism and Animal Faith*. New York: Dover Publication, Inc., 1955

SARTE, JEAN PAUL, *Being and Nothingness*, trans. by H. E. Barnes. New York: Philosophical Library, Inc., 1956

SCHELLING, F. W. J. VON, *Of Human Freedom*, trans. by J. Gutmann. La Salle, Ill.: Open Court Publishing Company, 1936

SCHOPENHAUER, ARTHUR, *The World as Will and Idea*, trans. by R. B. Haldane and J. Kemp, 3 vol. New York: Charles Scribner's Sons, 1950

SEXTUS, EMPIRICUS, *Philosophical Works*, trans. by R. G. Bury, 3 vol. Cambridge, Mass.: Harvard University Press, (Loeb Classical Library), 1933-36

SPINOZA, BENEDICTUS DE, *On the Improvement of the Understanding*, trans. by J. Katz. Indianapolis: The Bobbs-Merrill Company, Inc. (Liberal Arts Press), 1958; *Short Treatise on God, Man, and His Well-Being;* in Spinoza, *Selections,* ed. by John Wild. New York: Charles Scribner's Sons, 1930

VOLTAIRE, FRANÇOIS MARIE AROUET DE, *Philosophical Dictionary.* New York: Philosophical Library, Inc. (Wisdom Library)

WHITEHEAD, ALFRED NORTH, *Science and the Modern World.* New York: New American Library (Mentor); *Process and Reality: An Essay in Cosmology.* New York: Harper Torchbooks

WISDOM, JOHN, *Other Minds.* New York: Philosophical Library, Inc., 1952

WITTGENSTEIN, LUDWIG, *Tractatus Logico-Philosophicus.* London: Routledge & Kegan Paul, Ltd., 1961; *Philosophical Investigations,* trans. by G. E. M. Anscombe. New York: The Macmillan Company, 1953

B. Histories and Commentaries

BURNET, JOHN, *Early Greek Philosophy.* Cleveland: World Publishing Company (Meridian Books)

CASSIRER, ERNST, *The Philosophy of the Enlightenment,* trans. by F. C. A. Koelln and J. P. Pettegrove. Boston: Beacon Press, 1955

COPLESTON, FREDERICK, *A History of Philosophy,* 6 vol. Westminster, Md.: Newman Press, 1946-60

GILSON, ÉTIENNE, *History of Christian Philosophy in the Middle Ages.* New York: Random House, Inc., 1955

HALÉVY, ELIE, *The Growth of Philosophic Radicalism,* trans. by M. Morris. Boston: Beacon Press, 1955

HEGEL, G. W. F., *Lectures on the History of Philosophy.,* trans. by E. S. Haldane and F. H. Simson, 3 vol. New York: Humanities Press, 1955

HÖFFDING, HARALD, *History of Modern Philosophy,* trans. by B. E. Meyer, 2 vol. New York: Dover Publications, Inc., 1955

JASPERS, KARL, *The Great Philosophers,* trans. by R. Manheim. New York: Harcourt, Brace & World, Inc., 1962

RUSSELL, BERTRAND, *A History of Western Philosophy*, New York: Simon & Schuster, Inc., 1945

WINDELBAND, WILHELM, *History of Ancient Philosophy*, trans. by H. E. Cushman. New York: Dover Publications, Inc.; *A History of Philosophy*, 2 vol. New York: Harper Torchbooks

III. A Reading List in Aesthetics

ARISTOTLE, *On Poetics;* in *Great Books of the Western World*, Vol. 9

BELL, CLIVE, *Art*. New York: G. P. Putnam's Sons (Capricorn Books), 1959

BOSANQUET, BERNARD, *A History of Aesthetic*. Cleveland: World Publishing Company (Meridian Books)

CROCE, BENEDETTO, *Aesthetic, as Science of Expression and General Linguistic*, trans. by D. Ainslie, 2nd ed. reprint. New York: Noonday Press, 1953

DEWEY, JOHN, *Art as Experience*. New York: G. P. Putnam's Sons (Capricorn Books), 1959

HEGEL, GEORG WILHELM FRIEDRICH, *The Philosophy of Fine Art*, trans. by B. Bosanquet. London: Kegan Paul, Trench and Company, 1886

KANT, IMMANUEL, *Critique of Judgement*, Part I, "Critique of Aesthetic Judgement"; in *Great Books of the Western World*, Vol. 42

LANGER, SUSANNE, *Feeling and Form*. New York: Charles Scribner's Sons, 1955

LONGINUS, *On Great Writing (On the Sublime)*, trans. by G. M. A. Grube. Indianapolis: The Bobbs-Merrill Company, Inc. (Liberal Arts Press)

NIETZSCHE, FRIEDRICH, *The Birth of Tragedy*. New York: Doubleday Anchor Books

SANTAYANA, GEORGE, *The Sense of Beauty*. New York: Dover Publications, Inc.

SCHOPENHAUER, ARTHUR, *The World as Will and Idea*, Book III and Supplements to Book III, trans. by R. B. Haldane and J. Kemp. New York: Charles Scribner's Sons, 1950